THE SOCIETY FOR USEFUL KNOWLEDGE

THE SOCIETY FOR USEFUL KNOWLEDGE

*How Benjamin Franklin and Friends
Brought the Enlightenment to America*

JONATHAN LYONS

BLOOMSBURY PRESS
NEW YORK · LONDON · NEW DELHI · SYDNEY

Published by Bloomsbury Press, New York

Quotation from "Paterson," by William Carlos Williams, from *The Collected Poems: Volume I,
1909–1939*, copyright © 1938 by New Directions Publishing Corp. Reprinted by
permission of New Directions Publishing Corp.

All papers used by Bloomsbury Press are natural, recyclable products made
from wood grown in well-managed forests. The manufacturing processes
conform to the environmental regulations of the country of origin.

Library of Congress Cataloging-in-Publication Data

Lyons, Jonathan.
The Society for Useful Knowledge : how Benjamin Franklin and friends brought the
Enlightenment to America / Jonathan Lyons.—1st U.S. edition.
pages cm
ISBN 978-1-60819-553-4
1. United States—Intellectual life—18th century. 2. United States—Intellectual life—
1783–1865. 3. Franklin, Benjamin, 1706–1790—Philosophy. 4. Enlightenment—United
States. 5. Philosophy, American—18th century. 6. Political science—United States—
Philosophy—History—18th century. I. Title.
E162.L96 2013
973.3—dc23

2012051556

First U.S. edition 2013

1 3 5 7 9 10 8 6 4 2

Typeset by Hewer Text UK Ltd, Edinburgh
Printed and bound in the U.S.A. by Thomson-Shore, Inc., Dexter, Michigan

To Michelle, an Adept of Useful Knowledge from Day One

When speculative Truths are reduced to Practice, when Theories, grounded upon experiments, are applied to common Purposes of life, and when, by these Agriculture is improved, Trade enlarged, and the Arts of Living made more easy and comfortable, and of Course, the Increase and Happiness of Mankind promoted, Knowledge then becomes really useful.

—The American Society held at Philadelphia for
Promoting Useful Knowledge

TABLE OF CONTENTS

SIGNIFICANT EVENTS

These are some of the significant dates associated with the story of *The Society for Useful Knowledge*. More details are covered in the narrative that follows.

1620   The *Mayflower*, carrying William Bradford and other English and Dutch religious dissidents, arrives at Cape Cod.

1650   Restoration of the British monarchy under Charles II, ending republican rule.

1660   Royal Society of London for Improving Natural Knowledge is founded.

1681   King grants William Penn a charter for the American province of Pennsylvania.

1683   Englishman Josiah Franklin, father of Benjamin, emigrates to Boston.

1699   John Bartram, American botanist, is born in Darby, Pennsylvania.

1706   Benjamin Franklin is born in Boston.

1723   Franklin breaks his legal contract as an apprentice with his brother James, a Boston printer, and flees to Philadelphia.

1724   Franklin arrives in London on Christmas Eve in fruitless pursuit of money and equipment to go into the printing business back in Philadelphia. This is the first of four stints abroad, accounting for much of his adult life.

1726   Franklin returns to Philadelphia aboard the *Berkshire* to begin a short-lived career in business.

1727   Franklin and other like-minded craftsmen and mechanics form the Leather Apron Club, more commonly known as the Junto.

1731   Franklin and friends form the Library Company of Philadelphia.

1732   David Rittenhouse, mechanical and mathematical prodigy, is born outside Philadelphia.

1743   Franklin announces the formation of the American Philosophical Society. After a brief flurry of activity, it lies dormant for almost two decades.

1749   Franklin begins public campaign for creation of an academy and college in Philadelphia, the future University of Pennsylvania.

1751   Franklin publishes details of the lightning rod in his newspaper, the *Pennsylvania Gazette*. As with his other inventions, he declines to patent it.

1753   The Royal Society of London awards Franklin its Copley Medal, the world's most prestigious prize for science, for his experiments in electricity.

1754   Franklin proposes his Plan of Union, at a colonial conference in Albany, New York, anticipating many of the elements of the future independent American political structure.

1757   Pennsylvania legislature sends Franklin to London to represent its interests before the Crown. He does not return until 1762.

1761   Americans join the global effort to observe and record the transit of Venus, in an attempt to measure the size of the known universe.

1764   Franklin is sent back to London on behalf of the Pennsylvania legislature. He returns empty-handed in 1775.

1768   Treaty of union agreed between Philadelphia's rival knowledge societies, allowing the reconstitution of Franklin's original American Philosophical Society.

1769   The second transit of Venus acts as a powerful spur to the activities of the American Philosophical Society. The Americans win plaudits from abroad.

1773   Creation of the Virginia Society for the Promotion of Useful Knowledge is announced.

1774   First Continental Congress meets in Philadelphia's Carpenters' Hall, symbol of the power and influence of Pennsylvania's mechanics.

1775   United Company of Philadelphia for Promoting American Manufactures is created. Similar societies are soon active in Boston, Baltimore, New York, Richmond, Wilmington, and Newark.

1776   Congress approves final text of the Declaration of Independence, written by Thomas Jefferson and edited by Franklin and others.

        Franklin is sent to Paris to head the American diplomatic effort to win military and political support for the rebellion against the British. He returns in triumph in 1785.

1777   Botanist John Bartram dies, four days before the British begin their nine-month occupation of Philadelphia.

1780   John Adams and others form Boston's American Academy of Arts and Sciences, in emulation of Franklin's American Philosophical Society.

1783   The United States, represented by Franklin, John Adams, and John Jay, and Great Britain sign the Treaty of Paris that ends the War for Independence and recognizes American sovereignty.

1787   Franklin and colleagues form the Society for Political Inquiries. The circle provides a forum for Tench Coxe and his vision of an industrialized and technologically advanced America.

1787   Pennsylvania Society for the Encouragement of Manufactures and the Useful Arts is formed. It includes prominent members of the Society for Political Inquiries.

1788   Mechanics' associations take the lead in national celebrations of the new federal Constitution and demand government support for manufacturers.

1790   Franklin dies at the age of eighty-four, in Philadelphia. His funeral draws a crowd estimated at two thirds of the city's total population.

1791   Alexander Hamilton, secretary of the treasury, submits his Report on Manufactures to the Congress. The plan relies heavily on the work of Coxe, now Hamilton's deputy.

1791   The Society for Establishing Useful Manufactures (SUM) is incorporated in the state of New Jersey, leading to the foundation of the industrial city of Paterson.

1796   SUM ends manufacturing efforts and concentrates on business development and the sale of power to independent entrepreneurs. It survives until 1945, when it is absorbed into the city of Paterson.

1796   David Rittenhouse, self-taught instrument maker and astronomer, dies.

1796   Washington delivers his Farewell Address, warning of the dangers of political factionalism and extolling the diffusion of useful knowledge in a democracy.

Chapter One

THE AGE OF FRANKLIN

In the beginning, all the world was *America*.
—John Locke

BENJAMIN FRANKLIN DID not live to see the first full decade of American sovereignty. Yet he proved the central transformational figure in a transformative period of the nation's history. Born in 1706 into modest circumstances in Boston, then a mere outpost of fewer than nine thousand residents, Franklin capped his public career eight decades later, in the glittering capital of Paris, where he ushered the newly independent America onto the world stage. He died in 1790, not long after the ratification of the federal Constitution, a document he endorsed, albeit with a certain ironic detachment. Along the way, Franklin's ideas, actions, and achievements—in short, his own lived experience—helped set America on course for its steady journey from colonial backwater to world power.

It is no wonder, then, that at the age of seventy-eight Franklin saw himself supremely qualified to spell out the essence of the young republic, leavened with his own hopes and aspirations, for those beyond its shores. In the few short months after victory over the British, sealed by the Treaty of Paris on September 3, 1783, Franklin—the best-known American of his day—had found himself besieged by potential immigrants eager to learn more about this new society and, perhaps, to profit from it. His response was simple and direct. Newcomers must rely on their skills or a commitment to hard, honest work, he explained in the published essay "Information to Those Who Would Remove to America," for it was surely ill-advised for highborn Europeans to arrive on American soil in the hopes of simply trading on their breeding or conventional social standing.

"In Europe it has indeed its Value, but it is a Commodity that cannot be carried to a worse Market than to that of America, where People do not enquire concerning a Stranger, *What* is he? But *What does* he *do*?" Franklin wrote in March 1784. "If he has any useful Art, he is welcome; and if he exercises it and behaves well, he will be respected by all that know him; but a mere Man of Quality . . . will be despised and disregarded.*

"According to these Opinions of the Americans, one of them would think himself more obliged to a Genealogist, who could prove for him that his Ancestors & Relations for ten Generations had been Ploughmen, Smiths, Carpenters, Turners, Weavers, Tanners, or even Shoemakers, & consequently that they were useful Members of Society."[1]

Here, Franklin gives a concrete American voice to one of the most cherished notions of the Age of Enlightenment—that the value of learning and knowledge, of information and data, is directly proportional to its practical import or utility. In other words, to be of any real value, knowledge has to be truly *useful.* It cannot rest on blind acceptance of past tradition or rely on sanctification by entrenched authority. After an adolescent detour into what he later dismissed as dangerous "metaphysical Reasonings," Franklin enthusiastically adopted this notion of useful knowledge as his lifelong intellectual, social, and political standard, and he worked tirelessly to inculcate these values in the new American society that was beginning to take shape all around him.

In a letter to a young woman he was tutoring in science, Franklin wondered aloud, "What signifies Philosophy that does not apply to some Use?"[2] Elsewhere, he pointedly directed a scientific colleague not to waste his time on theoretical matters but "employ your time rather in making Experiments than in making Hypotheses and forming imaginary Systems, which we are all too apt to please ourselves with till some Experiment comes, and unluckily destroys them."[3] Faced with the riddle of the possible relationship between lightning and electricity that had so far stumped the finest minds in Europe, Franklin's response—one that would soon make him and his electric kite world famous— was disarmingly simple: "Let the experiment be made."[4]

Like many others in his day, Franklin was first drawn to the mysteries of electricity after attending a series of public demonstrations on the subject. In fact, he was so taken with the matter that he later purchased the lecturer's

---

* I have endeavored to preserve Franklin's preferred orthography in quotations from his works and those of his contemporaries. I have, however, generally adopted modern forms of spelling in place of the more informal usage of the period. Where necessary, punctuation has also been updated.

experimental apparatus for his own use. Such demonstrations attracted broad audiences in colonial America, while accounts of new experiments and fresh discoveries were the regular stuff of newspapers and magazines. Typically, these traveling electrical shows involved a brief overview of the latest theories of electrical phenomena and demonstrated the collection of an electrical charge by rubbing a glass tube or rotating a glass sphere against a piece of soft leather, or perhaps a piece of wool or a lump of rosin.

But the high point undoubtedly consisted of demonstrations that allowed members of the audience to experience the effects of electricity for themselves, either directly from the generator, the so-called electrical machine, or from a charged Leyden jar that could store the electrical fire until it was required. Popular handbooks presented numerous electrical diversions to be tried at home. In one of the most popular parlor games, the Venus electrificata, an insulated woman was given an electrical charge and any young gallant brave enough to give her a kiss was in for a nasty shock.

This commitment to useful knowledge, backed by experimentation and bodily experience, served as something of a common touchstone among the revolutionary generation, even as wartime unity and shared enthusiasm for an independent America gave way to bitter differences over the future direction of the new nation. Although generally cast in terms of competing economic and foreign policies, the emerging dispute in fact encompassed the entire republican vision that had rallied many to the revolutionary cause in the first place.

Drawing on their understanding of examples from classical times and keen to avoid the English path of heavy industrialization, Thomas Jefferson, James Madison, and their allies in the so-called Republican faction tended to view economic and political questions primarily in moral terms. America—in its ideal form, at least—should remain an agricultural nation, its rich and abundant lands able to absorb its remarkable population growth well into the future, without recourse to the development of industry and the accompanying dangers of social stratification and its associated ills. Untainted by luxuries and free of political or financial reliance on others, the new, virtuous citizen would be truly liberated to take full part in republican affairs. At the same time, America would freely export its agricultural surpluses to a hungry world but otherwise remain aloof from global affairs.

Alexander Hamilton and his fellow Federalists, for their part, had no time for throwbacks to an imagined republican utopia. They were intent on cementing a strong, centralized government with the glue of Revolutionary War debt repayment, a banking and credit regime, an expansive reading of federal powers in the new Constitution, an aggressive foreign policy, and ambitious industrial development. Human nature, Hamilton argued, was not motivated or shaped by republican virtue so much as by the pursuit of luxury, which would in turn fuel activity across the entire economy and prevent idleness, impoverishment, and vice from infecting the land.

So powerful were these divisive passions that they drove immediate postwar politics and gave shape to many of America's enduring governmental institutions, laws, and practices. America's publishers and printers labored mightily just to keep pace with the proliferation of pamphlets, polemics, and position papers proffered on all sides. Much to the alarm of George Washington—living symbol of victory over the British and the republic's first president—the emergence of competing tendencies portended the establishment of permanent political parties, invariably to be led, he warned, by "cunning, ambitious, and unprincipled men [out] . . . to subvert the Power of the People."[5]

Despite their very real differences, however, the most prominent figures and factions were united by more than just armed resistance to British domination. They also shared a fundamental—and revolutionary—view of the world, one grounded in popular eighteenth-century ideals of experimental science and experiential knowledge and generally ill-disposed toward received wisdom, classical authority, and religious mystery.

The true herald of this new America was not Jefferson, with his vision of a self-contained republican idyll resting on the shoulders of the virtuous yeoman farmer. Nor was it his chief rival, Hamilton, with his unshakable faith in mercantilism, industrialization, and direct economic and political competition with the world at large. Rather, we must look to the figure of Benjamin Franklin, whose long and varied life dovetailed with the most significant events in eighteenth-century America.

*   *   *

By the dawn of the American Revolution, Benjamin Franklin had already spent most of his adult life in the pursuit of knowledge that might profit society, improve the moral and economic standing of its individual members, and, not least of all, redound to the benefit of Franklin himself. Crucially, he saw such endeavors as primarily a collective pursuit rather than as the preserve of the solitary scientific genius, secreted away in his laboratory or hunched over his lonely workbench. Even his most famous contributions to science and technology—including the kite experiment that established the identity of lightning and electricity, the lightning rod, and the so-called Franklin stove—were the products of teamwork and the free exchange of information, ideas, and observations. For Franklin, true knowledge was both useful and social.

His quest for useful knowledge and self-improvement flourished within the precincts of the study circle and subscription library, amid the mysteries of the local Masonic lodge, and inside the collegiality of the coffee klatsch, the tavern gathering, and the drinking club. He created his own secret society, primarily of fellow artisans and craftsmen out to better themselves and their position within the hierarchical bounds of prerevolutionary society. And he eagerly adopted the eighteenth-century vogue for the exchange of learned correspondence and left behind an impressive archive of letters, in an array of European languages, with many of the leading scientists of his day.*

Over the decades, Franklin relied on these types of social networks to help forge what was in effect an American movement for useful knowledge. His overlapping colonial circles encompassed such figures as John Bartram, the cantankerous Quaker farmer and stonemason who ranged far and wide, from the pine barrens of New Jersey to the swamps of the Carolinas, on botanizing expeditions; Cadwallader Colden, a New York doctor and amateur scientist who boldly set out to challenge the world-famous Isaac Newton; the mathematical prodigy, watchmaker, and self-taught astronomer David Rittenhouse, who shared Franklin's zeal for Pennsylvania politics and American independence; the physician Benjamin Rush, surgeon general to the Continental Army, professor of medicine, and tireless campaigner on behalf of useful knowledge in American schools and colleges; and the fallen patrician-turned-apostle of American mechanization, Tench Coxe.

Fired by the potential for collective study and the exchange of information, many of these same men rallied around Franklin's long-running efforts to create America's first national institution, the American Philosophical Society, dedicated to the furtherance of useful knowledge. Over time, the association would also attract such prominent political figures as Washington, Hamilton,

---

* The term "scientist" was not adopted until the mid-nineteenth century or so, and the practitioners of science of Franklin's era referred to themselves as natural philosophers. However, in deference to modern usage, I employ the terms interchangeably.

Madison, John Adams, Thomas Paine, and John Marshall, as well as a number of foreign heroes of the revolutionary struggle: the Marquis de Lafayette, Friedrich von Steuben, and Tadeusz Kosciusko.

Thomas Jefferson later served as the Society's president for eighteen years— a post, say friends, that he greatly preferred to that of president of the United States. Jefferson was no mere dabbler in scientific subjects. He immersed himself in the study of fossilized mammoths, found across North America, and he even turned one area of the new White House into a "bone room" to hold his collection. He outfitted his Virginia residence, the stately Monticello, with technological innovations of his own contrivance, used the latest in mathematical principles to design a more efficient plow, and personally prepared scientific instructions for the Lewis and Clark expedition to the Pacific Coast.

Initial inspiration for an American philosophical society almost certainly came from John Bartram, but it was Franklin, by now a successful newspaper publisher and astute publicist, who seized the moment. It was high time, he proclaimed in 1743, that "Virtuosi or ingenious Men residing in the several Colonies" came together in a philosophical society in order to improve the collective lot of humankind. Grandly titled a "Proposal for Promoting Useful Knowledge among the British Plantations in America," Franklin's manifesto mandated that this new association—the first to draw membership from across the disparate colonies—be peopled, at a minimum, by a "Physician, a Botanist, a Mathematician, a Chemist, a Mechanician, a Geographer, and a general Natural Philosopher," or all-around scientist, as well as three administrative officers.[6]

The Philosophical Society was to be hosted in Franklin's adopted hometown of Philadelphia, then the largest urban center in North America and convenient midpoint of England's colonial territories. Distant members were encouraged to correspond with the Society and with one another through the regular exchange of letters, commentaries, and learned papers. Franklin offered his own services as the new association's secretary, placing himself at the very hub of colonial scientific exchange, at least until "they shall be provided with one more capable."[7]

After a few false starts and long stretches of outright inactivity, which Franklin blamed on the lassitude of others, the philosophical society gradually began to take root. Philadelphia steadily established itself as America's leading center of scientific inquiry and practical learning, a development that spurred other communities to form societies of their own. In the decades after 1776, nearly one hundred useful knowledge associations were founded across the former colonies, accompanied by a proliferation of journals, newspapers, and books aimed at disseminating the latest technological and scientific break-throughs to the general public.[8]

Among the earliest and most durable was Boston's American Academy of Arts and Sciences, formed in 1780 by John Adams and other local leaders, in a deliberate challenge to Philadelphia's intellectual preeminence. Adams had witnessed the American Philosophical Society firsthand during his tenure at the Continental Congress in Philadelphia, and he returned to his native New England determined that Boston, its largest city, deserved no less.

"In several Particulars they have more Wit than We," Adams admitted in a wartime letter to his wife and confidante, Abigail. "They have Societies, the Philosophical Society particularly, which excites a scientific Emulation, and propagates their Fame. If ever I get through this Scene of Politics and War, I shall spend the Remainder of my days in endeavoring to instruct my Countrymen in the Art of making the most of their Abilities and Virtues."[9] According to its charter of 1780, the mission of the American Academy was "to cultivate every art and science which may tend to advance the interest, honor, dignity, and happiness of a free, independent, and virtuous people."[10] Adams later served as head of the Academy, a position that overlapped with his term as America's second president.

Other useful knowledge societies of varying tenure and importance sprouted up as well. Most were local or regional in scope and intimate enough to allow for regular gatherings of the membership for lectures, to hear reports, and to discuss matters of mutual interest. This reflected the strong Enlightenment preference for scientific study and intellectual debate as personal, face-to-face experience, while at the same time providing a broad cross-section of local society with direct access to useful knowledge.[11]

The Society for the Promotion of Arts, Agriculture, and Economy in the Province of New York, in North America was patterned after the successful Royal Society of Arts, which used prizes and grants to promote new technolo-gies and agricultural innovation. The movement also took hold in Washington, the new national capital; Trenton, New Jersey; Albany, New York; Alexandria, Virginia; and as far south as Carolina and Mississippi and as far west as Kentucky.[12] More specialized knowledge associations, devoted to manufactures, improvements in agriculture, the study of natural history—even a Military Philosophical Society, founded at West Point by a grand-nephew of Franklin—appeared as well.[13]

From Rhode Island to Charleston, South Carolina, subscription libraries, driven by the same practical imperative that fueled the useful knowledge societies, opened their doors to eager readers. Many were inspired by Franklin's own Library Company of Philadelphia, founded in 1731. The charter of the Juliana Library Company of Lancaster, Pennsylvania—one of several libraries outside the provincial capital—proclaimed that the "Promotion of useful Knowledge is an Undertaking truly virtuous and Praiseworthy, and such as flows from the generous Breast alone."[14] Like its counterparts to the north and south, Lancaster's reading public eschewed the works of the classical authorities and Christian divines, the traditional province of the university collections, and gave precedence to books on agriculture, mathematics, mechanics, and other useful topics.

With Franklin's manifesto as its guiding spirit, the movement for useful knowledge left a profound mark on American society and culture, on the very idea of America itself, and, through it, on the world as a whole. Its echoes can be detected in the Declaration of Independence and other acts of the Founding Fathers; in the humming and hissing of the early steam engines on a London bridge that managed to captivate Thomas Jefferson, that dyed-in-the-wool pastoral idealist; in the emergence of grassroots democratic institutions; in the Great Awakening that challenged clerical tradition in the name of do-it-yourself faith; and in the rise of the nation's industrial and technological might, dwarfing anything that Alexander Hamilton and his partisans could have ever imagined. By the end of the nineteenth century, America led the world in both productivity and patented inventions, and the general outlines of its future technological and military supremacy were already clearly visible.

*   *   *

Beginning in Elizabethan times, Europeans habitually invoked the very name America to connote any kind of virgin territory or new field of endeavor. With the coming of the Enlightenment, from the mid-seventeenth century, the New World began to take on a new cast, one that went beyond mere novelty. The critical examination of social, political, and intellectual life during this Age of Reason introduced the search for universal laws that governed both man and the world around him. Among these newfound principles was the notion of a pristine natural order that lay buried under the rotten surface of European life.

The settlement of the New World seemed to offer the promise that man could at last strip away the artificial social and political structures imposed on Europe over the centuries and reveal the true State of Nature. The pursuit of this elusive natural order and the perfected social arrangements that would accompany it—whether the lost biblical Zion sought by the early Puritan colonists of New England or the "self-evident" truths grounded in "the Laws of Nature and of Nature's God" of the Declaration of Independence 150 years later—represents one of the central themes of the American experience.[15]

By breaking with the last remnants of the medieval notion of the universe as an immutable hierarchy, a Great Chain of Being reaching from God at the top, through the angels and man, to minerals and rocks at the bottom, republican theoreticians arrived at an American exceptionalism, one that operated outside outmoded European ideas of history. The Enlightenment philosopher John Locke had declared as early as 1690 that America was not so much new or novel, as it was *original*. Now, the American Revolution had liberated the colonies from Old Europe's ways, and set the stage for the realization of the natural order inherent to the New World. America could fully align itself with the latest scientific precepts of harmony, precision, and progress that paralleled Isaac Newton's revolutionary laws of celestial motion. In doing so, it would surely leave Old Europe behind.

"The learned say it [America] is a new creation and I believe them, not for their reasons, but because it is made on an improved plan," wrote Jefferson, one hundred years after Locke—one of the American's intellectual idols. "Europe is a first idea, a crude production, before the Maker knew his trade, or had made up his mind as to what he wanted."[16] The great seal of the independent United States—a project Franklin and Jefferson pursued together before handing it over to others—carries on its reverse the slogan Novus ordo seclorum, literally "a new order of the ages" and meant, said its author Charles Thomson, secretary to the Continental Congress, to herald the dawn of the American epoch. Four score and seven years later, Abraham Lincoln's most famous speech reminded his fellow citizens that America alone had been "conceived in Liberty."[17]

The roots of such republican certainty predate the long, grueling contest with the armies of the British Crown. First, Americans had to free themselves from a rigid European economy of knowledge that circumscribed their imaginations as surely as England's colonial rule restricted their economic autonomy and limited their political freedoms. America's intellectual grievances, it turns out, were virtually identical to its political and economic ones.

The botanist John Bartram for years felt the repeated sting of Europe's disdain for his efforts at original contributions to the field. Another early American naturalist complained bitterly more than a decade before the Revolution of the "dictatorial powers" exercised by Europe's philosophers and scientists.[18] Others saw their own work expropriated or otherwise plagiarized from across the Atlantic. Even Franklin's groundbreaking electrical experiments at first provoked only laughter and disbelief among the European men of science.

Seen in this way, the American Revolution represents less a turning point than a significant milestone in a journey that began not at Lexington or Concord in the spring of 1775 but in the study circles, public libraries, and the useful knowledge societies that first took shape in colonial cities and towns almost fifty years earlier. It was no accident, then, that the struggle to create *American* science and the struggle to create a free and independent America often went hand in hand.

It was widely accepted at the time that Europe's far-flung colonies would act merely as suppliers of raw materials—seeds of newly discovered plants, narrative accounts of strange diseases, the bones of unknown animals, and so on— for study, classification, and explanation by the natural philosophers back in the mother country. In the eyes of Enlightenment science, the colonists themselves were by their very essence unsuited to the intellectual rigors of natural philosophy. Any true scientific achievement on colonial soil would have to be the work of visiting Europeans, rather than at the hands of native-born Americans. One of the first accounts of North American plants, dating to 1635, was the work of a French botanist relying solely on specimens sent back to Paris.[19] This set the pattern for more than one hundred years.

One leading French naturalist, the Comte de Buffon, famously proposed that climate and other conditions in the New World had led to the inevitable degeneration of its fauna and flora. Buffon's more enthusiastic readers extrapolated from this argument to call into question the virility and intelligence of both America's European settlers and its native inhabitants, the Indians. That sparked a rousing defense of American virtue and vigor from Jefferson, spelled out in his only published book, *Notes on the State of Virginia*.[20]

Then an American diplomat at the French court, the future U.S. president defended colonial achievement in a range of endeavors, from the electrical breakthroughs of Franklin, to the mechanical wonders of David Rittenhouse and the military prowess of General Washington. "As in philosophy and war, so in government, in oratory, in painting, in the plastic arts, we might show that America, though but a child of yesterday, has already given hopeful proofs of genius."[21] He also arranged for the delivery to Buffon's residence of the hides and antlers from robust specimens of New England moose, elk, and deer to underscore his rebuttal. One imposing carcass stood seven feet tall.

Notwithstanding these protestations, however, there was a pervasive sense that the colonists could never aspire to anything more than a subsidiary role in a global economy of knowledge that mirrored Europe's imperialist system. Plants, animals, and other natural phenomena of the New World periphery, as well as their integration into taxonomies, studies, and disciplines—created and enforced in the European capitals and then reexported as scientific knowledge—followed the same pathways as the trade in basic commodities and their subsequent transformation into high-value finished goods for sale back to the colonies.

As early as 1629, the Dutch settlements in New York and New Jersey were formally barred from producing finished textiles or any other woven goods, forcing them to rely on imports from home. Under the British, initial aspirations for American industrial production, such as glassworks in Virginia or iron foundries in Puritan New England, were steadily eroded throughout the eighteenth century by an expanding body of English laws specifically designed to impede colonial manufactures and protect British ones. These trade restrictions paralleled barriers to colonial science erected and then maintained by the Europeans' intellectual prejudice.

✻   ✻   ✻

Like many things "American," the notion of useful knowledge enjoys a strong European—particularly English—pedigree. Franklin's "Proposal for Promoting Useful Knowledge" was inspired by the Royal Society of London for Improving Natural Knowledge, which he saw as both model and future partner. And his appeal to the colonies' "Virtuosi" was no accident, for members of the Royal Society used just that term to describe themselves and their fellow practitioners of scientific and philosophical inquiry.

Almost one hundred years old at the time of Franklin's 1743 manifesto, the Royal Society was then the world's premier scientific association. It had a well-established language, a particular intellectual outlook, and a specific notion of science, all of which Franklin adopted for himself and then consciously emulated in his "Proposal." As early as 1664, the first editor of the Royal Society's journal enthused over those "profitable discoveries" grounded in "solid and useful knowledge"—just the thing needed in the young American colonies, Franklin reckoned, as they sought to secure their place in a new and uncertain universe.

Yet ideas and trends long percolating in English society underwent profound transformation in the hands of the American colonists, for the physical, intellectual, and psychological landscape of the New World was unlike anything back home in Europe. America, it turned out to the surprise of many of the newcomers, was neither the Garden of Eden of the promoters' handbills nor anything like a microcosm of the world they had left behind. Enlightenment ideas of science and notions of useful knowledge, which accompanied many of the early, well-educated settlers, took on an increasingly American hue.

After completing a two-month voyage on the *Mayflower*, a dispirited William Bradford gazed at the American shore only to find himself confronted with a "hideous and desolate wilderness, full of wild beasts and wild men." Bradford lamented that the exhausted Puritans had "no friends to welcome them, nor inns to entertain or refresh their weather-beaten bodies, no houses much less towns to repair to, to seek for succor."[22] Another early settler, at Virginia's Jamestown, challenged his fellows to reconcile both the "felicities" as well as the "miseries" of this strange new land.

The unexpected hardships of famine, water shortages, fraught relations with the native peoples, the difficult and unfamiliar climate, and associated other miseries steadily took their toll on the Puritans' institutions, beliefs, and practices.[23] The first tight-knit religious communities began to disintegrate in the face of economic imperatives and competing responses to the struggle for daily existence. Where they had expected a new Zion graced with "sweet air, fair rivers, and plenty of springs, and the water better than in England," they found only dangerous wilderness, the subjugation of which they soon made a matter of religious duty.[24]

For many of these educated religious dissidents among the new arrivals such a state of affairs demanded a willful, disciplined, and intellectually rigorous approach that could tame the wilderness and secure man's mastery over such unruly lands. In this way, the Puritans tapped into the utilitarian sentiment that pervaded much of seventeenth-century Protestantism.[25] That which was useful in this effort was to be cherished, nurtured, and promoted, while that which simply recalled the Old World sensibilities or were maintained out of habit was best discarded.

Such attitudes steadily took hold across the colonies and were given concrete expression in the laws, institutions, and practices that sprang up in the New World. The development of natural philosophy, what we today call science, faced considerable resistance from the European establishment, with its deep attachment to classical studies and the humanities in general. This was not so in the New World, where the intellectual influence of the Puritans and other religious dissidents was generally unimpeded.[26]

In the towns and cities of North America, artisans, petty merchants, and workers, unfettered by the traditional guild system, eagerly sought to learn new skills through private instruction. Evening classes, created to allow students to attend after their day's work was over, offered training in such practical arts as surveying, bookkeeping, shorthand, and even foreign languages. Public lectures on scientific topics proliferated. Newspapers and specialty journals alike brought word of practical discoveries in science and the latest technology to an increasingly literate America.

One early South Carolina law, typical of the times, mandated instruction "in useful and necessary learning" in the local parish schools. Guidelines for the new province of Pennsylvania, written in 1682, established basic public education and called for bounties or premiums to be paid to "authors of useful sciences and laudable inventions."[27] William Penn, the province's Quaker proprietor, laid out clear views on colonial education: "I recommend the useful parts of mathematics, as building houses, or ships, measuring, surveying, dialing, navigation."[28]

The Reverend Hugh Jones of Virginia, meanwhile, urged an end to reading Greek and Latin works among his students at the College of William and Mary, to be supplanted by concentration on English, Christianity, mathematics, surveying, and navigation. "These are the most Useful Branches of Learning for them," writes Jones, "and such as they willingly and readily master, if taught in a plain and short Method, truly applicable to their *Genius*."[29] Newer institutions of higher learning, now beginning to open across the colonies, adopted a similar orientation toward useful knowledge.

In Philadelphia, the enigmatic Samuel Keimer, a transplanted English dissident and master printer who once employed the young Ben Franklin in his atelier, introduced his readers to useful knowledge in a bid to dispel "Ignorance and Superstition" and promote "the public Good." Keimer, a free spirit and on-again, off-again Quaker, announced that the publication of his forthcoming newspaper would offer subscribers "the richest Mine of useful Knowledge (of the Kind) ever discovered" in America.[30]

Such ideas were particularly welcome in Pennsylvania, where the Quaker sensibilities of William Penn and his associates predominated among the early elite. Quakerism developed amid the religious turmoil of seventeenth-century England, part of a broad response to the authoritarian and corrupt ways of the established Church of England. Central to Quakerism is the belief that God is directly accessible by all, without outside mediation. The intellectual attitudes of Philadelphia's Quaker community—in particular the prohibition on ornamental knowledge, the rejection of an effete clerical class, and support for the empirical study of nature—left its citizens sympathetic to attacks on both the classical canon of European learning and English social convention. In their eyes, the works of the ancient Greeks and those of the medieval Scholastic philosophers had usurped the rightful place of scripture in the imagination of the learned.

It was far better, reasoned the Quakers and other like-minded sectaries, to arm Americans with the practical information they required to make their proper way through the world and to equip them to read the holy book on their own. "Languages are not to be despised or neglected, but things are still to be preferred," declared William Penn.[31] In this same spirit, Franklin announced seventy-five years later, "And for one I confess that if I could find in any Italian Travels a Receipt [recipe] for making Parmesan Cheese, it would give me more Satisfaction than a Transcript of any Inscription from any old Stone whatever."[32]

Philadelphia proved a congenial home to Franklin, who sprang from a long line of independent artisans. There, he found a ready supply of like-minded tradesmen, craftsmen, and "mechanics" eager to engage in civic and political life, to discuss books and philosophical ideas, and to pursue the latest in practical learning. Contemporary English usage defined the mechanic as a practitioner of those "Arts wherein the Hand and Body are more concerned than the Mind," and the term—used at times to convey the sense of "base" or "pitiful"—carried with it residual class prejudice.[33] However, Franklin pointed out in his advice to would-be immigrants, things were very different in the New World.

The shortage of skilled labor in colonial America, the accompanying high wages, and the lack of restrictive regulations, meant that many a master craftsman or mechanic could aspire to become an independent entrepreneur, with considerable economic security, social standing, and political influence. Even the journeyman, noted Franklin, could hope to save enough funds to buy land and become an independent farmer, or to go into other business for himself. "Hence it is that Artisans generally live better and more easily in America than in Europe, and such as are good Economists make a comfortable Provision for Age, & for their Children. Such may therefore remove with Advantage to America."[34]

Franklin earlier based one of his most important economic tracts, "Observations Concerning the Increase of Mankind, Peopling of Countries, &c.," on the notion that America's plentiful supply of cheap land would keep labor scarce, encourage rapid population growth, and otherwise shape colonial society in profound ways. He went on to predict with remarkable accuracy that the American population would double every twenty-five years and surpass that of Great Britain within a century.*

These conditions created ample room for the rise of an independent American artisan class, something lacking at the time in Europe. With its emphasis on real-world problem solving over mathematical precision and on experience over tradition, the movement for useful knowledge in time helped elevate the skills and values of the mechanic to an American social and intellectual ideal. The conflict with Great Britain, in which mechanics' associations often took a leading role, only accelerated these advances.

To Franklin, a printer by trade and a lifelong admirer of skilled craftsmanship, the mechanic's vocation held particular meaning, for his was a self-regulating world, a wholly rational system of cause and effect, of physical laws. "The Husbandman is in honor there, & even the Mechanic, because their

* The essay, circulated first in manuscript form and then published in 1755, was framed as an attack on a new law that restricted iron manufacture in the colonies in order to prop up British exports. Franklin argued that inexpensive land would keep America a rural, agricultural society into the foreseeable future, thus posing no threat to British industry. His demographic projections were to prove far more prescient than his social and economic analysis.

Employments are useful," Franklin informed his foreign readers in "Information to Those Who Would Remove to America." "The People have a Saying, that God Almighty is himself a Mechanic, the greatest in the Universe; and he is respected and admired more for the Variety, Ingenuity and Utility of his Handiworks, than for the Antiquity of his Family."[35]

*   *   *

Amid the company of Revolutionary War figures, Benjamin Franklin stands out—for the range of his experience, the scope of his talents and interests, and the brute tenacity with which he pursued his interlocking goals of self-improvement, social betterment, and, once fully roused, independence from the mother country he had venerated. Franklin's place today as an American icon, reinforced by his comforting portrait on the hundred dollar bill, on postage stamps, in advertising, and on T-shirts, is arguably second to none.

Despite the familiarity that attends such ubiquity, he has long posed something of a literary and historical puzzle. His storied career, his rich symbolic meaning, and his voluminous writings together offer an embarrassment of riches for the reader, the historian, the researcher, or the critic. This has impelled many to parse Franklin into ever more narrow, and thus more manageable, tranches. A quick troll through any major library collection reveals the extent to which these many "Franklins"—scientist, diplomat, aphorist, patriot, humorist, educator, lover, and so on—have taken up permanent residence in the American consciousness.*

Compounding the challenge of locating the "real" Franklin is the looming presence of his unfinished memoir, written in four distinct stages over the course of two decades and never edited or harmonized by its author into a coherent whole.[36] The extant document has conflicting aims. At different times it presents private moral lessons directed at Franklin's family, his own bid for moral perfection, and his significant part in the intellectual life, civic affairs, and politics of the day.

In the assessment of its modern editors, *The Autobiography of Benjamin Franklin* is "not notably accurate." It glosses over some of Franklin's most important political and commercial missteps, frequently disguises his motives, and ignores

---

* The Library of Congress, where the present volume was completed, lists hundreds of titles devoted to distinct aspects of Franklin, his life, and his times, in addition to the flood of general biographies that appear with startling regularity.

serious shortcomings in his personal relationships, most importantly with his wife, Deborah, and estranged son, William.[37] Omissions, inaccuracies, and all, Franklin's autobiography furnished invaluable raw material for the popular, hagiographical accounts that began to appear shortly after his death, establishing the now-familiar outlines of a man who embodied the reassuring virtues of hard work, frugality, religious faith, social responsibility, and scientific curiosity, all wrapped up in an inspirational tale of rags to riches.[38]

Parson Weems, the traveling book salesman who bequeathed us the apocryphal morality play of George Washington and the cherry tree, mined Franklin's memoir in 1818 to produce an enduring portrait of the Philadelphia printer as self-made man, beginning with the *Life of Benjamin Franklin: With Many Choice Anecdotes and Admirable Sayings of This Great Man, Never Before Published by Any of His Biographers.* Other authors followed suit.

Even serious investigators have succumbed to the undeniable charms of Franklin's own story. Max Weber, one of the architects of modern social thought, relied solely on an early German translation of the *Autobiography* to cast Franklin as the exemplar of the Protestant "spirit" of capitalism.[39] Carl Van Doren, prize-winning author of an early scholarly biography of Franklin, called the autobiography a "masterpiece of memory and honesty."[40] However, Van Doren seems to have recognized the wide gulf that often separates the artist from his creation; he hints at one point that Franklin the man has nonetheless remained elusive, not so much a single, identifiable personality as a "harmonious human multitude."[41]

The early popularizations also set the stage for an anti-Franklin backlash. For Herman Melville, Franklin's undoubted accomplishments had come at the unacceptable cost to his soul. "Jack of all trades, master of each and mastered by none—the type and genius of his land. Franklin was everything but a poet," Melville wrote in his satirical novel *Israel Potter.*[42] Mark Twain lamented Franklin's ill effects on generations of young boys, whose fathers were certain to hold up the mythical figure as a salutary example of just how far they could go in life with sufficient hard work and self-denial.[43] D. H. Lawrence, the British novelist and critic, famously skewered him as that "middle-sized, sturdy, snuff-colored Doctor Franklin" out "to take away my wholeness and my dark forest, my freedom" and tuck it away neatly "into his kitchen garden scheme of things."[44]

Still, there is a fruitful path through these many Franklins, one that sets him firmly within the intellectual, social, and political context of his times. The eighteenth century was, in many ways, the Age of Franklin. Not only did his extraordinary life intersect with the great political, social, and intellectual developments of the times, including the birth of the American republic, but his relentless push to expand the reach of news and ideas helped fuel the rapid acceleration of intellectual life across the former colonies and America's rise as a technological and industrial power in its own right.

In this regard, Franklin was both harbinger and mouthpiece for the aspirations of an emerging middle class, educated and increasingly autonomous, and for the nation it would one day come to define. In the words of the eminent historian Carl L. Becker, "He accepted without question and expressed without effort all the characteristic ideas and prepossessions of the century—its aversion to 'superstition' and 'enthusiasms' and mystery; . . . its preoccupation with the world that is evident to the senses; its profound faith in common sense, in the efficacy of Reason for the solution of human problems and the advancement of human welfare."[45]

✻   ✻   ✻

For Franklin and many of the other Founding Fathers, the natural order to which they aspired was captured by the mechanical representation of the planets contained in a wondrous planetarium, or "orrery," crafted in the late 1760s by Rittenhouse, the self-taught astronomer. Here was a complete working model of the universe, its uniform motion humming along, untended, under a watchful system of checks and balances.

"The amazing mechanical representation of the solar system which you conceived and executed, has never been surpassed by any but the world of which it is a copy," wrote Jefferson in a letter to the inventor.[46] Like his comrades, Jefferson saw the Rittenhouse orrery as a product of natural American genius, untouched and untroubled by traditional learning.

In this same spirit, the Founding Fathers came to recognize that anything that interfered with the harmonious workings of American society and the pursuit of happiness by the individuals in it—such as the overreaching actions of the British Crown against its colonies—had to be swept aside. While the useful knowledge societies played no direct role in this revolutionary enterprise, they gave practical expression to the widespread ideas and attitudes that informed first the colonial rebellion and then the creation of a new nation and a new society. One need only glance at the interests, experience, and attitudes among the signatories to the Declaration of Independence and the Founding

Fathers—Franklin, Jefferson, Rush, Adams, Madison, Hamilton, and Charles Carroll among them—to recognize how deeply such notions went to the heart of the American Revolution.

In a letter to Adams in 1816, Jefferson summed up the prevailing sentiments of the revolutionary generation: "We are destined to be a barrier against the returns of ignorance and barbarism. Old Europe will have to lean on our shoulders, and to hobble along our side, under the monkish trammels of priests and kings, as she can."[47] With the final political break with Great Britain, America was now free to shake off the inept meddling of priests and kings and to realize the implicit dream of a natural order—one of harmony and reason—that had been perverted by an imperfect Europe.

Of course, the immediate exigencies of nationhood that followed the successful Revolutionary War left the citizens of this new nation facing an uncertain future. Bereft of many of the institutions of Old Europe, lacking in capital and manpower, without great libraries or universities, and cut off from traditional markets by lingering British hostility and the threat of naval blockade, the new "Free and Independent States" had little recourse but self-reliance and practical study. Franklin's society for useful knowledge, and his many imitators, collaborators, and successors among the "Virtuosi and ingenious Men" of the former colonies, pointed the way to the American future.

Chapter Two

BREAKING THE CHAIN

The great Uncertainty I found in Metaphysical Reasonings disgusted me,
and I quitted that kind of Reading & Study, for others more satisfactory.
—Benjamin Franklin

EVEN BY THE relatively unhurried standards of early eighteenth-century sea
travel, Benjamin Franklin's return voyage from London to Philadelphia in the
summer of 1726 was a long and trying affair. Franklin set off with his mentor
and would-be business partner, the Quaker merchant Thomas Denham, aboard
the *Berkshire* on July 21. Flush with the excitement of the impending journey
home, Franklin reveled in the early days at sea: "Sitting upon the quarter-deck,
I have me thinks one of the pleasantest scenes in the world before me. 'Tis a
fine clear day, and we are going away before the wind with an easy pleasant gale.
. . . On the left hand appears the coast of France at a distance, and on the right
is the town and castle of Dover, with the green hills and chalky cliffs of
England, to which we must now bid farewell."[1]

But Franklin's valedictory note was struck in haste. Poor weather imposed a
series of delays, and it was almost three weeks before the *Berkshire*, its small
cluster of passengers and crew growing more restless by the day, was able to
catch the favorable winds, free itself from the covetous grip of England's port
towns, and at last reach the open sea. Yet despite the tedium—or, perhaps,
because of it—Franklin churned out a "Journal of Occurrences" that relent-
lessly catalogued almost three months at sea.

Franklin, Denham, and their fellow passengers spent most of these first days
touring the little settlements where the ship was forced repeatedly to anchor.
When possible, they passed the nights in inns and took their meals in nearby
taverns, all the while fending off what Franklin had no doubt were the usurious
predations of local merchants dedicated solely to fleecing stranded travelers.

This was particularly the case in their first stop, that "*cursed biting* place" known as Gravesend: "If you buy anything of them, and give half what they ask, you pay twice as much as the thing is worth. Thank God, we shall leave it tomorrow."[2] Periodically, the passengers were rousted from their cozy landlubbers' beds and ferried back in rowboats after word that the *Berkshire* was about to set sail, only to find themselves becalmed once again.

On the Isle of Wight, the party marveled at the grandiose gravesite of a former governor who had drafted his own epitaph for a tomb fashioned from royal porphyry that had once been intended for use by the French king at Versailles. "One would think either that he had no defect at all, or had a very ill opinion of the world, seeing he was so careful to make sure of a monument to record his good actions and transmit them to posterity," sniffed Franklin.[3] Two years later, he took a page from the late governor's lesson in public relations and wrote the words that he proposed adorn his own gravestone. Such matters, Franklin had realized at a very early age, were too important to be left to the whims of history or the vagaries of public sentiment.

Once the *Berkshire* finally got under full sail, Franklin put the long hours of enforced leisure to good use. His nineteen-month stay in England had taught him many things—the fickle ways of love and friendship, the pitfalls of business, the social value of intellectual discourse, the raw power of ideas. Most of all, it had revealed the ways in which the pursuit of useful knowledge as practiced by the London virtuosi, carefully cultivated, documented, and communicated, could both contribute to society at large and advance his own prospects.

Franklin's shipboard activities set a pattern he was to follow in each of the six subsequent Atlantic crossings that he made in his lifetime. In fact, his last voyage—at the age of seventy-nine, after his diplomatic triumphs in Paris on behalf of the newly independent American states—yielded separate scientific papers on the phenomenon of the Gulf Stream, faster and more efficient rigging for sailing ships, and proposed life-saving equipment for mariners and their passengers.[4] For now, he bombarded the experienced officers and crew of the *Berkshire* with questions about naval science, navigation in particular, and placed wagers with his shipmates on the first sighting of land. He diligently recorded the ship's position across the Atlantic, tracked the prevailing winds and other meteorological details, studied an eclipse of the moon, and kept a tally of the fish and seabirds that came and went.

Franklin noted the particular beauty of dolphins, whose "glorious appearance" contrasted so markedly with the "vulgar error of the painters, who always represent this fish monstrously crooked and deformed, when it is in reality as beautiful and well shaped a fish as any that swims." Caught with lures made of candles and feathers to resemble their preferred prey, the flying fish, these creatures also "tasted tolerably well." And he ruminated on the psychological states of his fellow passengers under the stress of a long sea voyage, which, he concluded, reveals the true nature of a man better than any bout of heavy drinking could ever do.[5]

Franklin also made his first tentative foray into the realm of experimental science, a journey he would pursue for the rest of his life. As the ship gradually approached American shores, he fished a strand of seaweed from the ocean and found it encrusted with what he surmised to be embryonic crabs. To find out, Franklin began one of his earliest-known scientific investigations. "I have resolved to keep the weed in salt water, renewing it every day till we come on shore, by this experiment to see whether any more crabs will be produced or not in this manner," he recorded in his diary for September 28, 1726.[6]

The next day, Franklin notes, he "found another crab, much smaller than the former, who seemed to have newly left his habitation. But the weed begins to wither, and the rest of the embryos are dead. This newcomer fully convinces me, that at least this sort of crabs are generated in this manner."[7] This flurry of scientific activity drew to an end two weeks later, when Franklin and his fellow passengers, their bread ration long since reduced to two and a half biscuits per day, reached Philadelphia, exhausted but ecstatic that their ordeal, some eighty-two days in all, was finally over.

✳   ✳   ✳

Franklin, then age nineteen, had arrived in the British imperial capital on Christmas Eve, 1724, aboard the aptly named *London Hope* only to find that he had been betrayed by his putative patron, Pennsylvania governor William Keith. Taken with the young man's obvious talent and bursting ambition—and in need of a sympathetic printer and publicist to help revive his own fading political fortunes—Keith had offered to provide financial backing and letters of introduction to associates in London so that Franklin could refine his professional skills, procure a new press and sets of type, and then return to Philadelphia and go into business for himself.

Keith's offer proved disingenuous. There were no letters of credit, nor any of the other promised correspondence, in the official mailbags on board the *London Hope*, and Franklin now found himself in a strange town with few contacts and even fewer financial resources. On the advice of the fatherly Denham, whom he had first met on this same outbound voyage, Franklin secured work with the city's printers in order to support himself and—or so the plan went—to earn passage back to Philadelphia.

Franklin was already well versed in the printing trade, thanks to his older brother James, in whose workshop he had served a brief and troubled apprenticeship back in their native Boston. His legal assignment to James, formalized in 1718, was the culmination of a painstaking effort by the boys' father, Josiah Franklin, to make sure his sons each had a marketable trade to serve the burgeoning community of Boston. Here, Benjamin had proven a particular challenge, even to a man as resourceful as Josiah Franklin—immigrant tradesman, religious nonconformist, and the father of a prodigious number of children on both sides of the Atlantic.

Josiah was an astute observer of human nature, a clever, curious, and inventive man often sought out by neighbors and even his social betters for advice and counsel.[8] And he was eager to cultivate the best in his many offspring. "At his Table he liked to have as often as he could, some sensible Friend or Neighbor, to converse with, and always took care to start some ingenious or useful Topic for Discourse, which might tend to improve the Minds of his Children," Franklin later recalled.[9]

Josiah's own decision to leave Oxfordshire behind and emigrate to New England in 1683 had been more a matter of rational economic calculation than a direct response to religious persecution against his fellow Puritans, set in motion by the restoration of the monarchy under Charles II in 1650. There was simply not enough work in England, he reasoned, to support the extended Franklin clan, which sprang from a line of dyers, blacksmiths, and farmers.[10] Once in the colonies, Josiah coolly assessed the local market and jettisoned his own specialty as a dyer of silk and other fine cloth and adopted the less-esteemed but more profitable trade of making candles and soap from rendered animal fats, at the "sign of the blue ball" on Milk Street.

Observing that his youngest son was miserable working in the family soap-making business, Josiah began to shop around for an occupation that might catch the boy's fancy. At first, Josiah settled on a clerical career, and he dipped into the family's meager resources to provide the schooling necessary to prepare Benjamin for theological training at Harvard College. "My early Readiness in learning to read . . . and the Opinion of all his Friends that I should make a good Scholar, encouraged him in this Purpose of his," Franklin wrote years later, adding that he could not recall a time when he could not read.[11]

His uncle and namesake Benjamin Franklin, writing from England, celebrated the boy's bright future in sweeping, florid tones: "If the Buds are so precious what may we expect when the fruit is ripe?" Ezra Stiles, a biblical scholar and president of Yale, later recorded Franklin family lore that held that Benjamin was already reading the Bible by age five. He was, marveled Stiles, "addicted to all kinds of reading."[12]

Josiah's plan quickly began to unravel. He had never fully freed himself of nagging doubts about the heavy expense required for a clerical education, as well as the uncertain professional prospects that lay ahead for the boy. The educated man, Josiah reckoned, was often left with little more than "a mean Living" and would have done better to pursue a solid trade instead.[13] He soon pulled Benjamin from Boston Grammar School, despite the boy's sterling promise and rapid rise through the grades, and sent him to private lessons in basic writing and arithmetic. After a total of two years of schooling—the only formal education Franklin would ever receive—father and son were back where they had begun: young Benjamin still needed a suitable trade.

Haunting the father, no doubt, was the memory of one of his older boys, also named Josiah, who had run away to sea. A list of family birthdays compiled by Benjamin as an adult bore only the starkest notation beside the name of his long-lost brother: "Went to sea, never heard of."[14] Benjamin, too, had yearned for shipboard adventure, if nothing else to escape the drudgery of the candle-and-soap trade. His mother, Abiah Folger, was from a whaling family in nearby Nantucket, perhaps fueling the boy's romantic notions of a life at sea.

Already, Benjamin was an accomplished swimmer, a serious student of navigation, and a competent boatman, all of which greatly troubled Josiah, who was determined to find his precocious son a safer profession. "He therefore took me to walk with him, and see Joiners, Bricklayers, Turners, Braziers, &c. at their Work, that he might observe my Inclination, and endeavor to fix it on some Trade or other on Land. It has ever since been a Pleasure to me to see good Workmen handle their Tools."[15]

Josiah briefly attached Benjamin to a relative, a maker of knives and other utensils, before finally apprenticing his youngest son to James, just returned from England with a printing press of his own. After the trial and error of the previous months, it must have been a welcome move, although Benjamin, now age twelve, understandably harbored some reservations about being legally bound to a brother nine years his senior. In addition, he faced the standard restrictions on any apprentice of his day: "Taverns, inns, or alehouses he shall not haunt. At cards, dice, tables or any other unlawful game he shall not play. Matrimony he shall not contract."[16] In return, the master craftsman typically agreed to teach his apprentice the secrets of the trade and to provide "Meat, Drink, Apparel, washing & Lodging, and . . . a complete new suit of Clothes." He was also to instruct his charge in reading and writing.[17]

Benjamin's misgivings proved well-founded. The brothers quarreled frequently, mostly over matters of discipline, and the youngster cut short his apprenticeship in 1723, in violation of his legal obligations, by running away— first to New York and then to Philadelphia—and striking out on his own. But by then Benjamin Franklin had acquired a taste for the vocation that would remain central to his character, and dear to his heart, for the rest of his days. It was also the key to virtually every facet of his public and private lives, for the many aspects of the printing and publishing business proved essential to Franklin's multiple and overlapping careers as aphorist and essayist, scientist, diplomatist, postmaster, investor and patron, civic activist and politician, head of household, and well-to-do landlord.

Franklin himself expressed this organic link with the printing trade when he drafted his own mock epitaph, in 1728, more than six decades before his death:*

The Body of
B. Franklin,
Printer;
Like the Cover of an old Book,
Its Contents torn out,
And stript of its Lettering and Gilding,
Lies here, Food for Worms.
But the Work shall not be wholly lost:
For it will, as he believ'd, appear once more,
In a new & more perfect Edition,
Corrected and amended,
By the Author.[18]

---

* In accordance with his will, Franklin was buried in the Christ Church cemetery, next to his wife, Deborah. A plaque there simply reads, BENJAMIN AND DEBORAH FRANKLIN.

The opening words of his last will and testament put his profession ahead of his other worldly honors: "I, BENJAMIN FRANKLIN, of Philadelphia, Printer, late Minister Plenipotentiary from the United States of America to the Court of France . . ."

In many ways, printing was unique among the contemporary trades. By its very nature, its successful practitioners required something of a worldly outlook. They were, as a result, less insular than members of other craft guilds, which were fundamentally conservative and designed almost exclusively to preserve trade secrets among a limited number of apprentices, journeymen, and masters in order to limit competition.

True, printers also served apprenticeships and they had their own set of skills to protect and pass along to succeeding generations of craftsmen. Nevertheless, the scope of their activities—encompassing what we would distinguish today as the separate endeavors of publishing, marketing, editing, public relations, advertising, and journalism—and their reliance on technological innovation and trends in reading, writing, politics, and scholarship marked them out for greater interaction with society at large. And it was in many of these affiliated realms, all gathered under the general notion of the printer, where Franklin himself excelled.

Somewhat more prosaically, the printing trade also came to the rescue of this restless young man on those occasions when he found himself stranded in an unfamiliar town with no money and no prospects. Such had been the case when Benjamin fled his brother's high-handed behavior for a new life in Philadelphia. And such was the case upon his first arrival in England. Soon he was working as a journeyman in the studio of the respected London printer Samuel Palmer, where Franklin's speed and skill with learned texts—as a compositor, he was able to accommodate quotations in Greek, Latin, and even Hebrew—proved invaluable.

The sheer physicality of the work further enhanced its appeal in Franklin's eyes. Here was an activity worthy of both a strong mind and a strong body. The strapping young printer took after his father—"well set and strong"—and he kept fit by exercising regularly, dabbling in vegetarianism and watching his diet in general, getting plenty of fresh air, and largely abstaining from the bad habits of his workmates, most of whom were "great Guzzlers of Beer." At one point, Franklin positively crows as he recalls his displays of strength in front of his fellow workmen, who berated him over his preference for drinking only water.

"On occasion I carried up and down Stairs a large Form of Types in each hand, when others carried but one in both Hands. They wondered to see from this and several Instances that the Water-American as they called me was stronger than themselves who drank strong Beer."[19] He was also a regular at the theater and "other Places of Amusement" and chased the city women, at one point making an ill-fated attempt to seduce his best friend's mistress.[20] Franklin's London exploits were not limited to the purely physical or the sensual. He also threw himself into the political, social, and religious debates that animated the city's lively coffeehouses, the so-called Penny Universities where a lowly coin bought not only a cup of imported coffee but also access to pamphlets and gazettes, the latest news from café "runners" or criers, and seemingly endless discussion of the day's affairs, developments in science, and other intellectual pursuits.

By the turn of the century, coffeehouses had become a vital part of London's social and intellectual scene. Even the Royal Society lent their learned imprimatur. "The Coffee-Houses make all sort of People sociable, they improve Arts, and Merchandise, and all other Knowledge," concluded a report published in the Society's *Philosophical Transactions* in 1699.[21] These establishments took in mail for regular customers and hosted many of London's clubs, professional associations, and debating societies. Traders in commodities and securities, the so-called stockjobbers, met over coffee to swap shares, make deals, or compare rumors. City physicians—those "dispensers of life and death, who flock together like birds of prey watching for carcasses"—as well as local clerics and visiting American merchants all had their favorite haunts.[22]

As an institution, the coffeehouse provided patrons with something of a respite from the rigid and highly stratified social and economic system that awaited in the world beyond its doors. Here, the rising cohorts of urban professionals, intellectuals, independent merchants, and other businessmen could socialize, debate political, social, and religious issues, and transact business in relative freedom, outside the reach of church, state, or university. Wit, business acumen, political intelligence, and related gossip—rather than formal social standing or birthright—secured access to this café society's most sought-after tables and its liveliest clubs and discussion circles.

For a sharp young man with an impressive reservoir of book learning but little social standing—Franklin was, after all, still a lowly journeyman printer and a colonial hayseed to boot—the leveling atmosphere he found in the coffeehouses seemed made to order. Here, he discovered that his sharp pen and quick wit offered access to some of the city's leading lights, a phenomenon that soothed his vanity and addressed, if not quite quenched, his considerable ambition. On subsequent stays in the imperial capital, the mature Franklin became a mainstay of gatherings of Royal Society members at the Grecian Coffee House and of the progressive Club of Honest Whigs at St. Paul's café.[23]

*   *   *

London's coffeehouses also traded in controversy, reveled in argument, and, on occasion, smacked of sedition and heresy. By now, Franklin was familiar with the most contentious issues of the times, largely through his striking ability to tease complex ideas from the written word. Even as a youngster, Franklin spent what little pocket money he had on books. Later, he haunted the booksellers of Boston, Philadelphia, and London, and he regularly prevailed upon fellow apprentices and journeymen to surreptitiously borrow volumes from their masters' stocks so that he could read them at night and then return them unnoticed in the morning.

Such was the power of books that they often shaped Franklin's outlook on life. Delving into his father's modest collection of religious works, for example, had already led him, by age fifteen, to stray from the family's Puritan traditions. Instead, he numbered himself among the growing ranks of the deists, who believed in a supreme God but rejected any necessary role for revelation or for the infallible scripture said to have recorded it. "Some Books against Deism fell into my hands. . . . It happened that they wrought an Effect on me quite the contrary to that was intended by them: For the Arguments of the Deists which were quoted to be refuted, appeared to me much stronger than the Refutations. In short I soon became a thorough Deist."[24]

Here, young Franklin was not alone. The great Scottish philosopher David Hume underwent a very similar experience, turning to deism after reading polemics against it. In time, Hume would celebrate the philosopher in Franklin. "America has sent us many things—gold, silver, tobacco, indigo, and so forth; but you are the first philosopher, and indeed the first great man of letters, for whom we are beholden to her."[25]

Back home in America, Franklin had already learned that a bookish youth could attract the attention and the patronage of the rich and powerful, no matter his tender age or precarious position in society.[26] According to Franklin's memoirs, the governor of New York sought him out after hearing the extraordinary news that a young man had just arrived by ship from Boston accompanied by "a great many books," and he treated the boy with "great Civility" and showed off his own well-stocked library.[27]

James Logan, one of the founders of the Pennsylvania colony and an accomplished classical scholar, discussed books with Franklin and even allowed him to borrow from his personal collection—then the finest in colonial America. Governor Keith likewise took a personal interest in the abundant talents of the teenage lad, although it was the governor's deceptive offer to set him up in the printing business that had left the would-be protégé almost penniless in London.

What held true in colonial America, with its less-than-rigid social barriers and general, if imperfect, inclination to privilege talent over rank, likewise held true in the cafés and taverns of London. All Franklin needed was an entrée to this heady world of unorthodox ideas, freewheeling debate, and the latest in literary fashion. He found it in a curious little essay of his own contrivance that began as a stunt for a drinking buddy who had sought out Franklin's "*present* Thoughts of the *general State of Things* in the Universe."[28]

At the time, Franklin was setting type at Palmer's for a new edition of a bestselling religious work that argued that morality—and, by analogy, truth itself—is aligned with the natural world and may be discerned by man's reason. The book, *The Religion of Nature Delineated* by William Wollaston, hews closely to the Enlightenment vogue for so-called natural religion, which in keeping with the scientific tenor of the age sought evidence of God and his wisdom in the wondrous order of the natural world. Here, the orthodox Wollaston endeavors to outflank the deists by making room for both Isaac Newton's ironclad laws of motion—and the day's ever-new scientific discoveries in general—and traditional scriptural teachings.

Franklin got right to work on a response, adopting a style not unlike that of a Euclidean proof that establishes a set of propositions, in this case about the nature of God, from which then flows the entire argument, all laid out in what he later called a "Chain of plain Consequences." The finished pamphlet, *A Dissertation on Liberty and Necessity, Pleasure and Pain*, denied any real distinction between good and evil and sees pleasure and pain as binary opposites that control man's behavior as surely as Newton's new laws seemed to regulate the movements of the celestial bodies. In Franklin's youthful hands, then, God himself was little more than a machine. Samuel Palmer, on whose press Franklin discreetly printed one hundred copies, admired the boy's "undoubted Ingenuity" but nonetheless found his unorthodox ideas "abominable."[29]

No doubt anticipating just such a reaction, Franklin concludes his essay on a note of youthful defiance and ascribes the inevitable rejection of its arguments to humankind's natural vanity: "Whatever sooths our Pride, and tends to exalt our Species above the rest of the Creation, we are pleased with and easily believe, when ungrateful Truths shall be with the utmost Indignation rejected. . . . But, (to use a Piece of *common* Sense) our *Geese* are but *Geese* though we may think 'em *Swans*; and Truth will be Truth though it sometimes prove mortifying and distasteful."[30]

Among the very few copies of the *Dissertation* that circulated in the city, one came to the attention of William Lyons, a surgeon and regular at Batson's coffeehouse. He filled the pamphlet's margins with handwritten notes and other critical comments and set out to meet the author. "It occasioned an Acquaintance between us; he took great Notice of me, called on me often, to converse on those Subjects," writes a clearly gratified Franklin.[31] Lyons introduced his young interlocutor to the inflammatory moralist and philosopher Bernard Mandeville, who held court regularly at the Horns alehouse.

The Dutch-born Mandeville, steeped in the republicanism of his native land, had recently achieved considerable notoriety after a British grand jury sought to suppress his latest edition of *The Fable of the Bees*. In it, Mandeville argues that man's private vices, for example the profligate consumption of luxuries, confer important public benefits. More specifically, the pursuit of self-interest, when managed astutely and channeled effectively by political leaders, is vital to the material well-being and overall success of society at large. A lesser-known work, *A Modest Defence of Publick Stews*, endorsed legalized prostitution, albeit in a highly regulated form, and matter-of-factly numbered sexual services among the many commodities in any market economy.*

Later, Mandeville sought to clarify his central argument in *The Fable of the Bees* in an attempt to ward off further criticism or legal troubles: "Private Vices by the dexterous Management of a skilful Politician, may be turned into public Benefits."[32] The often subtle notions hidden beneath Mandeville's satirical

---

* In its archaic usage, stew, or stewe, referred to a brothel, a tavern, or other place of ill repute. Here, Mandeville employs the former meaning.

presentations influenced the works of Adam Smith, David Hume, and other leading Scottish intellectuals, and—with Mandeville's rough edges smoothed away—would later resonate among the rebellious American colonists, with their demands for life, liberty, and the pursuit of happiness.[33]

The pugnacious Mandeville and his circle at the Horns tavern clearly saw the youthful author of *A Dissertation on Liberty and Necessity* as one of their own. After all, Franklin had zeroed in ruthlessly on the essential human arrogance— "Whatever . . . tends to exalt our Species above the rest of the Creation, we are pleased with and easily believe"—that underpinned the orthodox approach to natural religion. For his part, Franklin rejoiced in his newfound celebrity friends. Years later he still fondly recalled Mandeville as a "most facetious entertaining Companion."[34]

Lyons also took Franklin to Batson's coffeehouse to meet Dr. Henry Pemberton, secretary of the Royal Society. Pemberton, who introduced Newton's complex works to a curious and enthusiastic general public, even held out the possibility of a meeting with the revered mathematician. To Franklin's lifelong regret, this never came to pass. Nevertheless, the young American had gained a seat at the table with some of London's most accomplished virtuosi— those philosophers, mathematicians, and inventors who dominated Enlightenment science—as well as its leading essayists and wits.

Through Pemberton, he made the acquaintance of Sir Hans Sloane, soon to succeed Newton as president of the Royal Society. Franklin cannot help but strike a certain note of self-satisfaction in the earliest section of his memoirs, written with a close eye on his personal legacy more than four decades after the event, when he recounts his first meeting with Sloane, a prominent court physician whose famed "Cabinet," or scientific collection, later formed the basis of the British Museum.

"I had brought over a few Curiosities among which the principal was a Purse made of the Asbestos. . . . Sir Hans Sloane heard of it, came to see me, and invited me to his House in Bloomsbury Square, where he showed me all his Curiosities, and persuaded me to let him add that to the Number, for which he paid me handsomely."[35] In fact, a surviving letter to Sloane, dated June 2, 1725, makes it clear that it was Franklin who solicited Sloane's interest in buying the purse and other items. He also resorted to something of a high-pressure sales tactic: "p.s. I expect to be out of Town in 2 or 3 Days, and therefore beg an immediate Answer."[36]

Franklin later numbered Pemberton and Sloane among the prominent acquaintances whom he began to encounter on his early forays into London's intellectual world, a world comprised largely of those physicians, clerics, artisans, scholars, nobles, and businessmen in and around the Royal Society. And it was from this circle that Franklin first gleaned a real appreciation for the value and power of science, and intellectual pursuits in general, as well as an understanding of how such inquiries were conducted, evaluated, and disseminated to one's colleagues.

According to the association's statutes, the Royal Society was formed "to improve the knowledge of natural things, and all useful Arts, Manufactures, Mechanic practices, Engines and Inventions by Experiments."[37] Despite the king's imprimatur, the Royal Society long retained the informal character of the irregular gatherings of scientists and inventors in London and Oxford— many of them dedicated amateurs—from which it had first sprung.[38] The broad scope of members' interests and their diverse social stations proved one of the Society's greatest strengths, and for decades these attributes shaped its investigations into matters well beyond the narrow boundaries of modern science.

"All places and corners are now busy, and warm about this Work," wrote Thomas Sprat, the Society's first historian, in 1667, "and we find many Noble Rarities to be every day given in, not only by the hands of the Learned and professed Philosophers, but from the Shops of *Mechanics*, from the Voyages of *Merchants*, from the Ploughs of *Husbandmen*, from the Sports, the Fishponds, the Parks, the Gardens of *Gentlemen*."[39] The index to that year's volume of the Society's journal, *Philosophical Transactions*, lists recent "undertakings" on everything from: A, "Air, being exhausted, vegetables do not grow" to Y, "Yellow Amber. See Amber."[40]

The success of the Royal Society's project did not depend on "perfect Philosophers" trained in science but relied instead on decidedly amateur enthusiasts. "It suffices," announced Sprat, "if many of them be plain, diligent, and laborious observers: such, who, though they bring not much knowledge, yet bring their hands, and their eyes uncorrupted: such as have their Brains infected by false Images. . . . Greater things are produced, by the *free* way, than the *formal*."[41]

Although Sprat was writing almost five decades before Franklin first began to roam London's coffeehouses and taverns, it is hard to imagine a better candidate for such work than the young colonial printer. Franklin was meticulous, hardworking, observant, broadly curious, and already skilled at recording nuance and capturing subtlety in the written word. What is more, his was a brain largely uninfected with the "false Images" implanted by formal education or tradition. And he would soon have access to the vast unstudied and uncataloged physical wonders of the New World, about which the fellows of the Royal Society—and European science in general—yearned to learn as much as possible.

But if Franklin had much to offer to the new scientific enterprise, so too did the emerging idiom of experimental science and observation have much to give in return. Here was an endeavor that promised to cut across social and educational boundaries, a project in which all who participated—even junior colonial artisans with just two years of schooling—could both advance themselves and contribute to the expanding storehouse of human knowledge. Franklin had already come into contact with such luminaries of British science as Sloane and Pemberton, and he narrowly failed to meet the great Newton himself. Clearly, the pursuit of scientific experimentation and observation promised access to a powerful social, intellectual, and political network that would otherwise remain unattainable.

Yet Franklin's newfound social and intellectual success in the taverns and coffeehouses, as well as his minor dealings in American "Curiosities" and the demand for his services among the city's better printers, could not obscure the growing realization that he was now effectively marooned in London, with few financial resources and no real future. He had left Palmer's printing house for higher pay at John Watt's more prestigious establishment, and he reduced his rent by moving to cheaper digs and negotiating aggressively with his new landlady. Still, he could save no money.

Franklin had recently broken with his American traveling partner James Ralph—later a London-based writer and critic—over his inopportune advances toward Ralph's mistress. This not only cost him Ralph's friendship but also the considerable sum of twenty-seven pounds, which the latter still owed him for living and travel expenses. Notes for the final section of Franklin's never-completed *Autobiography* reveal how much the affair still rankled, sixty years after the fact: "My Diligence and yet poor through Ralph."[42]

Franklin began to have other regrets, chief among them the publication of his underground pamphlet, the *Dissertation on Liberty*, which on reflection led to a disquieting world without any distinction between good and evil. It might make for impeccable logic but it was, he began to realize with alarm, completely unthinkable in moral terms and thoroughly unworkable in social ones. A clearly embarrassed Franklin later wrote to an old friend that he soon refuted the *Dissertation* and then put such matters behind him altogether. He went on to assure his correspondent that he had burned as many copies of the offending pamphlet as he could find to keep them from exercising an "ill Tendency" on his circle of intimates.[43] Just four copies are known to have survived intact.*

Preparing the first installment of his memoirs, an older, more reflective Franklin reached a gentler verdict on the *Dissertation*, dipping into his printer's lexicon to dismiss this "little metaphysical Piece" as one of life's "Errata"—in essence, a mistake in moral typography. Other youthful errata included running away from his legally binding apprenticeship to his older brother; misusing funds that had been left in his care by a family friend; propositioning his best friend's lover; and abandoning Deborah Read—temporarily, as it turned out, for they later married—after having "interchanged some Promises" back in Philadelphia.[44]

Nevertheless, Franklin would spend much of the rest of his long public life seeking to expiate the "great Uncertainty, . . . the wide Contradictions and endless Disputes" he had found in his early pursuit of "the metaphysical Way." And he confessed that he still rued "the horrible Errors I led myself into when a young Man, by drawing a Chain of plain Consequences as I thought them, from true Principles, [which] have given me a Disgust to what I was once extremely fond of."[45]

Here, the exploits of the Royal Society came to the rescue of the remorseful young author of the *Dissertation on Liberty*, for their approach to natural science offered a way out of the moral and ethical dead end posed by this troubling essay. By following his "Chain of plain Consequences," Franklin had worked out a conclusion on the basis of one of more premises or hypotheses—a method known as deductive reasoning—in this case about the nature of God.

Conversely, the inquiries of the London virtuosi tended to work in the other direction. They first made observations and collected experimental data and

---

*   The extant copies are housed at the British Museum, the Library of Congress, Yale University Library, and John Carter Brown University Library. Benjamin Franklin, *Autobiography* 2003: 96, n7.

only then proceeded to construct a reasoned argument or theory. This method, so-called inductive reasoning, has long tantalized philosophers: does it really lead to knowledge? Critics challenge both the reliability of generalizing from a limited number of observations and the underlying assumption that what we might term physical laws will continue to operate in the future as they have apparently always acted in the past.

Nevertheless, this approach is a good proxy for the way we humans perceive the natural world and act upon our experiences. As such, it appealed directly to Franklin and other educated laymen, for it allowed them to make observations and carry out experiments in the course of their daily lives without necessarily constructing "Hypotheses and . . . imaginary Systems." The farmer, the printer, or the carpenter, as much as the learned gentleman of leisure, could now contribute to the growing body of useful knowledge. Moreover, they were inspired by the fact that the leading scientists and philosophers of the Enlightenment had left no doubt that experimentation and observation could produce definitive truths.[46]

Franklin and his collaborators were avid readers of Newton's *Opticks*, published in 1704. This popular book clearly spelled out the value of experimentation, and it was far more accessible to these amateur scientists than his more complex theoretical work, with its heavy reliance on higher mathematics. Franklin was also a careful student of Theophilus Desaguliers's *A Course in Experimental Philosophy* (1734–44), an illustrated work that showed the use of different types of scientific apparatus.[47]

For the rest of his life, Franklin would eschew the deductive approach that had led him into such difficulties with the *Dissertation*. In its place, he championed the inductive methods of Europe's new scientists, applying them to his world-class research on electricity and sharing them with others at the forefront of the American pursuit of useful knowledge.[48]

But there were other things weighing on Franklin's mind. Foremost was the burning desire to better his modest station in life. On this score, Franklin's first road trip to London had been a failure: he would not after all be heading home as the proud owner of a new printing press and sets of type, able to go into business for himself in the fastest-growing city in the colonies. Throughout his stay in the capital, money had remained a steady worry. At one point, Franklin seriously considered a proposal to tour Europe and support himself by giving swimming lessons to sons of the nobility. He had already taught two friends, including a fellow printer, how to swim, and several London gentlemen sought instruction after witnessing Franklin's "many Feats of Activity both upon and under Water, that surprised and pleased those to whom they were Novelties."[49] Typically much of the inspiration had come straight from a book: *The Art of Swimming*, by Melchisédec de Thévenot, the much-traveled inventor of the spirit level and librarian to the French king.

Once again, Franklin turned for advice to Thomas Denham, the Philadelphia merchant, who headed off Franklin's teaching scheme. "I was once inclined to it. But mentioning it to me good Friend Mr. Denham, with whom I often spent an Hour, when I had Leisure. He dissuaded me from it, advising me to think only of returning to Pennsylvania, which he was now about to do."[50] The Quaker merchant then made Franklin a counter-offer. He would take on the young man as a clerk in his Philadelphia firm, with the prospect that one day Franklin could trade for his own account. He even offered to stake Franklin the ten pounds for ship's passage as part of their future business relationship.

"The Thing pleased me, for I was grown tired of London, remembered with Pleasure the happy Months I had spent in Pennsylvania, and wished again to see it," according to Franklin's account. "Therefore I immediately agreed, on the Terms of Fifty Pounds a Year, Pennsylvania Money; less indeed than my present Gettings . . . but affording a better Prospect."[51] The pair soon set about procuring goods and working out contractual arrangements for their new venture and then boarded the *Berkshire* for the return home.

Even after he left behind the charred remains of his *Dissertation* and set off for a new life back in Philadelphia, Franklin remained intent on exorcising the lingering effects of this particular erratum. The result was, in part, the moral code spelled out in what he called his plan of conduct, with which he busied himself during the long days of sea travel when he was not tending to his early experiments and recording his meticulous observations. This program ushered in a new and lasting turn in Franklin's outlook, activities, and pursuits, for its exhortations to do good—rather than to *think* well—brought a pronounced emphasis on the sociable and the workable at the expense of the purely logical.

"I grew convinced that *Truth, Sincerity and Integrity* in Dealings between Man and Man, were of the utmost Importance to the Felicity of Life, and I formed written Resolutions . . . to practice them ever while I lived."[52] In the assessment of one student of American thought, Franklin's only real recourse was to consign the metaphysics of his *Dissertation on Liberty* to the flames and start anew: "A world without a belief in virtue does not work. A machine that does not work is thrown out. . . . A philosophy that does not work is no philosophy at all."[53]

Despite the professional setbacks, ever-present financial worries, and a general feeling of disappointment at the time, Franklin would later come to recognize that his eventful year and a half in London had provided an important prelude to the scientific, social, and political successes to come. "Though I had by no means improved my Fortune. But I had picked up some very ingenious Acquaintance whose Conversation was of great Advantage to me, and I had read considerably."[54]

Chapter Three

THE LEATHER APRON MEN

Pennsylvania is heaven for farmers, paradise for artisans, and hell for officials and preachers.

—Gottlieb Mittelberger

THE CITY TO which Franklin returned in the autumn of 1726 was on the cusp of a remarkable boom. No longer the idyllic "green country town" in the mind's eye of its founder, William Penn, Philadelphia was now the fastest growing of the major British settlements along the Eastern Seaboard.[1] Soon, it would leave the others—Boston, Newport, New York, and Charleston—far behind in terms of commercial power, economic development, and political and cultural influence.

By 1730, Pennsylvania province was home to around 51,000 colonists. This population would more than double to almost 120,000 in 1751, and double again to 240,000 two decades later.[2] While the birthrate in the North American settlements was high in comparison with Europe, much of this rapid population growth was due to the tide of immigration, which by its very nature promised to upend the established social order. "The rich stay in Europe, it is only the middling and the poor that emigrate," reported J. Hector St. John de Crèvecoeur, a French immigrant and country gentleman in his *Letters from an American Farmer*, begun shortly before the Revolution and published in 1782.[3]

Philadelphia seemed to take this dizzying growth in stride. On its face at least, the city appeared an orderly, well-run sort of place, for it lacked much of the haphazard development and swelling urban chaos that characterized its northern rivals Boston and New York. The Scottish physician Alexander Hamilton (not the Founder of the same name), a transplant to Annapolis, Maryland, recorded impressions of Philadelphia in his travel account of 1744, the *Itinerarium*: "The plan or platform of the city lies betwixt the two rivers

Delaware and Schuylkill, the streets being laid out in rectangular squares which makes a regular, uniform plan, but upon that account, altogether destitute of variety."[4]

Other civic features of city life that caught the doctor's eye included the fashioning of painted cloth awnings to shield buildings from the sun and the regular practice of pouring cold water on the hot, dusty streets. "They are stocked with plenty of excellent water in this city, there being a pump at almost every 50 paces distant. There are a great number of balconies to their houses where sometimes the men sit in a cool habit and smoke."[5]

The German schoolmaster and organist Gottlieb Mittelberger, writing several years later in *Journey to Pennsylvania*, also remarked on Philadelphia's deliberate design: "The city is very large and beautiful, and laid out in regular lines, with broad avenues and many cross-streets. . . . It takes almost a whole day to walk around the city; and every year approximately three hundred new houses are built."[6] Among its most prominent features were the central market and the fine wharves—numbering sixty-six along two miles fronting the Delaware River by 1760—which were central to the city's economic health and thus carefully maintained.[7]

Like many other visitors, Hamilton was particularly struck by the residents' almost single-minded dedication to making money. At one point, he notes with alarm how the shops beneath his boardinghouse window regularly opened as early as five A.M. A member of a visiting delegation from Virginia esteemed Philadelphia as rich and vibrant a trading center as any in the colonies. "The days of Market are Tuesday and Friday," wrote William Black, "when you may be Supplied with every Necessary for the Support of Life throughout the whole year, both Extraordinary Good and reasonable Cheap, it is allowed by Foreigners to be the best of its bigness in the known World, and undoubtedly the largest in America."[8] And at least one quietist religious leader lamented the fact that Philadelphia's youth had long since forsaken the old "plain" ways of their forebears and adopted a worldly taste for cloaks and other clothes made of fine cloth, and "even velvet."[9]

Despite the hustle and bustle all around him, Hamilton, something of a bon vivant, found Philadelphia dour and its residents taciturn in the extreme, qualities he assigned to the town's Quaker origins. After one dinner party, he grouses that the guests simply grumbled about low prices for their grain and refused to be drawn on any other topic. "I never was in a place so populous where the *gout* [taste] for public gay diversions was so little. There is no such thing as assemblies of the gentry among them, either for dancing or music. . . . Their chief employ, indeed, is traffic and mercantile business which turns their thoughts from such levities."[10] Even the town's lone public clock sported nothing more than a plain dial, devoid of markings in keeping with the Quaker distaste for ornamentation.

All attempts by William Black and his colleagues to hold a farewell ball in the city failed miserably, for they "could find none of the female sex in a humor for it."[11] After one particularly trying day, a portion of which was spent auditing the "absurdities" of a Sunday sermon that he found "contradictory or repugnant to our human reason," Hamilton was only able to relax when he accompanied some fellow Scots to a tavern. "We dismissed at eleven o'clock after having regaled ourselves with music and good viands and liquor."[12]

The bright prospects that clearly lay ahead for the city and its surrounding province of Pennsylvania brought with them a number of important economic and political changes that began to open up new opportunities for social advancement, intellectual betterment, and personal enrichment. This transformation was driven by shifting demographics, the accelerating local economy, and the rapid expansion of foreign and intercolonial trade—all accompanied by steadily increasing demands for greater political and social power among emerging elements of this new society.

Penn, who in 1681 received the vast province in settlement of a royal debt owed to his late father, had proven a highly effective recruiter and entrepreneur. His promise of religious tolerance and relative political freedom in the colony, as well as the availability of land on favorable terms, attracted a steady flow of European immigrants into the city and, from there, into the rich farming regions of the valleys beyond. Large numbers of other religious nonconformists, chiefly from England, Ireland, and Germany, joined Penn's fellow Quakers.

Among the most notable of the early German arrivals was the pietist lawyer Francis Daniel Pastorius, local agent for the Mennonites and other religious dissidents seeking "a quiet, godly & honest life in the howling wilderness" of Pennsylvania.[13] Pastorius negotiated the purchase of land from Penn for the large immigrant settlement of Germantown, later absorbed into the city of Philadelphia proper. By one estimate, Germans comprised around one third of the province's population in 1775, by which time Philadelphia was already reckoned among the largest cities in the British Empire.[14]

As a result of such startling growth, the city's Quakers found themselves in the minority, representing just one quarter of the city's population by 1750, and considerably less twenty years later. Nevertheless, members of the Society of Friends long held their near monopoly on social and economic influence, even as the German influx brought with it a highly skilled agricultural and manufacturing workforce.[15]

This Quaker elite flourished along with the burgeoning volume of trade. Drawing on the rich production in the province's agricultural heartland, as well as that of neighboring colonies, including western New Jersey and the Delaware Valley, local merchants shipped wheat and flour, pork, beef, flax, and lumber, among other products, up and down the seaboard and overseas. The large southern plantations, which often relied on a single cash crop, such as tobacco or indigo, provided considerable demand for food and other necessities from the Middle Colonies, shipped from the thriving port at Philadelphia.

In return, the city's merchants imported quantities of molasses, rum, sugar, and wine. According to Franklin's own "surprising though authentic" reckoning, rum imports exceeded 212,000 gallons in 1728, and taverns outnumbered churches by ten to one. The favorite drink was known as cider royal, fresh cider fermented with applejack.[16] Philadelphia enjoyed a highly favorable balance of trade, in part due to its growing artisan class, which was largely able to meet local demand for finished goods without extensive reliance on expensive British imports. Black market—and thus highly lucrative—commerce with the Dutch and French settlements in the Caribbean, in violation of British trade regulations, further enriched these wily merchants.[17]

With their firm grip on much of this mercantile activity, the Quakers were able to retain considerable influence on everything from politics and defense policy to matters of public taste—in books and education, in manners and forms of address, and crucially in work habits, even as their proportion of the city population declined precipitously. It was membership in these same commercial circles to which Franklin had aspired when he entered into his business alliance with Thomas Denham, the Quaker merchant. However, Denham took ill after their lengthy return voyage from London on the *Berkshire* and later died. With Denham's support gone, Franklin's career in trade was over almost before it had even begun.

Once again at loose ends, Franklin returned to the printer's craft to seek his fortune, a development that thrust him firmly into the ranks of Philadelphia's middle class—the artisans, farmers, shopkeepers, mechanics, and other skilled workers—who were just beginning to carve out a prominent place for themselves in provincial society. The European guild system, which had allowed the ruling nobility to keep the artisans in check for centuries through rigid regulation, never really took hold in the American colonies.

With labor of all types in short supply, colonial tradesman, such as Franklin's father, Josiah, were increasingly free to choose their craft and pursue their business outside of any meaningful government or social control. This same freedom allowed those interested to acquire additional skills and supplemental knowledge through educational lectures, evening vocational courses, and similar projects aimed at artisans and workingmen.

In fact, notes historian Gordon S. Wood, the first third of the eighteenth century saw the rapid emergence of a colonial middle class that shattered what had long been a rigid social division between "gentlemen and plebes." Many in this rising social cohort acquired considerable wealth and, with it, greater intellectual curiosity and political sophistication about the world around them, as well as the necessary leisure time to devote to these new pursuits.[18] Printers such as Franklin stepped in to meet the growing demand for new information, ideas, and opinions expressed in pamphlets, books, and newspapers. This was particularly the case in Philadelphia, with its vibrant economy and seemingly boundless promise.

Equally important, William Penn had bequeathed the colony the strong humanitarian streak that ran throughout his Quaker faith, as well as through Franklin's later social activism: "True Godliness does not turn out Men into the World but enables them to live better in it and excites their Endeavors to mend it," Penn declared in *No Cross No Crown*, written while a temporary prisoner in the Tower of London.[19]

Traditional Quaker emphasis—shared by the Puritans in New England—on the dignity of labor, on a job well done, enhanced the social and political standing of the craftsman in Philadelphia and throughout the province.[20] And it was here that Franklin found not only talented and willing collaborators, particularly among other skilled artisans and mechanics, but also a host of public issues, social problems, and political matters that demanded attention.

This future metropolis was already suffering from considerable growing pains, exacerbated by a cumbersome political system that tended to suffocate decision making under the combined weight of the Penn family, by then its mostly absentee proprietors, and their entrenched local rivals. Politics in the province was also plagued by the hidebound attitudes of many of its leading citizens, who were ill prepared to manage the city's rapid transformation from modest colonial settlement to major urban center.

William Penn's son Thomas assumed active control of the province shortly after the death of his father in 1718, and he and his agents soon began to squeeze the colony financially in an attempt to get out from under the family's large debts. Thomas also turned his back on his father's idealized vision of religious liberty and pluralism. He even married an Anglican and left the Quakers for the establishment Church of England—moves that only exacerbated tensions between the increasingly assertive city fathers and the proprietary family. Whereas the younger Penn and his siblings saw the colony as little more than a cash cow, the province's homegrown commercial and political leaders, as well as its rising middle class, were determined to build a vital, pluralist, and increasingly autonomous community.

The resulting stalemate meant that the provincial government was generally unable to address many of the ills common to eighteenth-century city life. The streets were unpaved, poorly lit, and frequently a mess or, in bad weather, simply impassable. Police protection and fire service were sorely lacking. Sanitation was haphazard and disease was rampant, as were mosquitoes and other pests. Education remained firmly in the hands of the city's fragmented religious groups and rival denominations, greatly complicating efforts to create anything like a unified school system, a provincial university, or other institutions able to meet the needs of America's foremost city.

Hamilton's travel diary paints a picture of a boomtown punctuated with unseemly rubbish heaps, scrap lumber, and half-built houses. He also fretted that this wealthy trading colony was incapable of defending itself from the threat posed by pirates and privateers, or by England's increasingly jealous European rivals, France and Spain. "Here is no public magazine of arms nor any method of defense, either for city or province, in case of the invasion of the enemy," Hamilton noted with disapproval. "This is owing to the obstinacy of the Quakers in maintaining their principle of non-resistance. It were a pity but they were put to a sharp trial to see whether they would act as they profess."[21]

As with other itinerant chroniclers, Alexander Hamilton, the good-time doctor, and Gottlieb Mittelberger, the organ master, recorded their passing observations of Pennsylvania life, issued their judgments, and then quit the scene. The former returned to his country medical practice, while the latter sailed back to Germany. There would be no such withdrawal for Benjamin Franklin. Rather, his recent disavowal of "metaphysical Reasonings" now impelled him toward a new worldview, one that emphasized good works over clever words, action over theory, and collective, that is social, endeavors over the internal life of the mind.

Philadelphia appeared to offer particularly fertile soil for this newfound zeal for social action, that is, for those felicitous "Dealings between Man and Man." Coursing throughout Franklin's thinking were the broad notions of science, and of useful knowledge in general, that he had absorbed from the "very ingenious Acquaintance" made in London, as well as from the "considerable" reading that had already established itself as a lifelong habit. Virtually all of Franklin's subsequent public life—not just his famous investigations into electricity, the Gulf Stream, and other natural phenomena, but also his political and social writings, his civic participation and philanthropy, his publishing enterprise, the homespun aphorisms of Poor Richard, the relentless networking and knowledge sharing—would reflect the underlying Enlightenment idea of "science."

One of Franklin's favorite authors, the Englishman John Ray, once imagined God's charge to the natural philosopher as he sends him out into the world: "Go thither . . . and bring home what may be useful and beneficial to thy Country in general, or thyself in particular."[22] Ray, whose work Franklin later recommended as indispensible for the education of colonial youth, went on to align the work of the natural philosopher not just with observation, collection, and experimentation, but also with social action in the form of meetings, the sharing of information, and mutual assistance.[23]

✻   ✻   ✻

Franklin found in the work of John Ray a master blueprint for approaching the challenges facing both his adopted city and his fellow tradesmen, an approach dominated by the free and open exchange of ideas and findings, as well as a general preference for practical solutions over theoretical principles. He routinely declined to seek patents or otherwise profit directly from his various innovations, such as the Franklin stove.

On occasion, he took this enthusiasm for practical knowledge and experience to such an extreme as to privilege it over any search for underlying causes or physical laws: " 'Tis of real Use to know, that China left in the Air unsupported will fall and break; but how it comes to fall, and why it breaks, are Matters of Speculation. 'Tis a Pleasure indeed to know them, but we can preserve our China without it."[24]

By the autumn of 1727, Franklin was ready to launch his first significant social venture, the Leather Apron Club. This society grew out of an earlier grassroots organization, the Tiff Club, created by William Keith, the recently ousted governor of Pennsylvania and the unreliable patron of Franklin's first London adventure. Tiff Club members were known as leather aprons, a reference to their social base among the artisans, craftsmen, and petty merchants.* Keith's populist tendencies and general rabble-rousing alarmed the well-to-do Quaker grandees, prompting one of their number to dismiss these unwanted intruders in the political arena as "new, vile people . . . they may be truly called a mob."[25]

Franklin's own group, soon known simply as the Junto, combined the conviviality of a private drinking club with the advantages of a mutual-aid society, the moral and intellectual self-improvement of a discussion circle, and the altruism of a civic association. Membership was restricted to twelve and proceedings were conducted in secret, all the better to advance participants' projects, facilitate planning, and pursue career advancement; it also protected the Junto, argued Franklin, from awkward solicitations for membership from friends and associates.

From the outset, the club revolved around the printer Franklin and other proud wearers of the leather apron. These included the glazier Thomas Godfrey, a self-taught mathematician and inventor of an improved quadrant for navigation; the surveyor Nicholas Scull; the shoemaker, geographer, and sometime astrologer William Parsons; and William Maugridge, "a most exquisite Mechanic, and a solid, sensible Man."[26] Also taking part were the prosperous silversmith Philip Syng; a merchant's clerk; several journeymen printers from Franklin's professional cohort; and the odd gentleman of fortune. Most would remain in Franklin's inner circle for the rest of their lives.

Gatherings of the Junto were held initially at the Indian King Tavern on Market Street, one of the oldest of the drinking establishments that were

---

* To avoid confusion, I have capitalized Leather Aprons when referring to specific members of Franklin's club by the same name and used the lower case when referring more generally to the artisans, craftsmen, and mechanics who made up an incipient middle class in early America.

integral to Philadelphia civic life, not unlike the London coffeehouses of Franklin's youth. Here, out-of-town visitors could find lodgings and locals could hold meetings, attend concerts, or sample the latest news and gossip. The Masonic lodge, another Franklin project, later held some of its earliest meetings at the Indian King, and the final order to evacuate American forces and leave the town to the advancing British in September of 1777 was issued from the bar.

The Junto met each week to discuss the personal and professional advancement of its members, as well as the prevailing idiom of science, or natural philosophy, and the language of social improvement. "The Rules that I drew up required that every Member, in his Turn, should produce one or more Queries on any point of Morals, Politics, or Natural Philosophy, to be discussed by the Company," recalled Franklin.[27] In addition, each participant was expected to deliver an original paper once every three months.

Junto members also took a series of oaths: to affirm their unequivocal respect for their colleagues; to declare their sincere love for humankind, "of what profession or religion so ever"; to act doggedly and impartially in the search for truth; and to disavow the notion that anyone be harmed "in his body, name or goods, for mere speculative opinions, or his external way of worship." Each of these solemn pledges, Franklin suggested, should be preceded by a "Pause . . . while one might fill and drink a Glass of Wine." Once a month, except in wintertime, the Junto gathered outdoors on a Sunday afternoon for calisthenics, the physical embodiment of Franklin's lifelong concern with fitness and health. They even had their own club song, to be "hummed in Consort, by as many as can hum it."[28]

To help guide the meetings, Franklin drafted twenty-four questions to be reviewed by all in the morning as preparation for that night's session. "Have you met with anything in the author you last read, remarkable, or suitable to be communicated to the Junto? Particularly in history, morality, poetry, physic [medicine], travels, mechanic arts, or other parts of knowledge?" reads one. "Do you think of anything at present, in which the Junto may be serviceable to *mankind*? To their country, to their friends, or to themselves?" asks another. Additional queries focused more narrowly on personal advancement, soliciting accounts of extraordinary business acumen that might be emulated, or cautionary tales of moral failings and commercial missteps to be avoided at all costs.[29]

Among the most pressing problems facing the province of Pennsylvania at the time was a persistent shortage of currency, mostly in the form of gold, silver, and copper coins. This benefited the rentier class that generally presided over local affairs but acted as a serious barrier to the advancement of men such as Franklin and his fellow tradesmen, all of whom were forced to borrow to finance their businesses. The city's workers, frequently in debt and at times hard-pressed even to collect those cash wages due them, also suffered from the lack of ready currency, and the province's general economic activity lagged as a result. Not surprisingly, the Leather Apron Club took up agitation for the introduction of paper notes and discussed the topic in depth at their private meetings.

Franklin had only recently opened his own workshop, advertised to the public as "the New Printing-Office, near the Market," with financial support from his buddies in the Junto. One of the Quaker members further advanced this risky enterprise—Philadelphia already had two established printers and many in town expected the new venture to fail—by securing a lucrative printing job from the Society of Friends, at the expense of one of Franklin's business rivals. After the recent disappointments in London, particularly the failure of Governor Keith to provide promised financing, Franklin had at last realized his dream of going into trade for himself.

He wasted no time in seeking to establish his reputation as a competent printer and reliable business partner, not only working long hours into the night but also making sure he was seen to do so. Ever eager to promote himself in the eyes of the Philadelphia elite, Franklin would on occasion purchase paper stock from city shops and then parade it through the streets in a wheelbarrow, publicly underscoring his commitment to physical labor as well as his ability to pay for the supplies he needed.

Benjamin Rush, the prominent physician, revolutionary, and Franklin protégé, lampooned the prevailing class notions that separated the gentleman from other more honest walks of life: "If a merchant be a gentleman he would sooner lose fifty customers than be seen to carry a piece of goods across the street."[30] But Franklin's tactics began to pay off, and the Philadelphia business leaders who wined and dined at the Every-night Club began to take notice of the young man still in his workshop as they returned to their homes late in the evening.

Franklin now controlled an important public outlet for his ideas and those of the Junto. The immediate result was the anonymous pamphlet, *A Modest*

Enquiry into the Nature and Necessity of a Paper-Currency, one of the earliest publications from this new press. Here, Franklin and the Leather Aprons give powerful voice to the interests and aspirations of the city's artisans and workers on one of the most important questions of the day. They were also carrying on in the spirit of William Keith, the former governor, and the members of his Tiff Club, who had lobbied for paper money.[31]

A Modest Enquiry is a work of considerable economic sophistication in which Franklin formulates—to the delight 130 years later of no less a political economist than Karl Marx—a coherent labor theory of value: "Trade in general being nothing else but the Exchange of Labor for Labor, the Value of all Things is . . . most justly measured by Labor."* Franklin then asserted that it is the workmen and artisans—the leather aprons—who represent *"the chief Strength and Support of a People"* and that the present circumstances penalize them unfairly and will force them to leave the province, at great cost to society as a whole.

"For what can be more disheartening to an industrious laboring Man, than this, that after he hath earned his Bread with the Sweat of his Brows, he must spend as much Time, and have near as much Fatigue in getting it, as he had to earn it? . . . *A Plentiful Currency will encourage great Numbers of Laboring and Handicrafts Men to come and Settle in the Country,* by the same Reason that a Want of it will discourage and drive them out."[32]

The members of the Junto were well aware of opposition to the issuance of paper currency among the wealthy and powerful, who feared that this would lead to inflation and eat away at the value of the interest payments they received from their many debtors. And so the Leather Apron men also argued that easier credit flowing from an enlarged money supply would accelerate construction, enhance trade, and strengthen other commercial activity. This would more than make up for any losses in the reduced value of interest payments.

---

*   "The first sensible analysis of exchange value as labor-time, made so clear as to seem almost commonplace, is to be found in the work of a man of the New World," wrote Marx. "That man is Benjamin Franklin, who formulated the fundamental law of modern political economy . . . when a mere youth." Karl Marx, *A Contribution to the Critique of Political Economy* [1859], translated by N. I. Stone (Chicago: Charles H. Kerr, 1904), 62. It seems likely, however, that Franklin developed his thinking on the subject from the earlier work of the Puritan reformer William Petty. See I. Bernard Cohen, *Science and the Founding Fathers* (New York: W. W. Norton, 1995), 151.

The proposed currency would be in essence "Coined Land," that is, bills backed by increasingly scarce provincial land that would ensure the value of the new paper money. Throughout the *Modest Enquiry*, the Junto's yardstick is clearly social utility: "I think it would be highly commendable in every one of us, more fully to bend our Minds to the Study of *What is the true Interest of* PENNSYLVANIA."[33]

The partisans of paper currency eventually prevailed in the Pennsylvania Assembly over the interests of the province's financial elite, and the grateful victors gave a contract to print the notes to Franklin, their most articulate and persuasive advocate. "My friends there, who conceived I had been of some service, thought fit to reward me by employing me in printing the money: a very profitable job and a great help to me. This was another advantage gained by my being able to write."[34] Soon, he was also printing the Pennsylvania colony's laws, another lucrative commission, as well as producing currency for neighboring Delaware and New Jersey. Additional government contracts followed.

*   *   *

The successful efforts of the Leather Apron men on behalf of paper currency represented their initial foray into public affairs, and it set the pattern for Franklin's lifetime of social, political, and intellectual activism. First of all, the campaign itself represented a collaborative endeavor, with Franklin the driving force and ringleader but others playing vital supporting roles. Many of the points advanced in his pamphlet were hashed out at the regular meetings of the Junto, allowing members to sharpen their thinking and argumentation before going public. This soon became common practice among the Leather Apron men.

The Franklin stove first took shape after a debate within the Junto over how best to combat the persistent problem of smoky chimneys and to reduce the consumption of increasingly scarce firewood. This same circle later deliberated the appropriate use of another Franklin invention, the lightning rod, posing the question: "May we Place Rods on our Houses to guard them from Lightning without being Guilty of Presumption?" In other words, did the installation of a lightning rod on a home, church steeple, or ship's mast amount to interference in God's plan, or otherwise undercut his agency and power, as some conservative critics had charged?

The Junto did not dismiss divine providence but simply argued that "in Reason's Eye Lightning or Thunder is no more an Instrument of Divine

Vengeance than any other of the Elements." And it was unequivocal in its endorsement of this useful new technology: "So far from being Presumption to use [the lightning rod], it appears foolhardiness to neglect it."[35] Franklin propagated this same view in the second series of his famous almanac, *Poor Richard Improved*, in which he suggested a role for divine agency in the discovery of such useful protection against "Mischief by Thunder and Lightning."[36]

Franklin's New Printing-Office enabled him to present his views and those of the Junto directly to interested residents of the province. Franklin's subsequent publishing ventures, chiefly the *Pennsylvania Gazette* newspaper and *Poor Richard's Almanack*, cast even wider nets. "I endeavored to make it [the *Almanack*] both entertaining and useful. . . . And observing that it was generally read, scarce any Neighborhood in the Province being without it, I considered it as a proper Vehicle for conveying Instruction among the common People, who bought scarce any other Books."[37] *Poor Richard's Almanack* and its successor, *Poor Richard Improved*, sold as many as ten thousand copies a year and served as a virtual cash machine for the man who was literally printing money.

The newspaper was perhaps even more important for shaping public opinion. "I considered my Newspaper also as another Means of Communicating Instruction, and in that View frequently reprinted in it Extracts from the [British magazine] *Spectator* and other moral Writers, and sometimes published little Pieces of my own which had been first composed for Reading in our Junto."[38] Small broadsheet newspapers such as Franklin's *Gazette* proved increasingly popular in the colonies. Almost two dozen such publications were launched between 1713 and 1745.[39]

Likewise, Franklin's successful lobbying for the position of America's deputy postmaster was predicated, in part, on his desire to use its official privileges to dispatch his growing scientific correspondence free of charge. Of course, the steady salary and inherent prestige were very real inducements. But, as Franklin explained to a London colleague, this new, more senior office—he had been Philadelphia's local postmaster since 1737—offered considerable influence over colonial information flows and would place him at the center of America's most important exchange of news and information, including the latest in scientific discoveries. "It would enable me to execute a Scheme long since formed [for a philosophical society] . . . which I hope would soon produce something agreeable to you and to all Lovers of Useful Knowledge, for I have now a large Acquaintance among ingenious Men in America."[40]

Before the introduction of the postal stamp, recipients paid substantial fees when collecting their mail, while letters sent by the postmaster carried no such expense. This meant that Franklin could act as a convenient clearinghouse for scientific reports, receiving the originals and then distributing copies to America's virtuosi, precisely the task of secretary that he had already spelled out in his plan for a national philosophical society.

News and information that came to his attention in his official capacity—the Philadelphia post office was maintained at his print shop—routinely ended up in the *Pennsylvania Gazette* before it could reach competing publications. Franklin also established new, faster postal routes, including the introduction of stagecoach runs and overnight service between major cities, and pioneered delivery to the extremes of the British settlements. By the end of his tenure, post roads had been surveyed and established from New York into Canada, and from Maine to Florida. Ever the practical man, Franklin was willing to meet the going rate to purchase the office of deputy postmaster, but only within reason. "The less it costs the better, as 'tis an Office for Life only, which is a very uncertain Tenure."[41]

Other Junto projects followed the successful campaign for a paper currency. Each new enterprise emulated the pattern established by the club's initial success, and each was grounded in the related notions of social utility and social improvement. Thus, a debate within the Junto about the danger of fire in Philadelphia's narrow confines led to the formation of volunteer fire companies across the city and, later, to the creation of America's first fire insurance scheme, with Franklin at its head. Under the influence of the Leather Apron men, police protection was bolstered and a program of regular road repair and street cleaning was instituted. Franklin's design of an improved oil lamp that required less maintenance and cast a brighter light enhanced municipal lighting. Junto members also led the way in the creation of the city hospital and the founding of an academy that would in time become the University of Pennsylvania.

Most important among the Junto's early projects—especially for the development of science and technology in the American colonies—was the founding of the Library Company of Philadelphia in 1731. Initially, the Leather Aprons pursued a modest plan to pool their small private collections into a shared library for ready consultation by all. When that proved something of a disappointment—they were regularly losing track of their valued volumes or found too much overlap in titles—the Junto launched a subscription library, the backbone of America's first major public collection. Many of the early subscribers were artisans and craftsmen.

Naturally enough, the Library Company's early purchases reflected the central interests and concerns of its founders, directors, and subscribers, all of whom put a premium on self-improvement over classical conceptions of knowledge, wisdom, and mystery. Works of science, chiefly basic mathematics, as well as history and literature, predominated, together accounting for more than two thirds of the company's initial book order from London. Unlike the few American universities of the day, created to turn out an educated clerical class, the Library Company devoted little shelf space to theology, and almost none to the classic texts of the Greek and Roman authorities.[42]

Over the ensuing decades, Americans' taste in books coalesced securely around works of practical information. In an "examination of the state of literature in *North America*" published in 1789, the British lawyer and essayist Leman Thomas Rede reported that American letters lacked "those dignified literati, who in Europe obtain the adulation of the learned parasites" but more than made up for it through "the possession of all useful learning." Summing up the American book market, Rede concluded, "Whatever is useful, sells; but publications on subjects merely speculative, and rather curious than important . . . lie upon the bookseller's hands."[43]

Franklin and the small circle of Junto members were not alone, of course, in their interests or pursuits. There were stirrings of similar impulses toward self-improvement and practical knowledge across the province of Pennsylvania and throughout the British colonies. In Philadelphia, two dozen or so of the city's tradesmen, professional men, and craftsmen formed the Union Library Company in 1747, offering low-cost access to several hundred titles.[44] Another group of mostly Quaker artisans, including a cabinetmaker, a clockmaker, and a pharmacist, created the Association Library Company of Philadelphia, while the Amicable Company was formed around the same time by city laborers. These separate collections later merged with the original Library Company to form a single citywide system.[45]

This library movement, backed by improvements in communications, advances in education, and better domestic printing technology, resonated throughout the colonies.[46] The New York Corporation Library was created in 1730 and opened to the public sixteen years later. The oldest lending collection in the country, the Redwood Library and Athenaeum of Newport, Rhode Island, was founded in 1747 with a mission to create "a collection of useful Books suitable for a Public Library . . . having nothing in View but the Good of Mankind."[47] Charleston's Library Society dates to 1748. The few colonial colleges of the day gradually expanded their own holdings well beyond their traditional preserve of theology, while other private or subscription libraries flourished.

At all these institutions, directors and readers alike demanded access to up-to-date technical knowledge, contemporary political philosophy, and the latest accounts of scientific experimentation. Books on modern farming techniques were particularly popular, while only a single lowly Latin grammar graced the Library Company of Philadelphia's bookshelves. Much sought after were the writings of the British empiricist philosopher John Locke—"Esteemed the best Book of Logic in the World," according to a notation in the Library Company's first printed catalog. Works of cutting-edge science in the new collection included A View of Sir Isaac Newton's Philosophy, by Franklin's old coffeehouse acquaintance Henry Pemberton, and other similar texts.[48]

Thomas Penn invoked the utility of the Library Company when he pledged the full support of the proprietary family: "I shall always be ready to promote any Undertaking so useful to the Country, as that of erecting a common Library in this City."[49] Given the intense interest of the institution's founders in experimentation and the application of practical knowledge, the library soon expanded beyond a mere repository of the written word to become an early seedbed of scientific discovery. The Penns donated an air pump and later "a complete Electrical Apparatus" to the Company, allowing members to explore for themselves the composition of the atmosphere and the phenomenon of electricity, matters then being hotly pursued in England and on the Continent.

The Quaker merchant Peter Collinson, the Library Company's chief book buyer in London and an informal scientific adviser to Franklin and his circle, sent along accounts of the latest German research into the nature of electricity. He also included a special glass tube, for the generation of static electricity, with which members of the Company, prominent among them the founders of Franklin's Junto, began their own investigations.

"Your kind present of an electric tube, with directions for using it, has put several of us on making electrical experiments, in which we have observed some particular phenomena that we look upon to be new," Franklin replied to

Collinson, assuring him the gift was being put to good use.[50] Philip Syng, the Junto's silversmith, even built a hand generator of the Americans' own design—"like a common Grind-Stone"—to further their efforts, which culminated in the triumphal proof, later presented to the Royal Society of London, that lightning and electricity were one and the same.[51]

✳　　✳　　✳

By the age of forty, Benjamin Franklin had established himself at the very heart of commercial, civic, and political life of Pennsylvania. In addition to serving as local postmaster and publishing one of America's leading newspapers and the bestselling *Poor Richard* almanacs, he held the position of clerk to the Pennsylvania Assembly. This post effectively guaranteed valuable contracts to print public ordinances, currency, and other official documents. Business was going so well that Franklin began gradually to withdraw from day-to-day management of what was becoming a publishing empire, with interests and affiliates—primarily presses, newspapers, and paper mills—reaching from the Caribbean to New England. He could now afford to devote himself more fully to his many scientific and civic projects.

In a letter to Cadwallader Colden of New York, one of his scientifically inclined correspondents, Franklin announced his decision to hand his printing operations over to a business partner and accept a steady income in return. "Thus you see I am in a fair Way of having no other Tasks than such as I shall like to give myself, and of enjoying what I look upon as a great Happiness, Leisure to read, study, make Experiments, and converse at large with such ingenious and worthy Men as are pleased to honor me with their Friendship or Acquaintance, on such Points as may produce something for the common Benefit of Mankind."[52]

This same impulse had already convinced Franklin and a small circle of collaborators, including Colden and the botanist John Bartram, that the colonies could support their own useful knowledge society, modeled directly on the Royal Society of London. The result was Franklin's public appeal for formation of an American Philosophical Society, outlined in his "Proposal for Promoting Useful Knowledge among the British Plantations in America." In effect, he set out to create a Leather Apron Club writ large across the American colonial landscape.

In Franklin's vision, the scope of the Society's interests would range far and wide, from improvements in brewing and wine making to "all philosophical

Experiments that let Light into the Nature of Things." Also included were "all new Arts, Trades, Manufactures, &c. that may be proposed or thought of," as well as new mechanical inventions, the sampling and testing of soil, and the drawing of maps and coastal charts.[53]

This new society's endeavors revolved around one central guiding principle—the harnessing of man's intellectual and creative powers for the direct betterment of his estate, an idea that had been gently gestating in Europe for centuries. With the arrival of the Enlightenment, in full swing by the time of Franklin's birth, this principle was now completely bound up with the notion of the ineluctable scientific, social, and economic advancement of society under the benign influence of Reason.

All that was required to pursue these new arts, declared Franklin's "Proposal for Promoting Useful Knowledge," were sufficient economic resources, adequate time, and an efficient medium of intellectual exchange and social collaboration. Now that the "first Drudgery" of creating successful colonial cities and towns had been completed, Americans were ready to apply experimentation and their own powers of observation to the quest for useful knowledge. "To such of these who are Men of Speculation, many Hints must from time to time arise, many Observations occur, which if well-examined, pursued and improved, might produce Discoveries to the Advantage of some or all of the . . . [colonies], or to the Benefit of Mankind in general."[54]

Chapter Four

USEFUL KNOWLEDGE

It is idle to expect any great advancement in science from the superinducing and engrafting of new things upon old. We must begin anew from the very foundations, unless we would revolve forever in a circle of mean and contemptible progress.

—Francis Bacon

THE ROYAL SOCIETY for the Improvement of Natural Knowledge received its first official charter in 1662, but informal learned gatherings were already being held in London and Oxford more than fifteen years beforehand among "a small circle of diverse worthy persons, inquisitive into natural philosophy, and other parts of human learning: and particularly of what hath been called the *New Philosophy*, or *Experimental Philosophy*."[1] Whatever the Society's precise provenance, there can be no doubt that it was the intellectual stepchild of Francis Bacon, the English philosopher and one-time chancellor of England, who died in 1626.

Bacon had called for nothing short of a cultural revolution that would interdict the West's reflexive adherence to the outmoded teachings dating back to the Middle Ages and beyond. Such a revolution must be based on a new approach to knowledge, rather than simply "the engrafting of new things upon old."[2] To break a pattern that had sorely retarded human progress, Bacon advocated the pursuit of knowledge based on direct observation and experimentation. "The office of the sense shall be only to judge of the experiment, and . . . the experiment itself shall judge of the thing."[3]

Running throughout Bacon's thinking was a profound optimism at odds with much of prevailing opinion that nature and society were caught up in inevitable decay and doomed to unchecked degeneration. The world, argued the naysayers, could never again hope to attain the heights of the medieval or ancient thinkers. If today's philosophers had achieved anything worthwhile, it was only because they had relied heavily on the accomplishments of bygone eras. This same attitude tended to bolster unstinting reverence for the works of antiquity, in particular the great Greek and Roman authors.[4]

Bacon also emphasized the social application of knowledge, as well as the collective nature of its acquisition, analysis, and dissemination. An educated cohort of citizens, rather than the romantic, solitary figure of genius, offered the surest source of scientific intellectual advancement and civic success. Preference in schools and universities must be given to utilitarian subjects over the classics that had long dominated the traditional curriculum. "There is no collegiate education designed for these purposes," Bacon lamented, "where men . . . might give themselves especially to histories, modern languages, books of policy and civil discourse."[5] Other arts worthy of study included agriculture and cookery, chemistry, and the production of gunpowder, enamel, glass, and paper.

In short, Bacon proposed an entirely new intellectual project—he called his work the *Novum Organon*, or New Instrument, to underscore this point—and he sought to enlist the support of both state and society to see it through.* The complexities of such an ambitious program would clearly require a new social or collective orientation toward natural philosophy, as well as increased reliance on the kind of empirical evidence produced by experimentation and a simplified language of science that would reveal, rather than obscure, the matter at hand.

It would also, Bacon argued, alter the balance of power in intellectual life, opening up what had been the exclusive preserve of the small ruling class to a much broader cross-section of society. "The practical skills and diligence which characterized the approach of the artisan, freed from an attachment to immediate ends, must be carried into the realm of the intellect, itself freed from subservience to preconceived opinion."[6] Public encouragement and funding were required, as was the patience and organization to carry the work well beyond the span of "one man's life."[7]

The small circles of the learned and the inventive figures who responded to such a call—the future virtuosi—adopted Bacon's program, in particular what

---

* The title is a deliberate refrence to Aristotle's text on logic, cherished for centuries and known as the *Organon*.

they saw as his strong utilitarian streak, with enthusiasm. "I shall only mention one great Man, who had the true Imagination of the whole of this Enterprise, as it is now set on foot; and that is, the Lord Bacon," wrote the Royal Society's first historian, Thomas Sprat, in 1667. "If my desires could have prevailed . . . there should have been no other Preface to the History of the Royal Society but some of his Writings."[8]

Not only had Bacon proposed a new science, but he also had sketched out the prototype of the new scientist. Sprat's official account of the founding of the Royal Society, begun immediately after its formal incorporation, lauded Bacon throughout for creating a new breed of philosophers, "free from the colors of *Rhetoric*, the devices of *Fancy*, or the delightful deceit of *Fables*" and armed with a new, practical approach to nature. "They have attempted, to free it from Artifice, and Humors, and Passions of Sects, to render it an Instrument, whereby Mankind may obtain a Dominion over *Things*, and not only over one another's *Judgments*."[9]

Europe's first experimental scientific society, the Academia Secretorum Naturae, appeared in Naples as early as 1560, followed by similar endeavors in Rome, Florence, Leipzig, and Berlin. Others were later formed in Dublin, Paris, St. Petersburg, and elsewhere on the Continent.[10] Accompanying these new knowledge societies was the production of almanacs and other publications aimed at bringing the rudiments of science, technology, and word of new discoveries to the general public. In a similar vein, night schools, lectures, and reading rooms flourished, all serving to help break down traditional barriers that had restricted learning to only the most privileged elements of society.

Bacon's prescription represented perhaps the most ambitious and far-reaching attempt to date to come to terms with the social, political, and theological implications of the new scientific advances that came to characterize the seventeenth century. This was the age of scientific apparatus—the telescope, the microscope, the air pump, the pendulum, the barometer, and so on—that sealed Europe's final break with medieval notions of natural philosophy and marked the beginning of a recognizably "modern" science. The ever-expanding voyages of the European explorers, meanwhile, introduced the exotic flora of Africa and the Americas, prompting advances in botany and fueling early attempts at the classification of plant life as the basis for organized study.[11]

In the hands of the Royal Society's early members, the implicit utilitarianism running throughout Bacon's work was accentuated and pushed to the fore.

King Charles II, newly restored to the throne after the collapse of Puritan rule under Oliver Cromwell, signed the Society's first charter in the summer of 1662, charging its membership with "promoting by the authority of experiments the sciences of natural things and of useful arts."[12]

The king reinforced this practical mission with a decree that no patent would be issued for "any philosophical or mechanical invention, until examined by the Society." There would be, the Society promised in return, no "meddling with Divinity, Metaphysics, Morals, Politics, . . . or Logic."[13] This was an explicit pledge that the Royal Society, with its roots deep in the intellectual ferment of the Puritan Revolution, would steer clear of political and religious controversy now that the king and the Church of England were both fully back in power.

The emphasis on experimental science, direct experience, and useful knowledge in general flowing from the works of Bacon dovetailed neatly with the views of the Puritans and many of England's other sectaries, including the dissident Quakers who founded Pennsylvania. These movements shared a general stress on the utility of knowledge in the pursuit of religious truth and the general advancement of society. They were also eager to overhaul those institutions that supported the persecution of their members and acted as an impediment to social, religious, and political reform. This was particularly the case with the English universities, Oxford and Cambridge, which were closed to all dissenters from the official Church of England.

More broadly, the evangelical approach to reading scripture ushered in by the Reformation had already established the primacy, at least in theory, of the believer's own relationship to the written text over any intermediary role on the part of a priestly caste or other elite. For many of these new Protestant readers, common sense, not churchly tradition or academic philosophizing, was the best guide to understanding. George Fox, founder of the Quakers, took direct aim at the religious legitimacy of the universities, whose chief mission was the training of ministers for the state church. "Being bred at Oxford or Cambridge was not enough to fit and qualify men to be ministers to God," Fox wrote in 1646 after one of his spiritual insights or "openings," for all men are "born of God" and thus are capable of true religious understanding.[14]

Writing of his close friend Fox, William Penn reported that the Quaker founder was "ignorant of useless and sophistical science, . . . [and] had in him the grounds for useful and commendable knowledge, and cherished it everywhere."[15] Penn was a member in good standing of the Royal Society, and he was personally acquainted with many of his prominent contemporaries, including Isaac Newton and the philosopher John Locke, who forcefully advocated teaching "only what is most necessary."

With the establishment of his colony, Penn served as a powerful conduit for this zeal for educational reform and practical learning from the Old World to the new one. In a "Letter to Wife and Children," left behind for the edification of his family when he sailed for America in 1682, the Pennsylvania proprietor spelled out the essence of proper schooling: "Let it be useful knowledge such as is consistent with truth and godliness, not cherishing a vain conversation or idle mind. . . . Let my children be husbandmen and housewives; it is industrious, healthy, honest, and of good example."[16] As for ancient texts, rhetoric, and grammar—the stuff of a traditional English education—Penn shared Bacon's dismissive attitude and put the odds at "ten to one" to be of no use whatsoever.

Many of the Royal Society's most intransigent critics came from within the ranks of university professors, now purged of any sectarian leanings in the aftermath of the restoration of the monarchy. Those back in control of England's universities clearly recognized the threat to their authority and standing posed by any practical realization of Bacon's "New Philosophy" or by associated demands for educational reform.[17]

Joseph Glanvill, a clergyman and vociferous defender of the London virtuosi, denounced the universities' criticism as little more than knee-jerk reliance on the outmoded thinking of the Ancients and a general unwillingness to embrace new experimental technologies, such as the microscope and other "Optic Glasses." Glanvill even devoted a chapter of one of his works to "The Credit of Optic Glasses vindicated against a disputing man afraid to believe his own eyes against Aristotle."[18]

Not-so-subtle issues of class and privilege also intruded, for Bacon and his supporters recognized the potential contributions to scientific endeavor of the amateur inventor, the artisan, the mechanic, or even the simple laborer, in what was a direct affront to the exalted position of the academic class. Robert Hooke, the first curator of experiments at the Royal Society, likewise emphasized the value of including the practical talents of merchants and other businessmen in the pursuit of useful knowledge: "Their attempts," he argued, "will bring philosophy from words to action."[19]

Locke, a fellow of the Royal Society since 1688, pointed out that the "Commonwealth of Learning" had room for all, not simply for the rare genius such as Newton. "It is Ambition enough to be employed as an Under-Laborer in clearing the Ground a little, and removing some of the Rubbish, that lies in the way of Knowledge."[20]

Typical of this new thinking was the work of William Petty, a founding figure of the Royal Society and one-time personal secretary to Thomas Hobbes. Petty openly celebrated the artisan, the laborer, and the mechanic and contrasted them favorably with the elite universities' production of so many "Fustian and Unworthy Preachers in Divinity, so many pettifoggers in the Law, so many Quack-salvers in physic [medicine], so many Grammaticasters in Country-schools, and so many lazy men in Gentlemen's houses; when every man might learn to live otherwise in more plenty and honor."[21] One of Petty's reformist allies argued that men must "reject what is useless (as most of that which hath hitherto borne the name of learning, will upon impartial examination prove to be) and esteem that only which is evidently useful to the people."[22]

✻   ✻   ✻

The arduous Atlantic passage that transported the Puritans, Quakers, and other religious dissidents also carried the hopes and ambitions of the virtuosi that Francis Bacon's new science would produce a trove of curious discoveries in the New World. Prospects were buoyed by the fact that a number of the colonies were presided over by fellows of the Royal Society, such as William Penn or the Connecticut governor, John Winthrop the Younger. Yet like the early colonizers themselves, European notions of useful knowledge and experimental science, too, ran afoul of the demands of actual settlement, the slow and uncertain lines of communication across the vast ocean, and the trying matter of daily existence.

In 1667, the secretary of the Royal Society wrote to Winthrop, a colleague well versed in medicine and alchemy, to press for immediate implementation of the Society's scientific program. "Sir, I persuade myself that you . . . will make it a good part of your business to recommend this real Experimental way of acquiring knowledge, by conversing with, and searching into the works of God themselves."[23]

Winthrop's response was a measured one. On an earlier visit to England, he had presented the Royal Society's first scientific paper from the colonies, on the manufacture of tar and pitch from New England pine, and he promoted North

American shipbuilding and the cultivation of Indian corn. Winthrop, whose father and namesake was the first governor of Massachusetts, also owned New England's first "Optic glass," a ten-foot telescope, and later a smaller reflecting model.[24]

But now he had to concede that the practical challenges of life in the colony, even five decades after its founding, had largely overwhelmed the impulse for scientific inquiry. "Plantations in their beginnings have work enough, and find difficulties sufficient to settle a comfortable way of subsistence, there being buildings, fencings, clearing and breaking up of ground, lands to be attended, orchards to be planted, highways and bridges and fortifications to be made, and all things to do, as in the beginning of the world."[25]

Such obstacles were exacerbated by the hostility of the virtuosi to the idea of homegrown American science. It was one thing for Royal Society veterans like Winthrop or Penn, both of whom went back and forth from Europe to America, to engage in the pursuit of useful knowledge in the New World. It was quite another for the colonies to produce their own scientists, or to otherwise threaten the European monopoly over the economy of knowledge. For the Royal Society, members of this tiny American vanguard were little more than helpmates in a global enterprise, best suited to the collection and description of the New World's plants, animals, and other wonders but ill prepared for the rigors of true natural philosophy. Europe was to remain the primary source of economic, political, and intellectual power.

The first serious native-born challenge to this monopoly on science issued from a remote farmhouse on the banks of the Schuylkill River, a dozen or so miles outside Philadelphia. There, the Quaker John Bartram—in his habitual wide trousers and large leather apron—quietly wrestled a living from the land and immersed himself in the medicinal properties of the plants that dotted the nearby forests and meadows. Visitors reported that Bartram carved the foundation for the family home out of solid rock—the structure stands to this day—and painstakingly drained the surrounding marshlands to reveal fertile soil for his crops and good grazing land for livestock. Particularly striking were Bartram's sophisticated use of fertilizer and practice of crop rotation in the wilds of Pennsylvania, as well as the well-ordered botanical garden he assembled by trial and error.

Bartram's grandfather had followed William Penn, his fellow Quaker, to the New World in 1682 and settled in Darby, just outside the young town of

Philadelphia. John was born there, on May 23, 1699, but his father, William, soon left his son in the care of the boy's grandparents and moved to the Carolinas after a series of run-ins with other members of the Darby Quaker meeting. Fiercely independent like his father, John, too, clashed with the religious opinions and social mores of his community throughout his lifetime. Yet he stayed put, affixing a sign above the door to his greenhouse reflecting both his steadfast nature and core beliefs: "Slave to no sect, who takes no private road, But looks through nature, up to nature's God."[26]

Bartram was, by necessity as well as by inclination, largely self-taught. "Being born in a newly settled colony, of not more than fifty years' establishment, where the sciences of the Old Continent were little known, it cannot be supposed, that he could derive great advantages or assistance from school-learning or literature," recalled his son, William. Besides, Bartram preferred to take matters into his own hands, generally to great effect. He absorbed what he could as a young boy from the modest local school, but as an adult he studied on his own, reading late into the night. When possible, he sought out "the society of the most learned and virtuous men."[27]

Gradually, Bartram was drawn into the intellectual life of Philadelphia, where Enlightenment ideas of science and knowledge held sway. James Logan, colonial agent for William Penn and then the province's most learned resident, taught Bartram how to examine the fine details of his specimens under a microscope. Logan also helped Bartram with his study of Latin, then the international language of botany and other sciences, and allowed him to use his well-stocked library, a privilege Logan likewise granted to the young Franklin.[28]

A member of Franklin's Junto put Bartram in touch with the Royal Society of London, perennially on the lookout for North American agents to collect and ship back specimens of plants, animal pelts, fossils, and other "curiosities," for study by the natural philosophers of England and the Continent.[29] As a token of its esteem for Bartram's work, the Library Company of Pennsylvania waived the relatively high cost of membership and bestowed on him free access for life to their growing collection, which included a number of fine works on botany and natural history in general.

The Junto at one point took up a subscription to underwrite some of Bartram's botanizing expeditions, which took him farther and farther from home. A notice in Franklin's *Pennsylvania Gazette* to solicit contributions reminded readers of the utility of such a project: "Botany, or the Science of Herbs and Plants, has always been accounted in every Country, as well by the Illiterate as by the Learned, an useful Study and Labor to Mankind, as it has furnished them with Cures for many Diseases, and their Gardens, Groves and Fields with rare and pleasant Fruits, Flowers, Aromatics, Shades, and Hedges."[30] Soon, Bartram was exploring the forests and mountains, ranging from Canada to Florida, and dispatching seeds, dried plants, and other items, all accompanied by written accounts of his adventures to aristocratic patrons—the king of England, among them—across the Atlantic.

Despite these successes, Bartram's relations with the European men of science were often difficult. He was easily provoked, sensitive to the smallest slight, and increasingly resentful of his assigned subsidiary role in their great project. The virtuosi treated Bartram and a handful of other colonial naturalists as little more than extensions of their own scientific will, ideal for carrying out explicit orders but incapable of any original work. They regularly flattered these agents in print, or named the odd discovery in their honor, but they had no intention of sharing the glory or allowing them to make their own scientific contributions. When a useful invention of early American provenance did surface, as was the case with the reflecting navigational quadrant created by Franklin's Junto partner Thomas Godfrey, the Royal Society hushed up word of the breakthrough and then awarded initial credit for a similar device to its own vice president.[31]

At the outset, Bartram seemed to harbor little ambition to enter the ranks of the virtuosi presided over by the European knowledge societies, and he never fully mastered the skills, idiom, or attitudes of Enlightenment science. Nor did he show much interest in experimentation, although he did perform several tests at the behest of the Royal Society to help confirm the sexual nature of plant reproduction. He also practiced plant hybridization.

This reticence may have stemmed, in part, from a lifelong sensitivity to his lack of formal education, a lack Bartram may have felt all the more acutely as he began to correspond with some of Europe's leading scientists. Among them was the great Swedish botanist Linnaeus, who in 1735 proposed a remarkably durable system for classifying and naming plants and animals by genus and species. "Good grammar and good spelling may please those that are more taken with a fine superficial flourish than real truth," wrote Bartram to a contact in London, as he tried to turn his literary vices into scientific virtues.[32]

Whatever his educational shortcomings, real or imagined, Bartram clearly applied enormous intelligence, boundless energy, and strong powers of observation to the marching orders from members of the Royal Society, chiefly in the person of Peter Collinson, the London merchant. Bartram and Collinson never met but their steady correspondence across four decades bears witness to the latter's enormous influence over the man generally regarded as America's first botanist. In a tribute to Collinson after his death in 1768, one colleague wrote, "That eminent naturalist, JOHN BARTRAM, may almost be said to have been created such by my friend's assistance; he first recommended the collecting of seeds, and afterward assisted in the disposing of them in this country [England], and constantly excited him to persevere in investigating the plants of America."[33]

Collinson's letters from England, beginning in the 1730s, include seemingly endless wish lists of seeds, cuttings, and dried leaves or other specimens, more often than not accompanied by a great deal of false modesty and a fair amount of wheedling: "I only mention these plants; not that I expect thee to send them. I don't expect or desire them, but as they happen to be found accidentally: and what is not to be met with one year, may be another."[34]

He at first plied Bartram with presents in return for regular shipments of native American plants—a calico gown for Bartram's wife and some "odd little things" for the children.[35] Only after some gentle grumbling from Bartram did the two put their working relationship on a firm business footing, with the American's increasingly arduous and expensive botanizing expeditions covered by regular stipends from Collinson and his circle of European scientists and gardening enthusiasts. By 1765, even the court of King George III helped fund Bartram's travels.

Collinson's directives to Bartram were always very precise, but he was uncharacteristically vague about the terms of this royal appointment, in particular the formal title—if any—that may have accompanied Bartram's court stipend of fifty pounds a year. Collinson initially had referred to his American friend as "King's Botanist," but a later note cautioned Bartram against exploiting such a title without the court's explicit permission. This suggests the entire arrangement may have been more of a private affair.[36] And he readily admitted that the British monarch paid no real attention to Bartram's painstaking deliveries of rare New World flora, although the promised stipend would continue all the same. "I wish the King had any taste in flowers and plants; but as he has none, there are no hopes of encouragement from him, for his talent is architecture."[37]

The arrangement with the court, brokered by Collinson over many months through his extensive network of powerful contacts, was the source of sniping within America's small coterie of naturalists. In Charleston, South Carolina, the Scottish physician Alexander Garden—an avid botanist for whom Linnaeus named the gardenia flower—could not believe the news. Surely, the king had agreed only to underwrite Bartram's expenses and perhaps a small stipend rather than to offer the self-taught American a true royal appointment, a nonplussed Garden groused to a British colleague.[38]

With the establishment of a regular salary came increasing requests from London, including a detailed commission for Bartram to carry out a search for the headwaters of Philadelphia's Schuylkill River. Collinson oversaw each of these trips in the most minute detail, leaving little to chance and virtually nothing to the American's own initiative, experience, or local knowledge. He demanded Bartram maintain a daily journal and outfit his horse with special specimen boxes, and he even sent along a new suit of clothes to wear when visiting the Royal Society's contacts in Virginia. "Virginians are a very gentle, well-dressed people—and look, perhaps more at a man's outside than his inside," wrote Collinson, worried that Bartram's homespun jacket and plain ways might offend his hosts.[39]

From time to time, Collinson called on Bartram to provide evidence that might shed light on some of the scientific controversies debated back in London. How did the beaver fashion his dam? Did the rattlesnake simply bite and poison its prey? Or was there an element of "power it has over creatures, by *charming* them into its very jaws?" Similarly, members of the Royal Society had heard reports from New England of periodic outbreaks of locusts. "Pray has thee heard, or observed, that a certain species of locust returns every fifteenth year?"[40]

By all accounts, Bartram bore up remarkably well under such exacting demands, ranging far and wide and enduring numerous hardships in the wilderness to fulfill his missions. On an expedition to the Cedar Swamp of New Jersey to collect pine cones for the Duke of Norfolk, Bartram struggled against the elements. "I climbed the trees in the rain . . . and lopped off the boughs, then must stand up to the knees in snow, to pluck off the cones," he informed Collinson.[41]

On another trip, Bartram devoted two weeks of "painstaking effort" to tracking down the rare willow-leafed oak, only to have most of its treasured acorns "devoured by the squirrels and hogs."[42] No request was, it seems, too demanding or too daunting. The American furnished muskrat skins, a hornet's nest, samples of native ginseng for a proposed export scheme to China, even live turtle eggs that Collinson received just in time to see one hatch.

The grateful virtuosi began to sing Bartram's praise. Linnaeus celebrated the self-taught Bartram as "the greatest natural botanist in the world." Gardening and its more exacting cousin botany were then all the rage in Europe, fueled in large part by the sudden availability of exotic plants from America, and many of the wealthy and powerful competed with one another to populate their private gardens with the rarest of New World specimens. In Linnaeus's native Sweden, Queen Ulrika, herself an avid gardener, wrote a warm letter to Bartram, and the Royal Academy of Science of Stockholm made him a member in 1769.[43]

Collinson was always careful to fill his letters to Bartram with praise and encouragement, and the two men—linked by their shared Quaker faith and enthusiasm for plants—appear to have established a personal bond over their decades of correspondence, even as they bickered over expenses, missed shipments, or lost letters. In less guarded moments, however, Collinson allows his condescension, and that of the European virtuosi in general, toward his stalwart American partner to peek through.

"I am persuaded you would have been pleased with him," Collinson wrote to Cadwallader Colden, a fellow botany enthusiast in New York, after a failed attempt by the two Americans to meet. "You would have found a wonderful natural genius, considering his education, and that he was never out of America, but is an husbandman, and lives on a little estate of his own about five or six miles from Philadelphia."[44]

For the most part, Collinson and his colleagues were not particularly interested in what Bartram might think or what firsthand experience might tell him, but only in what he could collect and then send back to Europe for their study and analysis. In fact, Collinson openly discouraged the American from engaging in scientific speculation. "The box of seeds came very safe, and in good order," he reported in one letter. "Thy remarks on them are very curious, but I think take up too much of thy time and thought. I would not make my correspondence burdensome, but must desire thee to continue the same collections over again."[45] Later, when Bartram on his own arranged for the publication of a fine edition of one of his expedition journals, Collinson scoffed that he was wasting his time. Clearly, few would "buy so dear a book."[46]

Throughout their lengthy correspondence, Collinson is explicit that it is only the opinions of the experts back in Europe that carry any weight, and he dismissed Bartram's own views on the existence of two separate varieties of American cedar, the red and the white, until details of the plants could be examined by the natural philosophers of London, Oxford, Berlin, or Uppsala. "Half a dozen, by way of specimen, will be sufficient; *for though you call it white cedar, we are in doubt* what class it belongs to, until we see its seed-vessels."[47]

Collinson regularly forwarded some of Bartram's samples to his expert colleagues, who assigned them Latin names in accordance with the latest thinking on plant classification, and then returned these rulings to Bartram for his own edification. "Send more seed," Collinson requested in a letter of March 14, 1736. "All the specimens went to Oxford. When they are sent back, with their names, thee shall hear from me."[48] Collinson also provided American specimens for classification by the Dutch botanist Jan Frederik Gronovius, whose publication of the *Flora Virginica* was essentially an uncredited reworking—plagiarism might be a more apt term—of an extensive catalog of Virginia plants carefully compiled by Bartram's fellow American naturalist, John Clayton.

✳   ✳   ✳

The attitudes of men such as Collinson, Gronovius, and Linnaeus were in keeping with the established view of the colonial naturalists as handmaidens to their own grand scientific work, so it is not surprising that the Europeans fought to maintain their control over useful knowledge. When Bartram proffered the seemingly reasonable suggestion that perhaps the time was at hand for the American colonies to assemble their own scientific infrastructure, in imitation of the Royal Society, Collinson moved to quash the idea.

"As to the Society that thee hints at, had you a set of learned, well-qualified members to set out with, it might draw your neighbors to correspond with you," Collinson wrote in the summer of 1739. "Your Library Company I take to be an essay towards such a Society. But to draw learned strangers to you, to teach sciences, requires salaries and good encouragement; and this will require public, as well as proprietary assistance—which can't be at present complied with—considering the infancy of your colony."[49]

Collinson's initial assessment of the colonials' ability to create and then sustain a scientific organization of their own was not far off the mark, for Franklin's American Philosophical Society, announced publicly several years after Bartram first suggested it, struggled to get off the ground and it lay, essentially moribund, for years. Despite Collinson's early opposition, Bartram had refused to give up on the idea, which he shared with Colden, the patrician politician-cum-scientist from New York, as well as with Franklin and a few other like-minded colleagues in and around Philadelphia. The American naturalist seems to have been the early driving force behind the 1743 manifesto, which appeared under Franklin's name.[50]

Joined by the Philadelphia physician Thomas Bond, the circle made a number of attempts to spark interest in their venture, including the proposed publication of a scientific journal, the *American Philosophical Miscellany*, which they hoped would serve as a rallying point for participants from around the colonies. Franklin also tapped into his growing network of Europeans, and he offered to use his position as postmaster to assist the colonial members with their scientific correspondence.

In a breathless note to Colden, dashed off on April 5, 1744, Franklin reported that the new society "is actually formed, and has had several Meetings to mutual Satisfaction." Bartram would serve as botanist, with Franklin's old colleague from the Junto, the glazier and inventor Godfrey, in the mathematician's chair. Thomas Bond would fill the post of physician. Correspondent members from New York and New Jersey were also in place, and participants from Maryland, Virginia, Carolina, and New England were expected "as soon as they are acquainted that the Society has begun to form itself," Franklin reported, ending with a promise of "a short Account of what has been done and proposed at those Meetings."[51]

The project, however, was virtually stillborn. The proposed *Miscellany* languished, although Franklin eventually managed to collect enough material to fill several issues, primarily on medical matters.[52] The promised update on the Society's progress never appeared, and by the summer of 1745, Franklin had resigned himself to failure. He blamed the habits of his fellow colonials, in particular those from the upper crust whose discipline, he suggested, compared unfavorably to that of the Leather Aprons. "The Members of our Society here are very idle Gentlemen, they will take no Pains," he conceded in a letter to Colden.[53] The dour Bartram agreed but expressed the vague hope that success might yet be attained "if we could but exchange the time that is spent in the Club, Chess and Coffee House for the Curious amusements of natural observations."[54]

More than a century earlier, Francis Bacon had spelled out the necessary conditions for the successful realization of his New Philosophy project, laying the foundation for the Royal Society. These included, among other factors, the notion of science as continuous, collective action and the steady support of both the state and society as a whole. In his initial, discouraging response to Bartram, Collinson had dutifully reiterated Bacon's analysis as well as his own experience as a longtime fellow of the Royal Society, whose ranks included not only those expert in natural philosophy but also vital elements drawn from among the more "curious" of the merchants, artisans, and country gentlemen.

The British Crown, too, had provided important political backing to the virtuosi, many of whose Puritan tendencies might otherwise have been subjected to far more critical scrutiny after the restoration of the monarchy. In Pennsylvania of the 1740s, Bartram and his circle could count on little support from either their fellow citizens or the proprietary family, increasingly at odds with local public opinion—often in the person of the formidable Franklin himself—over the future direction of the province.

Other domestic obstacles plagued the early days of the American Philosophical Society. Despite the advances since the colonies were first settled, Franklin's America still suffered from acute shortages of labor and currency, the lack of great universities, libraries, and other cultural institutions, a dearth of domestic capital, the enormous distance from the mother country, and the absence of significant urban centers that could concentrate intellectual activity into a single, workable space. Philadelphia was by now America's leading city, but it was unable to offer anything like the sophisticated urban society or vast private financial resources that London provided to the Royal Society. Colonial life was still overwhelmingly rural and would remain so for many, many decades.

Meanwhile, the logic of imperial development, with England as the undisputed source of power, ideas, and privilege, meant that the individual colonies naturally directed their attention eastward across the Atlantic rather than toward one another. Meaningful cooperation among the various colonies was virtually nonexistent. The New World's status as supplier of raw materials—whether iron ore, lumber, or foodstuffs—and the mercantilist preference given to finished goods from British manufacturers at the expensive of domestic colonial production further contributed to this centripetal tendency.

Even the torturously slow lines of communication, whether for mail, goods, or personal travel, between the nascent American cities and England were often more reliable than those among the distant colonial settlements themselves. The diary of Alexander Hamilton, the Scottish physician, reveals in detail the challenges he faced throughout a tour of the middle and northern colonies that took four months; in just the first leg, one hundred and thirty miles from his home in Annapolis, Maryland, to Pennsylvania, the good doctor endured lame horses, disreputable travel companions, uncertain ferry service, unmarked roads, and cramped lodgings, including one public house where he was forced to sleep in the same room as the proprietor, his wife, and daughters. Travel and communications were especially important to the eighteenth-century way of doing science, which revolved around the learned society with its regular face-to-face meetings, its complex exchanges of correspondence among members, and its publication and distribution of a journal that could communicate claims to invention and originality and express the organization's collective judgment on all important questions of the day.[55]

As late as the momentous summer of 1776, officials in London were informed of the decision by the Second Continental Congress in Philadelphia to declare independence about the same time that the news reached the residents of Savannah, Georgia. It is not surprising that in the preceding decades Bartram, Franklin, and Colden found it easier to correspond with the European virtuosi than to organize the members of their homegrown American Philosophical Society.

Chapter Five

SENSE AND SENSIBILITY

Electricity has one considerable advantage over most other branches of science, as it both furnishes matter of speculation for philosophers, and of entertainment for all persons promiscuously.

—Joseph Priestly

PETER COLLINSON GRADUALLY began to soften his opposition to an American scientific society, and in a rare flush of enthusiasm the phlegmatic Quaker even permitted himself to muse aloud that America might one day pick up the torch of intellectual advance from an increasingly "exhausted" Old World.[1] Perhaps inadvertently, Collinson went on to play a key part in helping to establish a true place for colonial science by nudging Franklin and friends toward the series of experiments that would electrify the scientific world.

His correspondence provided the Americans with regular updates from Europe on the latest findings and fads, ranging from the enigma of the hydra, a plantlike creature then known as the polypus, to the mysteries of the electrical fire. "As this may very justly be styled the age of wonders, it may not be disagreeable just to hint them to you," Collinson wrote to Cadwallader Colden in the spring of 1745. "The surprising Phenomena of the Polypus Entertained the Curious for a year or two past but Now the Virtuosi of Europe are taken up in Electrical Experiments."[2] A separate missive to Franklin's Library Company was accompanied by a two-foot glass tube and a basic account of how to use it to produce static electricity.

Franklin and his circle needed no further encouragement. They equipped themselves with the basic apparatus, pored over published reports from abroad, built their own crude generator, and otherwise buried themselves in explorations of this mysterious new subject. "I never was before engaged in any study that so totally engrossed my attention and my time as this has lately done, for what with making experiments . . . I have, during some months past, had little leisure for any thing else," Franklin admitted.[3]

Following the lead of the itinerant "electricians," whose public lectures captivated European and American audiences by allowing onlookers to experience the power and wonders of electricity, the Philadelphia investigators even experimented on themselves. So, too, did one of the inventors of the Leyden jar, the Dutchman Pieter van Musschenbroek, who suffered numerous injuries from accidental discharge from this simple condenser.

Outlining a series of "Conjectures" that arose from these early experiments, Franklin invoked the decisive nature of bodily sensation to decide an important scientific point about the behavior of the electrical fire. "If any one should doubt, whether the Electrical Matter passes through the Substance of Bodies, or only over and along their Surfaces, a Shock from an electrified large Glass Jar, taken through his own Body, will probably convince him."[4] This physical experience of electricity on the human body was central to the contemporary idea of knowledge, which was validated by both reason and experimentation, by both sense and sensibility.

It was an article of faith among Franklin and his colleagues that science has the power to open up the world of wonders all around us. It could also explain those wonders as the product of orderly natural laws, debunk superstition, and tame unreasonable fears of nature.[5] In the eyes of the virtuosi, wonders and marvels were not a threat to the moral, social, or religious order, as they had often appeared in earlier times; the only danger lay in the imperfect ways in which the untutored mind apprehended and then sought to explain them. The function of scientific institutions such as the Royal Society and France's Académie des Sciences was, according to the latter's secretary Bernard de Fontenelle, as much to "disabuse the Public of false marvels as to report on true ones."[6]

The "true marvel" of electricity spawned a vibrant cottage industry. Craftsmen on both sides of the Atlantic began to produce glass tubes and other specialty equipment, as well as custom-made generators, hand-powered devices that used a spinning wheel to create a static charge and widely known as electrical machines. Handbooks and manuals of electrical experimentation, aimed more at the layman and hobbyist than the serious investigator, proliferated. One popular volume, John Neale's *Directions for Gentlemen, Who Have Electrical Machines, How to Proceed in Making Their Experiments*, published in London in 1747, dispenses with the theoretical niceties from the very outset, no doubt to the relief of his audience.

"I shall not take up my reader's time with enquiring into, or defining what electricity is. . . . Nor shall I go about to enumerate its several laws and properties," Neale writes. Instead, he simply sketches out the basic equipment and precepts required and then immediately turns his attention to the real business at hand. "A good part of the most entertaining phenomena in electrical experiments arises from electrifying human bodies."[7]

The subject, of course, must first be insulated from the earth to avoid discharging the electrical fire prematurely. Neale reports that the Germans preferred to suspend silk cords from the ceiling and create a sort of bench or small hammock, a method he says condemns the subject to swaying "inconveniently." The French and English, meanwhile, tended toward construction of insulating platforms made of pitch and rosin. Neale himself recommends that readers construct their own electrical stand by using three bottles made of glass, a nonconductor, to serve as legs for a triangular wooden stool.

Neale then leads his readers through twenty exercises with "electrised" bodies.* Experiment XII, for example, illustrates the body's conductivity, as well as the use of pointed rods, in this case a long needle, to draw down the charge and render it harmless. "If an electrised person draws his sword and extends it, a brush of blue fire will be seen to issue from the point in the dark. But let an un-electric person present the point of a needle against the sword's point though a yard from it, and the fire will instantly disappear."[8] In another scenario, the "electric mine," an unsuspecting observer holding a rod or wire attached to the generator felt a sudden jolt from an electrical contact hidden under the carpet, after unwittingly closing the circuit.

Jean-Antoine Nollet, the leading French authority on the subject, tended toward lavish public demonstrations to illustrate the enormous speed of electrical transmission. Formally the head of a monastery but best known for his scientific work, Nollet once sent a virtually instantaneous shock through a mile-long line of hundreds of monks, each linked to his neighbor by iron wire.

---

* The early English lexicon of electricity included both the verb "electrise," as well as today's accepted usage, "electrify." For a considerable time, the two were used interchangeably, and I have tried to preserve the preferred usage of individual writers wherever possible.

He later repeated the experiment for the edification of the French king, this time using a chain of 180 royal soldiers.

The Philadelphians were not to be outdone. They invented the game of Conspiracy, in which anyone rashly attempting to remove an electrified gilt crown from a portrait of the British king received a powerful shock for his temerity. On one well-planned outing, Franklin led a celebratory picnic during which they toasted their fellow electricians worldwide with electrised gilt glasses and then slaughtered a turkey with an electrical charge and roasted it with electrical fire. "I conceit that the Birds killed in this Manner eat uncommonly tender," Franklin later recounted.[9]

Franklin also began to promote traveling electrical shows as a sideline to his growing publishing business. These and similar diversions were not simply frivolous pastimes for idle ladies and gentlemen. The electrical shows and their offshoots introduced the new scientific wonders to a growing audience that extended well beyond the traditional educated elite. Franklin's investigations also established a direct connection between controlled experimentation for public consumption and the wider world beyond the walls of the laboratory, the salon, or the lecture hall. His famed electric kite, for example, applied the logic and techniques of experimentation to nature itself, which could now seemingly be studied and even manipulated almost at will.[10]

Franklin encouraged one of his most valued experimental collaborators, the out-of-work Baptist minister Ebenezer Kinnersley, to take their latest findings on the road as a way to earn a living and to spread the gospel of science and useful knowledge. "Among these the principal was Mr. Kinnersley, an ingenious Neighbor, who being out of Business, I encouraged to undertake showing the Experiments for Money, and drew up for him two Lectures," Franklin wrote in his *Autobiography*.[11]

Kinnersley first came to public attention with his condemnations of the evangelical enthusiasm unleashed in the Great Awakening, the religious revival movement in full swing across American colonies by the 1740s. He used the pulpit of Philadelphia's Baptist Church to dismiss the emotional preaching of the revivalists as "unbecoming a Minister of the Gospel." Such holy histrionics, Kinnersley warned the congregation, proceeded "not from the Spirit of God, for our God is a God of Order, and not of such Confusion."[12]

Franklin shared this distaste for displays of religious fervor, and he recognized a kindred spirit in Kinnersley, with his strong identification with an orderly universe—that is, one whose natural laws were the legitimate subject of scientific investigation. Franklin used his *Pennsylvania Gazette* to advance this notion, even as he drummed up public enthusiasm for his collaborator's commercial displays of the electrical fire. "As the knowledge of Nature tends to enlarge the human Mind, and give us more noble, more grand and exalted ideas of the Author of Nature, and if well pursued seldom fails producing some things *useful* to man, 'tis hoped these Lectures may be thought worthy of Regard and Encouragement."[13]

Despite the reserved demeanor of Kinnersley the preacher, Kinnersley the itinerant electrician proved something of a sensation. He was, says his biographer, "the greatest lecturer in colonial America."[14] With Franklin's backing, Kinnersley roamed the British colonies, from New England to the Caribbean, sharing with his audiences the latest findings of the Philadelphia circle. These included the first public hints of the identification of electricity with lightning, presented in Annapolis, Maryland, in the spring of 1749.

Meanwhile, Franklin and his associates back home continued their basic research with the use of iron shot, small cork balls, glass bottles, and a long bodkin or similar piece of pointed metal. The American electricians discovered that the electrised iron shot, resting on the mouth of a glass jar as an insulator, would unfailingly repel a nearby cork ball suspended from the ceiling by silk thread. "When in this State, if you present to the Shot the Point of a long, slender, sharp Bodkin at 6 or 8 Inches Distance, the Repellency is instantly destroyed, and the Cork flies to it." Further investigation revealed that the bodkin could both "*throw* off, as well as *draw* off the Electrical Fire"—a first important step toward what would become Franklin's most famous invention, one that stood at the intersection of science and utility.[15]

For the time being, however, Franklin was not satisfied with the results of this intensive study of electricity. The newly established uniformity in nature, backed by reason and confirmed by bodily experience, had already opened the way to another of the central notions of the Age of Enlightenment—that the value of learning and knowledge could be determined by its practical utility and its contribution to the common good. After all, an orderly, uniform, and efficient universe was certainly worthy of a more orderly, uniform, and efficient society.

Ever since his return from England, Franklin had faithfully honored this claim on utility, so much so that he even invoked it when giving way to initial frustration at the complexity of electrical phenomena and his seeming inability to understand and master them. "If there is no other Use discovered of Electricity, this, however, is something considerable, that it may *help to make a vain Man humble*," he confessed in 1747 to Collinson, the invaluable go-between for the Royal Society and the Philadelphians.[16]

Franklin concluded a detailed list of his latest findings, forwarded to Collinson for distribution to the European virtuosi, with a doleful note of failure: he and his colonial colleagues had so far been unable to hit upon any practical applications of their work on the electrical fire. As a result, they decided to call a temporary halt to their research. Besides, the imminent arrival of the hot Philadelphia summer meant the air would soon be too humid to permit efficient production of the static electricity that was central to their experiments. "Chagrined a little that We have hitherto been able to discover Nothing in this Way of Use to Mankind, and the hot Weather coming on, when Electrical Experiments are not so agreeable; 'tis proposed to put an End to them for this Season."[17]

*   *   *

Ever since his early days as a printer and publisher, Franklin had been acutely aware of the hazards surrounding extreme weather. The colonial economy rested on the twin pillars of agriculture and shipping, both vulnerable to dangerous climactic conditions. The towns and cities, their homes made almost exclusively of wood, were particularly susceptible to terrible fires ignited by a stray lightning bolt. The readers of his *Poor Richard's* almanacs, largely farmers, demanded long-range forecasts of heavy storms, cold fronts, and frosts, while the *Pennsylvania Gazette* regularly chronicled the deaths and destruction produced by lightning, floods, and other natural phenomena.

In fact, Franklin harbored something of a forensic interest in lightning strikes, personally inspecting homes, churches, and other damaged buildings in order to trace the burn marks and other clues to the path of this fearsome force. At other times he sent his son, William, to report back on particularly damaging cases. He was also intrigued by accounts of visible electrical disturbances in the rigging of ships at sea, what mariners called St. Elmo's fire.

As part of his continuing investigations, Franklin appealed for assistance from readers of the *Gazette*: "Those . . . who may have an Opportunity of observing any of the Effects of Lightning on Houses, Ships, Trees, &c. are requested to take particular Notice of its Course, and Deviation from a straight

Line, in the Walls or other Matter affected by it, its different Operations or Effects on Wood, Stone, Bricks, Glass, Metals, Animal Bodies, &c."[18]

For some time now, the Philadelphians had been steadily noting ways in which electricity in the laboratory and lightning in the great outdoors appeared to share a number of distinct qualities. According to their laboratory notes of November 7, 1749—that is, less than seven months after he bemoaned the lack of progress toward practical applications—this list of common properties had already grown to a dozen. Among the most notable were a "crack or noise in exploding," the emission of a "Sulphurous smell" and "swift motion [and a] crooked path."[19]

The colonial researchers had already discovered the ability of bodkins or other pointed rods to "draw off," or attract, the electrical charge. Might not lightning also be subject to such an effect? The time had come, Franklin declared, to find out. "We do not know whether this property is in lightning. But since they agree in all particulars wherein we can already compare them, is it not probable they agree likewise in this? Let the experiment be made."[20]

It was also possible to use a silversmith's sturdy iron punch to draw off, or neutralize, a substantial charge held by a powerful collector fashioned from a pasteboard tube some ten feet long, producing the characteristic "snap" of an electrical strike. "If a Tube only 10 Foot long, will strike and discharge it's Fire on the Punch at 2 or 3 Inches Distance, an electrified Cloud of perhaps 10,000 Acres may strike and discharge on the Earth at a proportionally greater Distance," Franklin reckoned.[21]

The eventual result was, of course, the development of the lightning rod, essentially a grounded metal point or needle that could protect buildings and anyone inside from the dangers of lightning bolts by safely discharging the electrical strike into the earth. In the spring of 1751, a notice in Franklin's *Gazette* alerted the general public to the workings of this new invention: "How to secure Houses, Ships, &c. from being hurt by its destructive Violence."[22]

Franklin affixed a lightning rod to his own home and even rigged up a series of bells and clappers that would ring out whenever an electrical current ran through the system—to the acute alarm of the rest of the household. "If the ringing of the Bells frightens you," he later wrote to his wife, Deborah, from London, "tie a Piece of Wire from one Bell to the other, and that will conduct the lightning without ringing or snapping, but silently."[23]

Given the slow pace of eighteenth-century communications, as well as the need for further experimentation, testing, and verification, it would take several years before the lightning rod became a common feature in the colonies and in Europe. Adoption of the new technology was also delayed by scattered opposition. Religious traditionalists tended to see lightning as a weapon of divine retribution and worried that the electricians were meddling in God's affairs, although many clerics, eager to preserve their church steeples from lightning damage, expressed support for the new invention.[24]

The superstitious joined the fray, many fearing that the newfangled rods would merely attract dangerous lightning bolts and thus increase the danger rather than ward it off or actively protect against it.* They generally preferred the old method of ringing church bells during thunderstorms to invoke God's protection and deter any danger. Even some prominent electricians, including one of the creators of the Leyden jar, thought that loud noises—the peal of bells or perhaps thunderous cannon fire—might better disperse lightning.[25]

Franklin himself later became embroiled in an almost comical debate over whether his pointed rods were more effective than "blunted" versions preferred by his leading British critic. With the War for Independence looming, political considerations impelled King George III, by then fed up with the increasingly obstreperous Americans, to overrule Franklin and the near-unanimous views of the virtuosi of the Royal Society, and order rods with blunted ends be erected to protect such valued buildings as St. Paul's Cathedral and the government powder magazine at Purfleet.

The king became the immediate target of London's coffeehouse wags, who savagely lampooned his ruling in satiric verse while at the same time extolling the views of Franklin:

---

* In a side note to the history of the coming French Revolution, the lawyer Maximilien Robespierre first came to public attention with his successful defense of a provincial landowner who had erected a lightning rod on his property, thereby unsettling his neighbors. "The Arts and Sciences are the richest gifts that God can give to mankind," argued Robespierre, later to be one of the leading figures of the revolution's Reign of Terror. "What perverse fate has then put so many obstacles in the way of their progress on earth?" Quoted in I. Bernard Cohen, "Prejudice Against the Introduction of Lightning Rods," *Journal of the Franklin Institute* 253: 36, n99.

> While you, great GEORGE! for safety hunt,
>   And sharp conductors change for blunt,
>   The Empire's out of joint.
>   FRANKLIN a wiser course pursues,
>   And all your thunder fearless views,
>   By sticking to——*the point.**

By then an ardent convert to the American revolutionary cause, Franklin noted coolly that protecting the gunpowder that helped fuel the British war machine was no longer his concern. For John Pringle, president of the Royal Society, the dispute over pointed or blunt rods proved a more serious matter. Royal prerogative was one thing, but, as he reportedly told the king, the "laws and operation of nature" were quite another.[26] Caught between the immovable power of the throne and the irresistible forces of physics, Pringle resigned his position.

✳   ✳   ✳

On the last day of November 1753, those men of science and invention at the Royal Society of London did something they had never done before: they awarded their highest honor to a complete outsider—and not just any outsider, but a resident of a colonial outpost, some thirty-five hundred miles to the west of the British imperial capital. Delivering the ceremonial oration, the president of the Royal Society took pains to point out that the absentee winner of the year's Copley Medal, albeit neither "a Fellow of this Society nor an Inhabitant of this Island," was nonetheless a British subject as well as a member of that more expansive republic, peopled by "learned Men and Philosophers of all Nations."[27]

The recipient of the Society's award for 1753, then the world's greatest prize for scientific achievement, was none other than "Benjamin Franklin Esqr. of Pennsylvania," in recognition of his "curious Experiments and Observations on Electricity." These included the "easy method" of confirming the identity of electricity and lightning, later memorialized in the Currier and Ives print of Franklin wielding his electric kite in a thunderstorm, as well as a host of related

---

*   Despite the running scientific and political dispute of the day over the relative efficacy of blunt and sharp points in lightning rods, either will work equally well outside the laboratory, given the enormous power of a lightning bolt. However, sharp points remain standard practice to this day.

findings on a subject that was then the latest fashion in salons, workshops, and lecture halls across Europe.

The adulation of the Royal Society marked a quick reversal of fortune for Franklin and for colonial science. The initial reception toward the work of the Philadelphian electricians had been dismissive, a fact that still rankled Franklin many decades later, while their subsequent findings were "laughed at by the Connoisseurs."[28] The Frenchman Nollet, whose own theories and scientific reputation were seriously undermined by Franklin's new approach, refused to believe his eyes. Overwhelmed by the absurdity of an *American* scientist, Nollet confided to an ally that this "Benjamin Franklin" was surely the fictitious creation of his own jealous rivals in England.[29]

With the success of the Philadelphia experiments, the Europeans were forced to take notice of the colonials as scientists in their own right. This marked the start of an American revolution against an economy of knowledge that had been in place for centuries. Unlike Bartram, Garden, and the other North American naturalists, whose work could be absorbed seamlessly into existing European conceptions of plant and animal life, Franklin and his fellow electricians presented a true achievement in basic science, one that featured a revolutionary theory to explain observations derived from experimentation. This, says Brooke Hindle in his classic study of early American science, represented "the most important scientific contribution made by an American in the colonial period."[30]

Among Franklin's recognized innovations were the distinction between positive and negative electrical charges; a plausible explanation of the workings of the mysterious Leyden jar, a simple condenser capable of storing electricity; the design and naming of the electrical "battery"; and the use of bodkins and other sharp points to "*throw* off, as well as *draw* off the Electrical Fire," the first step toward his development of the lightning rod.[31]

Franklin was showered with honors, awards, and public acclaim. In addition to the Copley Medal, the Royal Society elected him a fellow, in an unprecedented unanimous vote and after waiving the usual formalities. The Académie des Sciences, in Paris, made Franklin just one of eight foreign members. Allies on the Continent helped ensure that his theories and findings crowded out competing views, including those of the Nollet. Harvard, Yale, and William and Mary all awarded him honorary degrees, and henceforth he would be known universally as Dr. Franklin.

The ever-ambitious Franklin was delighted to go along. He had already met the Europeans more than halfway by studiously structuring his ideas and their presentation in ways acceptable to the members of the Royal Society and their Continental colleagues. And he would spend much of the rest of his life, whatever his other pressing political, commercial, or diplomatic duties, gladly playing the part of America's first scientist, and serving as intermediary between the upstart colonials and the Old World virtuosi.

Yet, the experiments of the Philadelphia electricians and the later work of their American heirs contained the seeds of a new approach to useful knowledge, one that challenged the increasing demands of the Europeans that it be subordinated—tamed, even—through application of quantitative methods, mathematical modeling, or mechanical representation. Before Franklin's groundbreaking experiments, researchers in England and France had already proposed the same, as yet untested, analogy between lightning and electricity. Nollet had noticed that the innards of a sparrow electrocuted in his laboratory closely resembled those of a man killed by lightning.[32] It was, however, the particular genius of the Americans that allowed them to cut through the theoretical disputes and arrive at a workable solution.

Distrustful of systems and unbeholden to the centralized political, social, and economic interests that held sway over the Royal Society and the Académie des Sciences, Franklin and his fellow Leather Aprons felt free to draw on a lifetime of common sense and experience as independent craftsmen and mechanics to solve the riddle of lightning. In a flurry of creativity unleashed by Franklin's discoveries, a new generation of American experimenters such as the itinerant physician Dr. T. Gale and the medical inventor Elisha Perkins began to apply electricity to everything from medical therapies and psychological treatments to spiritual regeneration. All the while they spurned formal scientific theory, which they equated with dangerous, centralized power.[33]

This American approach, essentially a victory of common sense over elite science, came at a time when the Europeans were moving to eliminate the wonder at the heart of natural phenomena and to remove such knowledge from the drawing room, the public lecture hall, and the mechanic's workshop and preserve it instead in the disciplined world of the university, the academy, and the professional laboratory. It was not until the middle of the nineteenth century that American science at last began to come under firm institutional authority.[34] By then, this resistance on the part of early American practitioners of useful knowledge to centralized control had carved out lasting space for the independent tinkerer, the inventor, and the industrial visionary—future Edisons, Taylors, and Fords—and inspired the revolutionary generation that would overthrow British rule in the name of "self-evident" truths.

No doubt, members of the Royal Society were only marginally aware of the full implications of their decision, and it is only in hindsight that we can recognize an early demarcation in the coming shift in the balance of scientific and technological power from Old Europe to the New World. To smooth over what was in truth a radical overhaul of the established intellectual order of things, the Royal Society bent over backward to portray Franklin and his circle of American experimenters as citizens of very same "learned Republic" already peopled by the European virtuosi.

The Royal Society could also rely on the shared notion of the uniformity and regularity of nature, one of the most dearly held ideas of the Enlightenment. This marked a significant departure from the older, more traditional worldview, in which nature and its mysteries expressed God's awesome power and as a result were to be feared and respected rather than examined, analyzed, and understood. Isaac Newton sealed this metaphysical transition at the dawn of the 1700s by establishing that nature obeyed certain identifiable physical laws that operated identically on earth and in the heavens.

True, opinion was divided over whether God would—or even could—override natural laws of his own creation, a point on which Franklin himself was deeply ambivalent. But this controversy did little to undermine the general unanimity among the learned that the physical world was knowable, quantifiable, and efficient. The rise of natural philosophy based on experimentation completed this gradual refutation of medieval and early modern ways of thinking.

But if nature's laws were one and the same, on earth as in the heavens, then surely any findings from Franklin's Philadelphia experiments, albeit carried out in colonial obscurity, were equally valid, and thus to be equally valued in London, Paris, Leipzig, or St. Petersburg. In this way, Newton's claim on the universal application of natural philosophy essentially freed Franklin and his fellow Philadelphians to challenge the imperial economy of knowledge and to stake their own claims on scientific inquiry.[35]

And, in fact, Franklin's experimental protocols—both the famous electric kite and an earlier version using a soldier's sentry box to attract lightning and capture some of its power—were soon performed to great acclaim across the scientific world, from England, France, and the Netherlands to Russia and as far away as Japan. His collected writings on the subject, drawn primarily from his letters to Collinson between 1747 and 1750, were published in London under the title, *Experiments and Observations on Electricity, Made at Philadelphia in America*. Subsequent editions appeared in French, German, and Italian.[36] Given Franklin's lifelong antipathy for classical learning, it is fitting that a planned volume in Latin was never completed.

Among the public at large, the dissemination of Franklin's curious observations and specifically his proposal for the use of lightning rods was, well, nothing short of electric. He was widely hailed as both a genius and the true philosopher of nature, and his accomplishments were celebrated in verse and commemorated by university professors, government ministers, and the press. His collaborator Kinnersley predicted that as a result of the lightning rod Franklin's name would go down in history alongside that of the incomparable Isaac Newton: "May this method of security from the destructive violence of one of the most awful powers of nature ... extend to the last posterity of mankind, and make the Name of FRANKLIN like that of NEWTON, immortal."[37]

The French economist Anne-Robert-Jacques Turgot, who served as finance minister when Franklin was representing the rebellious American colonies in Paris, wrote a Latin epigram that captured something of the popular sentiment toward the electrician-turned-politician: "He snatched the lightning from the sky and the scepter from tyrants." Franklin's image as a simple colonial sage—which he did nothing to discourage and in fact everything to advance—resonated with the French public in particular. A French translation of sayings from his *Poor Richard's* almanacs became a bestseller under the title, *The Way to Wealth*, while his homespun clothing provided the alluring air of the frontiersman amid the over-the-top finery and foppery of the Paris salons and the royal court.

Soon, his likeness accompanied by Turgot's inspirational motto was being reproduced on silk, porcelain, and other fine materials across France. Understandably, King Louis XVI was nonplussed by the sudden ubiquity of this potent symbol of democratic rebellion, even if Franklin and the Americans did represent useful allies against the hated British. In a fit of petulance, the king had a porcelain chamber pot fashioned for his mistress with Franklin's portrait prominently painted on the inside.[38]

Popular enthusiasm for the lightning rod tended to overshadow the advances in basic science achieved by the Philadelphia circle. The virtuosi, too, elevated the new Franklinist principles of electricity to almost unassailable heights and effectively blocked out opposing views. Several important elements united the public and the natural philosophers in their adulation. First, Franklin's work grew directly from the contemporary fad in Europe and the colonies for electrical phenomena. As a result, the man in the street, not just the specialist, was well aware of the theoretical problems and practical issues involved.

Second, Franklin's findings provided a seemingly straightforward example of the ways scientific knowledge could arm man with power over the forces of nature, as reflected in Turgot's epigram. Third, they comported with contemporary sensibilities regarding common sense and bodily experience as vital complements to rational investigation. Perhaps most important of all, the development of the lightning rod appeared to validate the widely held faith, traceable back at least to Francis Bacon more than 130 years earlier, that the work of the natural philosophers would ultimately lead to practical applications.[39]

✣   ✣   ✣

The two colonial cities that shaped Franklin's outlook, the Boston of his early years and the Philadelphia of his commercial and political successes, proved particularly hospitable to the exploration into "the Nature of Things." By the time of Franklin's birth, the Puritan founders of the Massachusetts Bay Colony had long since carved out space for reason and argumentation, in contrast to what they saw as the unthinking, implicit faith of their sectarian rivals.

They also saw the utility of knowledge as part and parcel of God's providence. To be sure, the divine plan was contained fully within the Puritan creed, but this did not absolve man from responsibility to carry out his own investigations into the world of nature.[40] John Norton, a leading figure among the New England Puritans, made this link between faith and knowledge explicit: "The end of the Gospel is to be known, the duty and disposition of the Believer, is to know."[41] Besides, noted his fellow cleric John Cotton, "Zeal is but a wildfire without knowledge."[42]

The Puritans also nurtured something of an intellectual tradition within their clergy, reflected in the founding of the early New England universities, Harvard and Yale. The Puritan cleric Increase Mather, who read deep religious portent into the appearance of a pair of spectacular comets in 1680 and 1682, took up astronomy and formed a small circle of his own, the Philosophical Society of Agreeable Gentlemen.

This modest enterprise, which apparently never had more than a handful of active members, faded within several years amid the press of religious and political controversies surrounding the Puritan community. Yet, Increase and his son Cotton Mather contributed regular reports of New World phenomena to the virtuosi in London, and Cotton was elected to membership in the Royal Society after the publication of a long series of his scientific letters, collated as the *Curiosa Americana*.

In time, the other main religious groups in colonial America followed the example of the New England Puritans and established their own educational institutions: the College of New Jersey (later Princeton) and the informal "log colleges" among the Presbyterians; Queen's College (Rutgers) for the Dutch Reformed; King's College (Columbia) and the College of William and Mary for the Anglicans. While the central thrust was devoted to education of the faithful and the grooming of the clergy, other subjects gradually began to make inroads into the traditional curriculum.

Among the Philadelphia Quakers, who had no place for a trained priesthood, or any other formal religious authority for that matter, education naturally flowed toward recognizable secular subjects that could improve society and produce better citizens.[43] Such attitudes often clashed with the social ambitions of the city's leading families, who demanded the social prestige that a classical education would confer upon their sons. The ensuing struggle long plagued another of Franklin's favorite civic projects—the creation of a proper college befitting the largest and richest city in the colonies—and eventually forced him to withdraw from any meaningful role in an institution that later became the University of Pennsylvania.

International acclaim for Franklin camouflaged the deeper significance of the arrival of colonial science, just as it compensated for any regret he may have felt over the early setbacks suffered by the American Philosophical Society. Besides, Franklin still had the felicitous company of his friends and collaborators in the Junto, as well as those from the larger Library Company, to discuss the latest ideas, try out new experiments, and pursue useful civic improvements.

However, the immediate prospects for other scientifically inclined Americans were somewhat less promising. Cadwallader Colden, one of Franklin's early partners in the proposed philosophical society, confessed in a letter to Collinson that their transatlantic correspondence was his only true source of intellectual stimulation. "I take you to be one of my own taste, and I have often wished to communicate some thoughts in natural philosophy, which have remained many years with me undigested, for we scarcely have a man in this country that takes any pleasure in such kind of speculations."[44]

Farther south, in Charleston, the young Scottish doctor Alexander Garden likewise bemoaned his own isolation, despite the heavy concentration of fellow physicians drawn to South Carolina by the high incidence of illness induced by the hot, steamy climate. Garden had emigrated in 1752, and he, too, sought to make his fortune from the miseries of the region's rampant disease: yellow fever, malaria, dengue fever, and diphtheria were all common afflictions. Carolina, recounted one eighteenth-century European visitor, was "in the spring a paradise, in the summer a hell, and in the autumn a hospital."[45]

Still, it was almost impossible for Charleston's several dozen physicians—some formally trained in Europe, others simply quacks out for a quick buck—all to earn a living. Patients rarely paid on time, if at all, and more and more doctors kept arriving to try their luck. An attempt by the town's practitioners to band together in a "Faculty of Physic" and demand regular payment for services rendered only provoked disdain among the local populace, a number of whom took to the pages of the *South Carolina Gazette* to ridicule the entire profession. Some pilloried the physicians in verse, capturing the general public animus for American medicine.[46]

Garden, who sniped reflexively at his friend John Bartram's lack of learning after the latter began to supply the British crown with plant specimens, was appalled by the low level of scientific knowledge among his new Carolina colleagues, particularly in matters of medicinal herbs and other aspects of botany. Nor were the rest of the city's inhabitants much better.

"In Charleston we are a set of the busiest, most bustling, hurrying animals imaginable, and yet we really do not do much, but we must appear to be doing," he complained to one of his regular European correspondents. The local "gentlemen planters" were the worst of all, their entire existence taken up simply with "eating, drinking, lolling, smoking, and sleeping."[47] South Carolina was "a horrid place," the ill-tempered Garden added in a separate letter, "where there is not a living soul who knows the least iota of Natural History."[48]

To ease their shared predicament, men like Bartram, Colden, and Garden devoted enormous energy to cultivating contacts among the European scientists, often through amateur intermediaries such as Collinson and later through Franklin as well, and then to carrying on a regular correspondence over the course of many years. At times, their entreaties make painful reading as the Americans seek to curry favor among the Europeans by underscoring their own lowly status in the intellectual pecking order. "May you, Sir, who are the favored priest of Nature, and already deeply initiated into her mysteries, go on to inform yourself more and more, to examine and discover everything that is possible, and to instruct us in your invaluable writings," wrote Garden in his tireless campaign to win over Linnaeus.[49]

The Swedish naturalist eventually responded with a number of letters of his own, and he gladly accepted Garden's help in collecting specimens, for which he later credited his colonial correspondent in his masterwork, the *Systema Naturae*. But Linnaeus had to be pressed by a mutual friend to reward the American's many years of contributions to the field of botany before agreeing to assign the name *gardenia* to a genus of tropical flowering shrubs.

Maintaining such a correspondence was not a simple endeavor in the eighteenth century. The slow pace of the transatlantic mail packets and other vessels, and the very real chance that important items would miscarry or fail to arrive altogether, required a great deal of organization, effort, and planning. Correspondence frequently crossed, confounding sender and recipient alike, or was lost to the fortunes of war, accidents at sea, or plunder by privateers. The time-consuming production of multiple copies of particularly important correspondence was routine, as was the keeping of special letter books, or ledgers, to record both incoming and outgoing mail, organized by date, subject, or perhaps recipient. On top of that, the naturalists had to arrange with friendly sea captains to ensure that their precious cargoes of plants, animal bones, fossils, or other specimens safely reached their destination.

Garden agonized throughout his lifetime over fears that he had failed to keep up his side in this exchange of letters, notes, and observations, often begging his correspondents' indulgence toward his obvious shortcomings. By contrast, the organized, efficient, and single-minded Franklin, who recognized at once the power inherent to directing the flows of information and ideas, effortlessly took to the art of the scientific letter and kept at it faithfully until his death.

Despite these handicaps, the Americans slowly managed to work their way into the fabric of European scientific discussions. Such communication was the stuff of eighteenth-century science, and these advances represented a vital step for the colonials, all the more so as there were virtually no prospects the Americans would ever meet their distant interlocutors.[50] Equally as important, the style of learned correspondence adopted from the European model, with its distinct protocol, mores, and ideals, helped integrate North America into the worldwide scientific project and introduced a system that was soon applied with equal success among the slowly swelling ranks of the colonial virtuosi.

But the imperfect exchange of ideas and information provided by the scientific correspondence of mid-eighteenth-century America could not replace the very real need for a critical mass of like-minded colleagues, as well as the invaluable amateurs, supporters, and hangers-on who made possible the success of a learned society. The lack of intellectual stimulation in Charleston, as well as the relentless heat and humidity, gradually wore down Garden's resistance. In 1754, the doctor diagnosed his own malady as "acute inflammatory distemper," and he prescribed for himself a leisurely trip to recover his health amid the cooler air to the north.

Despite the difficulty of long-distance travel up and down the Eastern Seaboard, Garden could not resist the chance to seek out some like-minded souls. In New York, he visited Colden, living in luxury on his fine estate of Coldengham, while in Pennsylvania he called on both Bartram and the seemingly ubiquitous Franklin, finding the latter "a very ingenious man."[51] Restored by his journey and back in Charleston, Garden redoubled his efforts to remain in contact with Bartram, Colden, and John Clayton, of Virginia. After all, he admitted glumly, these were "the only botanists whom I know of on the continent."[52]

Poor communications and a shortage of like-minded souls were not the only problems facing early attempts at the formation of a colonial knowledge society. Also missing were a number of associated institutions—well-stocked libraries, established universities, and regular scientific books and journals—as well as sufficiently large and wealthy population centers to host and finance such efforts, and the habit of cooperation and communication among residents of the various colonies. In short, America so far lacked the social and political bases for such an enterprise.

❊   ❊   ❊

The founders of the American Philosophical Society and individual natural philosophers of the day, such as Bartram and Garden, all had to contend with the same fundamental obstacles that bedeviled other aspects of American life in the mid-eighteenth century. Even in such a potentially grave matter as a common defense in time of war, there was nothing like a consensus among the colonies and no mechanism that might secure one. With his Philosophical Society largely dormant after several false starts, including a failed publishing venture designed to attract new members, Franklin turned to the world of politics to address some of the broader issues facing the British settlements. He drafted a far-reaching and ambitious "Plan of a Proposed Union of the Several Colonies," which he put forward in 1754 at a conference in Albany, New York.

That same year, he also published his famous "Join, or Die" cartoon—a snake representing the American colonies, severed into their constituent parts—to accompany an editorial in the *Pennsylvania Gazette* on the importance of unity. Here was an early recognition that the only way forward for the thirteen colonies—some of which were ruled directly by the Crown, others by special charter, and still others, such as Pennsylvania, controlled outright by proprietors—lay in some degree of coordinated legislation and executive administration.

The proximate inspiration for the Albany conference, and for the Franklin plan, was the latest flare-up in imperial rivalry between France and Britain, which spilled over into North America in the form of the French and Indian War, running from 1754 to 1763. Franklin, among others, recognized the military and economic vulnerabilities of the fragmented colonial settlements. Delegates to the conference voted for his plan, only to see it fail to win support from any of the individual colonial assemblies, each eager to defend its own position and privilege. "Its Fate was singular," Franklin wrote in his *Autobiography*. "The Assemblies did not adopt it as they all thought there was too much *Prerogative* in it; and in England it was judged to have too much of the *Democratic*."[53]

In fact, the matter was a great deal more complicated than Franklin lets on, something he surely realized at the time. The political maneuvering around such a notion, both in London and across the colonies, was murky at best. Franklin himself was deeply involved in a running controversy back home in Philadelphia over the creation of a militia to defend the province and its valuable port, a move that set him at odds with both the pacifist Quaker elite on religious grounds, and with the proprietary Penn family and its supporters on political and economic ones.

British officials were ambivalent toward the Albany plan and a number of similar schemes put forward by others. They could see the utility of any project that would aid the colonial war effort against the French and their allies among the Indians, but they also recognized the long-term dangers posed by anything that smacked of a union of interests among the disparate American provinces.

Such fears on the part of the British were not ill founded. Franklin's blueprint for closer cooperation among the colonies called for proportional representation to a grand council, with a president, appointed by the British crown, to preside over the "General Government." This new legislature and executive officer would have responsibility for commerce, treaties, colonial expansion, and relations with the Indians; the raising of land and naval forces and the construction of forts "for the Defense of any of the Colonies"; and the collection, management, and allocation of those funds collected by duties or taxes.[54]

Mindful of the concerns back in London, Franklin and the assembled delegates in Albany were careful to provide guarantees of British sovereignty, most notably a three-year period during which the Crown could review and nullify any of the colonial legislature's laws. Further, the Albany plan promised that any "Laws made . . . for the Purposes aforesaid, shall not be repugnant but as near as may be agreeable to the Laws of England."[55] Still, it is not hard to see the early outlines here of what would emerge three decades later with the writing and ratification of the U.S. Constitution.

Tensions between the colonies and the mother country were already coming into focus, as the American settlements steadily matured into fully fledged political and economic entities, each with its own interests and challenges. Problems of trade, currency, executive powers, military protection, and popular representation—that is, the entire range of relations between governor and governed—surfaced with regular frequency, with each new instance underscoring the growing gulf between the two sides.

Franklin found himself more and more drawn into politics, and away from those pleasurable hours devoted to experimentation, further undermining prospects for the swift revival of the moribund American Philosophical Society. He had already served in local office, as both a Philadelphia city councilman and as a justice of the peace, and in 1751 he was elected to a seat in the

Pennsylvania Assembly. Six years later, the assembly dispatched him to England as provincial agent, charged with negotiating a series of sweeping political reforms with the proprietors, the heirs to William Penn. Franklin sailed in November for London; he would remain abroad, representing first Pennsylvania and several other colonies and then the newly independent United States, for twenty-three of the next twenty-eight years.

Chapter Six

DEAD AND USELESS LANGUAGES

Do not men use Latin and Greek as the cuttlefish emit their ink, on purpose
to conceal themselves from an intercourse with the common people?
—Benjamin Rush

LOOKING BACK OVER the course of his life, the octogenarian Franklin
reported that by the 1740s he had "on the whole abundant Reason to be satisfied with my establishment in Pennsylvania." His printing business was flourishing and he had begun a series of successful commercial partnerships in the
other colonies. He was ensconced in the comforting embrace of the interlocking social and intellectual circles provided by the Junto, the Library Company,
and the Masonic lodge.

Franklin busied himself with the study of French, Italian, and other
languages in order to gain access to the latest scientific developments coming
from Europe. His civic ventures—improved police protection, more efficient
public lighting, better street cleaning, a fire brigade and an associated fire insurance company—were in the works or already thriving. Still, he remained as
restless as ever. "There were however two things that I regretted: There being
no Provision for Defense, nor for a complete Education of Youth; No Militia
nor any College."[1]

Franklin's dogged efforts to create a Pennsylvania militia damaged beyond
repair his already difficult relationship with the provincial proprietors. They
were alarmed by his success in bypassing their appointed governor and raising
a large private force, complete with cannon wheedled from the governor of
New York after many shared glasses of sweet Madeira wine.[2] Thomas Penn,
now the leading voice of the proprietary family, saw in this expression of
autonomy, and in Franklin's accompanying argument that a government that
failed to protect its people could not depend on their obedience, a direct threat

to his authority. "He is a dangerous man and I should be glad if he inhabited any other country, as I believe him of a very uneasy spirit," Penn wrote to one provincial aide. "However as he is a Sort of Tribune of the People, he must be treated with regard."[3]

The militia project also placed Franklin at odds with influential elements of the province's old-line Quakers, whose pacifist principles barred them from taking part in, or financing, any armed force. At the same time, it helped cement his ties to the artisans and the independent farmers, who saw membership in the militia as an avenue to greater civic and political participation. Many of these same men would later take up arms together in the rebellion against the Crown, but for now Franklin's militia units were less military formations than social and political clubs.[4]

By contrast, the campaign for a provincial school and college, with a curriculum composed of useful knowledge, proved a much more drawn out and subtle affair, one that divided Philadelphia more along lines of class and social status than those of religious doctrine and proprietary politics. Unlike most of the other civic projects closely associated with Franklin and his circle, the creation of what would one day become the University of Pennsylvania remained an enduring source of frustration and bitterness and provoked a sense of failure to the end of his days. It was only many years after Franklin's death that the educational philosophy propounded in his early vision for a Philadelphia academy slowly began to take root in the young nation's schools, colleges, and universities.

According to notes for his never-completed autobiography, Franklin dated his first musings on a Philadelphia academy to a paper that he first drew up as early as 1743: "Go again to Boston. . . . Propose a College, not then prosecuted."[5] However, no such document has yet been found among his voluminous papers.* The first extant public reference to the fully formed idea of a provincial school appeared only six years later.

It is clear that Franklin had already given the matter of education a great deal of thought, perhaps colored by his own experiences back in Boston. His formal schooling, a brief spell at age eight at Boston Grammar School in preparation for planned theological training at Harvard, came to a sudden end with

---

* This was the same year in which he cooperated with John Bartram to publish their proposal for a learned association, the future American Philosophical Society. In his memoirs, Franklin says he set aside his initial education plan for several years after his first choice to run the school declined to take the post. *ABF*, 182.

his father's change of heart. After some rudimentary tutoring in sums and writing, young Benjamin was back at work in the family soap and candle business. Every other subject that Franklin mastered over his lifetime—and there were many—was self-taught, allowing him to escape the rigid curricula of his day and instead pick and choose only those works he found most useful and satisfying.

At age sixteen, as the pseudonymous author of the widow Silence Dogood letters in his brother's newspaper, the *New England Courant*, Franklin had savagely lampooned the scholars at Harvard for their classical pretensions. Dogood describes her dream of young college men scattered among the veiled figures of Latin, Greek, and Hebrew, with whom they falsely "pretended to an intimate Acquaintance." At the center of the scene sits Learning, perched on her high, almost inaccessible throne but otherwise in an "awful State."[6]

Now Franklin approached the creation of a Pennsylvania college with considerable planning and deliberation. First, he discussed the idea with his associates in the Junto and the Library Company. Next, he took separate soundings among "some public-spirited Gentlemen" and consulted the works of prominent thinkers, including "the famous Milton" and "the great Mr. Locke."[7] Only then did he begin to prepare the public to support the scheme through notices in the press and the publication of a thirty-two-page pamphlet, replete with footnotes and a list of references, which he distributed free of charge with the *Pennsylvania Gazette*.

The slim volume, *Proposals Relating to the Education of Youth in Pennsylvania*, offers a detailed roadmap to the foundation and management of an academy and college. The pamphlet, and several subsequent publications along similar lines, all demonstrate just how much stress Franklin and his fellow leather aprons laid on the value of a practical education, taught in English rather than in the traditional classical languages, and with an emphasis on mathematics, natural philosophy, agronomy, accounting, and mechanics.

"As to their Studies," Franklin wrote of the incoming students in his *Proposals*, "it would be well if they could be taught *every Thing* that is useful, and *every Thing* that is ornamental. But Art is long, and their Time is short. It is therefore proposed that they learn those Things that are likely to be *most useful* and *most ornamental*, Regard being had to the several Professions for which they are intended." Toward that end, the proposed curriculum was heavily weighted toward the proper use and understanding of the English language."[8]

Addressing the classical tongues, which had formed the basic medium of advanced European education for centuries, Franklin instead emphasized the absolute primacy of English and scientific instruction. Forcing the children of the lower and middling classes to devote the time and expense needed to master Greek and Latin before proceeding with their advanced schooling posed an unreasonable burden and effectively limited access to education.

After all, his own father, Josiah, had balked at the looming costs the family faced with Benjamin's enrollment at the classically oriented Boston Grammar School, and quickly yanked his son from his formal studies. It appears that Franklin may have initially favored a ban on Greek and Latin, reversing himself in the face of opposition from powerful donors and other supporters of the overall plan, and his published proposal accepted with some reluctance their place in the classroom. "And though all should not be compelled to learn Latin, Greek, or the modern foreign Languages; yet none that have an ardent Desire to learn them should be refused; their English, Arithmetic, and other Studies absolutely necessary, being at the same Time not neglected."[9]

Leisure time would be best spent attending to practical matters. "While they are reading Natural History, might not a little *Gardening, Planting, Grafting, Inoculating,* &c. be taught and practiced; and now and then Excursions made to the neighboring Plantations of the best Farmers, their Methods observed and reasoned upon for the Information of Youth. The Improvement of Agriculture being useful to all, and Skill in it no Disparagement to any."[10]

Central to Franklin's vision was a dedicated English School as the central component of the academy. There, the language of everyday American (and British) life was to be given scholarly attention typically reserved for Latin and Greek. Students would address the works of "the best English Authors," including Milton, Locke, Addison, Pope, and Swift—the very writers that had shaped Franklin as a voracious young reader and an aspiring essayist.[11] The great books of the Ancients would be read in translation, saving students from many years of preparatory language study that could now be devoted to more useful subjects.

The emphasis on the cultivation of practical skills—those of the farmer, the mechanic, the small merchant, the government functionary—echoed the social reformer and Puritan philosopher William Petty's exaltation of the tradesman and the artisan at the expense of those "lazy men in gentlemen's houses" turned out by the universities of seventeenth-century Britain. It also echoed one of the fundamental laws of William Penn's original colonial project—long since abandoned by Franklin's day—for the mandatory education of the young "so that they may be . . . taught some useful trade or skill, that the poor may work to live, and the rich if they became poor shall not want."[12]

Franklin reckoned that completion of his proposed curriculum would leave graduates well prepared to lead useful and productive lives. "Youth will come out of this School fitted for learning any Business, Calling or Profession, except such wherein Languages are required; and though unacquainted with any ancient or foreign Tongue, they will be Masters of their own, which is of more immediate and general Use."[13]

The proposed social basis for the Franklin's new school was also noteworthy, for it was to be under the management of an independent board of trustees, a self-styled "voluntary society of founders," with no direct reliance on any existing power or institution. Historically, European colleges and universities, and their American imitators, had been founded or controlled by religious orders seeking to train ministers and instruct believers, or by rulers eager to provide skilled workers for their state bureaucracies and to enhance their own prestige.[14] In contrast to the other colonial institutions of the day—Harvard, William and Mary, Yale, newcomers Princeton and Columbia*—the Philadelphia academy and college was understood from the outset to be nonsectarian, and its program of study made little direct reference to the study of religion in general.

*　　*　　*

Although the future University of Pennsylvania would remain true to this nondenominational mission, its very creation owed much to the Great Awakening, a wave of grassroots religious sentiment that injected greater participation of the lower and middling classes into organized religion and public life in general. In the South and along the frontier, the movement brought many new believers into the churches. In the Northeast and mid-Atlantic, it mobilized the artisans, the mechanics, and the petty merchants who began to assert themselves at the expense of the wealthy and powerful who dominated America's religious and social institutions. Accompanying this new

---

* Princeton received its charter in 1746 as the College of New Jersey. It was formally renamed Princeton in 1896, in honor of its host community, Princeton, New Jersey. Columbia was originally chartered in 1754 as King's College. It reopened in 1784, after the disruption of the Revolution, as Columbia University.

social prominence were increasing demands for an education that met their specific needs for useful knowledge and vocational skills, in what amounted to a rebuke to traditional notions of elite schooling.[15]

Franklin had long since left behind any attachment to organized religious practice. This view was bolstered by his own experiences growing up in Puritan-influenced Boston, which he fled at the first opportunity; his youthful romp through London's free-thinking coffeehouses; and then professional and public life in Philadelphia, where he drifted toward the deists and the more independent minded among the Quakers and where he openly clashed with the city's rigid Presbyterian clerics. Toward the end of his days, Franklin used his last major public address to urge ratification of the Constitution of the new United States, a document heavily influenced by deist currents.

Franklin was baptized in Boston, in what later became known as the Congregational Church, a close cousin to the Presbyterians of Philadelphia. But he soon turned his back on many of its central teachings. "Some of the Dogmas of that Persuasion, such as the Eternal Decrees of God, Election, Reprobation, &c. appeared to me unintelligible, others doubtful, and I early absented myself from the Public Assemblies of the Sect, Sunday being my Studying-Day."[16]

Defending himself in an emotional letter to his parents, who were openly distraught at the idea that their son had forsaken the teachings of his youth, Franklin spelled out the essence of his evolving religious views: "I think vital Religion has always suffered, when Orthodoxy is more regarded than Virtue. And the Scripture assures me, that at the last Day, we shall not be examined what we *thought*, but what we *did*; and our Recommendation will not be that we said *Lord, Lord*, but that we did Good to our Fellow Creatures."[17]

Yet, Franklin assures us that he was never without religious principles, including firm belief in "the Existence of the Deity, that he made the World, and governed it by his Providence."[18] For many years he remained a paid-up member of Philadelphia's Presbyterian congregation although he only rarely attended meetings. He even composed his own "New Version of the Lord's Prayer with Notes," modernizing the language and accounting for contemporary understandings of religious faith and practice. But Franklin was insistent that religion contribute to the public good in general and not merely to narrow sectarian interests or purely personal needs.

Attempts by the head of Philadelphia's Presbyterian congregation, Jedediah Andrews, to bring Franklin back into the orthodox fold foundered after the latter reluctantly agreed to sit through five consecutive Sundays on a trial basis. "Had he been, *in my Opinion,* a good Preacher perhaps I might have continued. But his Discourses were chiefly either polemic Arguments, or Explications of the peculiar Doctrines of our Sect, and were all to me very dry, uninteresting and unedifying, since not a single moral Principle was inculcated or enforced, their Aim seeming to be rather to make us Presbyterians than good Citizens."[19]

For Franklin, the chief value of religious practice, whatever the tradition, was the advancement of man's virtue and protection of the weak against the natural, human inclination toward vice. Seen in this way, he argued, religion was positively necessary. "If Men are so wicked as we now see them *with Religion* what would they be if *without it?*" Franklin asked rhetorically in a letter to an unnamed author who had sought his opinion on the matter.[20] He used more colorful language in his *Poor Richard Improved* of 1751 to warn against the dangers of undermining religion: "Talking against Religion is unchaining a Tiger; the Beast let loose may worry his Deliverer."[21]

Franklin set aside his general distaste for preachers when it came to George Whitefield, perhaps the most effective evangelist of the Great Awakening, and the two became fast friends and collaborators.* Franklin regularly published Whitefield's best-selling sermons and journals, contributing to the latter's fame and swelling his own coffers at the same time. Whitefield, in return, was more than generous with his fund-raising prowess in support of projects close to Franklin's heart, including the Philadelphia academy and college and the city hospital.[22]

Whitefield never tired of trying to convert Franklin, while the latter was in awe of the preacher's rhetorical skills and his ability to influence public behavior for the better. "It was wonderful to see the Change soon made in the Manners of our Inhabitants," recalled Franklin, and he compared Whitefield's soaring public oratory to the transporting experience provided by "an excellent Piece of Music."[23] At another meeting, a clearly embarrassed Franklin inexplicably found himself emptying his pockets "wholly into the Collector's Dish,

---

* Earlier, Franklin had taken on the Philadelphia's Presbyterian establishment in defense of another outspoken cleric, Samuel Hemphill, whose sermons "inculcated strongly the Practice of Virtue" at the expense of orthodox dogma. Franklin lost that battle and he retreated more or less permanently from church life after that. *ABF,* 167.

Gold and all," despite his firm vow in advance not to contribute a penny. A like-minded friend, who had accompanied Franklin that day, avoided the same fate only by virtue of having left his wallet behind.[24]

Franklin never succumbed to Whitefield's evangelical entreaties, with their unwavering demands that the Christian first undergo a personal crisis and come face-to-face with sin before breaking through to the promise of salvation. But he and his allies did take advantage of the new space that Whitefield and other revivalist preachers created in the relatively stratified world of Philadelphia society.

The Great Awakening discomfited America's religious elite and it energized workers and artisans in the towns and cities by giving them a greater voice in matters of faith, practice, and the administration of the churches. The movement also exposed deep differences within congregations and often provoked splits into warring factions. Outspoken itinerant preachers, such as the hugely popular Whitefield, further challenged the established clerics and pushed the boundaries of religious debate. Emboldened by the accompanying breakdown in traditional clerical authority, the layman was increasingly empowered to take positions and choose sides.[25]

This same activism spilled over into civic life in general, and the leather apron men began to demand greater political and social influence. Fifteen years earlier, Governor William Keith had sought to exploit these same class griev-ances in his struggle with the proprietary family and its local supporters, a campaign that led directly to the founding of Franklin's Junto. Now, religious turmoil accelerated this trend toward a more inclusive system, a development that would assume its definitive, populist shape in Pennsylvania with the coming of the Revolution and the drafting of the radical provincial constitu-tion. Of course, it helped that Pennsylvania had no established church with which to contend.

At the heart of the Great Awakening was an emphasis on personal religious experience and authentic feeling at the expense of textual or clerical authority. "An increase in speculative knowledge in divinity is not what is . . . needed by our people," wrote Jonathan Edwards, Whitefield's fellow preacher and the movement's leading intellectual. "Our people do not so much need to have their heads stored, as their hearts touched."[26] This paralleled the demands of the leather aprons for a practical education that bypassed received wisdom and rested instead on useful knowledge, common sense, and experimentation. After all, the motto of the Royal Society of London was *Nullius in verba*—"take no man's word for it!"

Fueled by religious fervor and social activism, the province's artisans, craftsmen, and laborers enthusiastically backed a growing charity schools movement, which had begun in England and Scotland. These institutions, funded by subscription and often built by volunteers, provided for "Instruction of Poor Children gratis, in Reading, Writing and Arithmetic, and the first Principles of Virtue and Piety."[27]

A circle of mechanics began to build one such school in Philadelphia. Commonly known as the New Building, it would also double as a large auditorium for visiting preachers, such as Whitefield, who were either too controversial, too popular, or both, to be accommodated in Philadelphia's existing churches. "Both House and Ground were ... expressly for the Use of any Preacher of any religious Persuasion who might desire to say something to the People of Philadelphia," Franklin claimed years later with some exaggeration, "the Design in building not being to accommodate any particular Sect, but the Inhabitants in general, so that even if the Mufti of Constantinople were to send a Missionary to preach Mahometanism to us,* he would find a Pulpit at his Service."[28]

A special committee of trustees, consisting of two carpenters, a bricklayer, and a weaver, managed the construction, while a second body, made up of Whitefield, several merchants, and a shoemaker, were to see to it that the school's charitable mission was fulfilled. Another charity school project, led by local coal miners, began to take shape in Bristol, Pennsylvania, about twenty miles northeast of Philadelphia.[29]

Gradually, the religious enthusiasm of the Great Awakening eased into remission. The itinerant Whitefield, busy raising funds for an orphanage in Georgia, began to spend less and less time in Philadelphia, although he did preach a memorable sermon in the future school and auditorium, its unfinished walls reaching only to his shoulders. Its star attraction largely absent, the complex gradually fell into disuse, its educational programs largely abandoned.

It remained so until Franklin and his backers, primarily his fellow artisans and mechanics, stepped forward to pay off the project's debts and convert the

---

*   In fact, the associated trust stated explicitly that the building was restricted to the use of orthodox Christian preachers. See Cheyney, 24, n1.

structure into classrooms for the new Philadelphia academy, which would absorb the charity school and set aside a certain number of places for the indigent. "The Care and Trouble of agreeing with the Workmen, purchasing Materials, and superintending the Work fell upon me, and I went through it the more cheerfully, as it did not then interfere with my private Business," the management of which Franklin had already entrusted to his partner, the printer David Hall.[30]

✳   ✳   ✳

Having readied the classrooms, the mechanics, artisans, and craftsmen enjoyed less success in establishing their desired curriculum, grounded in useful knowledge and practical training, at the heart of the new academy and college. Between the presentation of these ideas in *Proposals Relating to the Education of Youth in Pennsylvania* and the opening of the school, much of the novelty and power of the Franklin scheme was eroded by opposition from social conservatives and other traditionalists.

This largely reflected the composition of the board of trustees, controlled by what Franklin, who never shed his strong class identification with the leather apron men, later referred to as a cabal of "the principal Gentlemen of the Province."[31] Schooling in Greek and Latin was still seen in both Europe and America as the mark of a true gentleman, and the powerful figures who dominated the board—founding members included Philadelphia's richest businessman, the mayor and several of his predecessors, city councilmen, and the province's chief justice—were determined that their own offspring should receive a fitting classical education in the new academy.[32] Furthermore, the creation of a cohort of educated tradesmen and other middling sorts, who might then be better positioned to demand a real say in provincial affairs, held little appeal to the majority of board members.

These same artisans had taken the lead in the planning, construction, and early financing of the provincial academy. Franklin's innovative educational program had generated considerable excitement among a wide swath of Pennsylvania society, including workers and mechanics, many of whom responded enthusiastically with pledges of financial support for his explicit notion of a practical education. The project also garnered backing among members of Franklin's expanding circle of European virtuosi, eager to inculcate their experimental philosophy in young New World minds.

However, conservative local notables wound up with most of the twenty-four seats on the school's board of trustees, reflecting their influence and connections to the world of provincial politics and business. Franklin and his old Junto partner Philip Syng were the only artisans to obtain seats on the board, although Franklin's prowess in public advocacy secured him the relatively weak position of board president. The board assigned Tench Francis, the province's attorney general, to work with Franklin in drawing up bylaws for the new institution, and at a meeting on November 13, 1749, the trustees approved the formal "Constitutions for a Public Academy in the City of Philadelphia."

These bylaws set aside many of Franklin's progressive precepts and gave clear precedence to the teaching of the Latin and Greek, with the study of English relegated to a subordinate position. Day-to-day authority for running the school was assigned to the Latin master. He was to be paid twice as much as the English master and to be responsible for the instruction of only half as many students. Over time, the trustees lost interest in the English program and shirked their duties toward its students and faculty; they even attempted to abandon it altogether in 1769 but were forced to reverse the decision after a close reading of their own bylaws, which mandated that such instruction be offered by the institution.

Despite these headwinds, Franklin immersed himself in the project throughout much of the 1750s. He further refined his thinking on education, set forth in the *Idea of the English School*, and he engaged in a furious effort to persuade the respected American clergyman Samuel Johnson (not the great English lexicographer and essayist of the same name) to run the new academy. Johnson declined the offer and later became the first president of King's College, in New York, but not before he had delivered high praise for Franklin's ideas. "Nobody would imagine that the draft you have made for an English education was done by a Tradesman." There was little, he noted graciously, that he would add to Franklin's proposed curriculum by way of improvement.[33]

In a notice in the *New York Gazette* of June 3, 1754, Johnson publicly endorsed Franklin's philosophy of education and laid out very similar thinking in his own aspirations for the new King's College: in addition to the classical languages, students would learn "the arts of *numbering* and *measuring*; of *Surveying* and *Navigation*, of *Geography* and *History*, of *Husbandry*, *Commerce* and *Government*, and in the Knowledge of *all nature* in the *Heavens* above us, and in the *Air*, *Earth* and *Water* around us, and the various kinds of *Meteors*, *Stones*, *Mines* and *Minerals*, *Plants* and *Animals*, and of Every Thing *useful* for the Comfort, Convenience and Elegance of Life, in the chief *Manufactures* relating to any of these Things."[34]

Franklin also worked hard to protect the day-to-day interests of the English and science programs from the hostility of the board. He arranged for a majority of the funds first set aside for school materials to be spent on "mathematical and philosophical" apparatus ordered from London through his primary contact Collinson. And he seems to have been behind a successful effort to increase the pay for the English master, although it remained considerably less than that of the chief Latin instructor.[35] Franklin saw to it that his fellow Junto member, the mathematician Theophilus Grew, and his old partner in the electrical experiments and public lecture series, Ebenezer Kinnersley, both joined the faculty, giving considerable heft to the school's teaching of science.

Most significant for the future course of the institution, Franklin successfully recruited the ambitious clergyman William Smith to teach a course in logic, rhetoric, ethics, and natural philosophy. With Franklin's blessing, Smith soon assumed the top administrative job as provost and ushered in the promotion of the academy to the formal rank of a college, allowing it to grant degrees. Smith would remain the driving force at what was now formally known as the College, Academy and Charitable School of Philadelphia in the Province of Pennsylvania for almost twenty-five years.

Educated in Aberdeen and ordained in the Anglican Church, Smith first caught Franklin's eye with his own tract, *A General Idea of the College of Mirania*, which presented the fictional province of Mirania as a vehicle for his progressive views on schooling. The twenty-six-year-old Smith, a private tutor on Long Island, had formulated the ideas contained in the essay as part of his own campaign to be named president of King's College and to shape its curriculum, then in its final planning stages.

When that failed to pan out, he turned his attention to the Philadelphia academy and even enrolled the two wealthy boys under his charge in the new school. He then set out to woo Franklin and he included in his pamphlet hearty praise for Franklin's own ideas. Smith even sent Franklin a personal copy on the very first day of publication.[36] Flattery aside, Franklin must have felt that he had found both a kindred spirit and the ideal candidate to manage the academy, although it still took several years to round up the financial and institutional support required to complete the appointment.

As Franklin recognized, Smith's utopian College of Mirania was a direct attack on traditional educational practice. "We must not then . . . wilder [bewilder] ourselves in the Search of Truth, among the Rabbis, Commentators and Schoolmen," wrote Smith, in the voice of his fictional narrator Evander. "Nor in the more refined Speculations of modern Metaphysicians concerning Spirit, Matter, &c., nor yet in the polemic Writings about Grace, Predestination, moral Agency, the Trinity, &c. &c. which so inflame the World at this Day." Rather, the goal was to turn out "better Men and Citizens."[37]

Toward this end, Smith's idealized college offered two distinct tracks, one for students preparing for divinity, law, or medicine, and one for "those designed for Mechanic Professions," each with its own plan of education. This latter Mechanics School "is so much like the English School in *Philadelphia*, first sketched out by the very ingenious and worthy *Mr. Franklin*."[38] Among the other innovations the two men endorsed were an emphasis on the English language— "taught grammatically, and as a Language, with Writing"—as well as the general exclusion of outright religious instruction and the pursuit of "Accounts, Mathematics, Ethics, Oratory, Chronology, History, the most plain and useful Parts of natural and mechanic Philosophy . . . to which is added something of Husbandry and Chemistry."[39]

By almost any standard, Smith's long tenure at the head of the Philadelphia academy should be considered a success. He oversaw its swift advance to the thin ranks of colonial colleges in 1755, introduced medical education in 1765, and established the institution as a university six years later. Early on, he implemented an ambitious new curriculum, one that mirrored many of the reforms he had witnessed in his own university days in Aberdeen. There, much of the medieval Scholastic tradition had been jettisoned to make way for the study of chemistry, natural history, and other aspects of natural philosophy.[40]

Smith's three-year program of study—a fourth college year was added later to American higher education—allocated one third of the coursework to mathematics and science, one third to the classics, and a like amount to logic, ethics, metaphysics, and oratory.[41] The central emphasis, wrote Smith in his formal proposal to the trustees, was on "Thinking, Writing and Acting well, which is the grand aim of a liberal education." Time would be set aside at the end of each of the year's three terms "for recreation, or bringing up slower geniuses."[42]

Even when it came to his beloved classical languages, Smith was prepared to address Franklin's concerns by casting them simply as tools for advanced learning and not as ends in themselves. Latin and Greek, he acknowledged in one of his college sermons, were to be seen "rather as an Instrument or Means of science, than a Branch thereof."[43] Smith also became an early and enthusiastic member of the American Philosophical Society, and many of his ideas owed no less to Francis Bacon and the Royal Society than did those entertained by Franklin. At his very first commencement as provost in 1757, Smith appealed to the college's benefactors and assembled guests on behalf of both the new graduates and their successors: "I beseech you, let their minds be seasoned with useful knowledge."[44]

In Franklin's eyes, however, Smith's tenure at the head of the school—*his* school—was little short of disaster. He was particularly bitter over what he saw as ill treatment of the English curriculum and its intended audience of students from the lower and middle classes. Not long after Smith's arrival in Philadelphia, the provost's social and political ambitions led to increasingly close collaboration with Thomas Penn, Franklin's great adversary, and Smith's support for the so-called proprietary faction put him at odds with the concerns of the Leather Apron Club and their supporters among the other artisans, the petty merchants, and the more progressive Quakers.

Finding himself in a natural alliance with Pennsylvania's ruling elite, who shared his own taste for the classics, Smith began to shed his public enthusiasm for Franklin's English School. Over time, funding levels for the English-language program dropped, enrollment suffered, and the best of the faculty, including Franklin's scientifically-minded allies, began to slip away or were forced to leave.

Smith's proposed reorganization of the curriculum, outlined in 1754 in the *American Magazine and Monthly Chronicle*, did not even mention the English School. Rather, he focused all his attention on the classical program.[45] Nor did Smith offer any acknowledgement of Franklin's seminal role in the founding of the academy itself and the creation of its first course of study. Perhaps most damaging of all, Smith used the pages of this same short-lived magazine, of which he was the editor, to question Franklin's rightful claim on the electrical discoveries that had won him such fame at home and abroad, ascribing them instead to Ebenezer Kinnersley, then a teacher at the school. Kinnersley, ever loyal to his friend and associate, publically denied the honors and backed Franklin as the leading figure among the Philadelphia electricians, but by then the Smith-Franklin rift was complete.

At the same time, Franklin's increasing involvement in Pennsylvania politics and other projects began to limit his influence at the school. Amid the press of other business, he resigned as board president. In 1757, the Pennsylvania legislature sent him on the first of two lengthy missions to London to negotiate the future governance of the province. Two years later, Franklin was forced to acknowledge that his absence from Philadelphia meant that he was no longer in a position to assist Kinnersley, his fellow electrician, in the teacher's struggles with the college administration, or to defend the principles of practical education.

"Everything to be done in the Academy was privately preconcerted in a Cabal without my Knowledge or Participation and accordingly carried into Execution," Franklin wrote from London by way of commiseration with his fellow electrician. "The Schemes of Public Parties made it seem requisite to lessen my Influence wherever it could be lessened. The Trustees had reaped the full Advantage of my Head, Hands, Heart and Purse, in getting through the first Difficulties of the Design, and when they thought they could do without me, they laid me aside."[46]

Franklin's anger that his educational project had been hijacked never subsided. Toward the very end of his life, back in Philadelphia after his diplomatic triumphs in Paris on behalf of the new United States, he prepared a detailed, six-thousand-word indictment of the trustees. The central fault, he argued in his "Observations Relative to the Intentions of the Original Founders of the Academy in Philadelphia," completed in the summer of 1789 but never published, lay with those "Persons of Wealth and Learning" who forced him to water down the stress on English instruction in useful knowledge in favor of a traditional program of classical education.[47]

Despite failing health that often left him bedridden, Franklin painstakingly combed through the minutes of the board over the intervening decades to support his contention that both the letter and the spirit of the academy's original constitutions had been systematically contravened, in violation of promises made to the majority of contributors. As the last of the founders still alive, it was incumbent upon him to try to right the wrongs done to the institution and its fundamental ideals. "I seem here to be surrounded by the Ghosts of my dear departed Friends, beckoning and urging me to use the only Tongue now left us, in demanding that Justice to our Grand children that our Children have been denied."[48]

Franklin acknowledged that he, too, had made mistakes. He unwisely permitted a number of the trustees' initial moves against the English School to go on unchecked when it might still have been in his power to reverse them. The essay also betrays a separate note of bitterness that his tireless diplomatic efforts abroad on behalf of the new nation had not received the public recognition he felt was his due.

Franklin's contributions to the future direction of American education, however, should not be slighted by his self-professed failure to realize the radical vision of the original Philadelphia academy. True, he had allowed himself to get entangled in personal disputes with William Smith. This had hindered his ability to lobby effectively for the so-called English program and related educational reform, and to ensure the productive education of lower- and middle-class students. Likewise, his political activism in the province further undercut these efforts by setting him against the establishment figures on the board, whose cooperation on educational matters he needed.

Yet the institution he left behind remained true throughout its history to its nonsectarian roots; unique among the colleges of the day, it was never under the direct influence of any single denomination. From the outset, it offered the nation's most progressive program of mathematical and scientific studies and paid great attention to the study of the English language, putting it decades ahead of the other colonial institutions of higher education.[49] One hundred years later, Franklin's impulse toward useful education was reinvigorated with the foundation of America's great land-grant universities, created under the federal Morrill Act of 1862 to provide training in agriculture and the mechanical arts "to promote the liberal and practical education of the industrial classes in the several pursuits and professions in life."[50]

*   *   *

Franklin's political mission to London, beginning in 1757, cost him what little remained of his influence at the Philadelphia academy, but he could still actively promote practical education and the movement for useful knowledge in the American colonies. The move to England and subsequent travels around the country and on the Continent allowed him to meet for the first time many of the European virtuosi, including Peter Collinson, with whom he had built up a steady correspondence over the years. The scientific fame surrounding his electrical experiments and invention of the lightning rod gave Franklin easy access to the upper echelons of British society and opened doors to the most interesting intellectual circles, coffeehouse clubs, and political discussion groups.

His successful navigation of the social networks that spanned the intimate world of European science provided an important channel by which the latest thinking on experimentation and useful knowledge could penetrate the American colonies. Among the beneficiaries of Franklin's knowledge and contacts was Benjamin Rush, fresh from medical studies at the University of Edinburg and in London to attend scientific lectures and visit the local hospitals.

It is easy to see why Franklin would take to the young American, whose social background, education, and enthusiasm for experimental science complemented his own experience, ideas, and values. For the rest of his life, he would continue to act as mentor, promoter, and a source of patronage and outright financial support for Rush and others like him.

The son of a Philadelphia gunsmith with family roots among the early Puritans and Quakers, Rush attended the rural West Nottingham Academy, one of the so-called log colleges in New Jersey. The schoolmaster Samuel Finley, who was Rush's uncle, integrated animal husbandry and other aspects of outdoor life with more traditional subjects. "All his scholars shared in the labors of harvest and hay-making. . . . These exercises were both pleasant and useful. They conduced to health, and helped to implant more deeply in our minds the native passion for rural life," Rush later recalled fondly, despite a lasting scar on one hand from a schoolboy accident with farm machinery.[51]

The academy's pedagogical philosophy was largely a conservative one, but it did place particular emphasis on the English language and on the study of arithmetic, geography, and geometry. As schoolmaster, Finley instilled in his students strong notions of public service, temperance, and modesty, and he steered Rush away from "the temptations" of a career in law and toward a more useful vocation as a physician and, later, a professor of medicine.[52] "I might have acquired more fortune and rank in life in the profession of law . . . but I am sure I have been more useful in the latter profession."[53]

Rush left the academy for Princeton and completed his undergraduate degree in 1760. He then returned to Philadelphia where he apprenticed himself to a local physician—typical practice for an aspiring colonial doctor—and attended lectures at the Pennsylvania Hospital. But by his own account, his true education only began with his arrival in 1766 in the cosmopolitan world of

Edinburgh, then in the powerful grip of Enlightenment ideas on the place of human reason in science, society, politics, and religion.

This was the Scotland of the skeptic David Hume, the political economist Adam Smith, and many other eighteenth-century luminaries of philosophy, experimental science, and invention. Rush, whose great-great-grandfather led a cavalry force under English revolutionary Oliver Cromwell, was also exposed to radical republicanism by a fellow descendant of a Puritan commander. These heady experiences helped set the American on a course that would make him one of the leading colonial voices for both useful knowledge and the revolt against the British monarchy. He would also go on to make original contributions to medical education and to the new field of psychiatry. "The two years I spent in Edinburgh I consider as the most important in their influence on my character and conduct of any period of my life," Rush records in his memoirs.[54]

This European sojourn included periodic visits to Franklin, who introduced Rush to London's intellectual world. He had dinner with Samuel Johnson (the famed lexicographer), met one of Cromwell's great-grandsons, and found his way into one of the city's leading literary circles, "a kind of Coffee house for authors." Franklin also provided his countryman with a much-needed loan and letters of introduction to his scientific contacts in Paris, including the French electrician Nollet, with whom he had now reconciled. Throughout his time in London, Rush took in the public attractions, attended the odd theater performance, and paid special interest to the city's burgeoning industrial enterprises. "I . . . visited most of the large and curious manufactories that were carried on in London, and wrote down descriptions of them."[55]

Rush returned to his hometown in 1769 at the age of twenty-four and opened a modest medical practice, initially serving indigent patients ignored by his fellow physicians before slowly expanding his business to include paying clients drawn by word of mouth. He was also named the first professor of chemistry at the Philadelphia college, founded by his mentor Franklin twenty years earlier, and joined a scientific circle that had grown out of Franklin's American Philosophical Society.

Philadelphia was already astir with anti-British sentiment. Rush's university days in Edinburgh had forced him to "exercise my reason upon the subject of government," and he soon concluded that "no form of government can be rational, but that which is derived from the suffrages of the people who are subjects of it."[56] He found some sympathy for his radical republican views among the Philadelphia branch of the clandestine Sons of Liberty, a colonial movement to resist Britain's increasingly harsh tax and trade policies.

Benjamin Rush was also among the first of the American revolutionaries to realize fully that a successful break with England would also entail a knowledge revolution, one that would immediately apply the latest scientific findings in botany, chemistry, mineralogy, and the like to uncovering the country's full potential in agriculture, industry, and trade. This sense of urgency lay behind Rush's lifelong campaigns against the study of Greek and Latin in America's schools and colleges.[57]

As Rush no doubt had suspected, the social, political, and economic upheaval that accompanied the Revolution provided a boost to the American movement for useful knowledge. Faced with the enormous challenges of battling the global superpower of the day, the colonists found that traditional learning was not the best preparation for armed rebellion in the face of vastly superior economic and military force. "In these times of action, classical education was found of less service than good natural parts, guided by common sense, and sound judgment," David Ramsay of South Carolina, one of the war's earliest historians, wrote in 1789. "It seemed as if war not only required, but created talents."[58]

Thomas Paine, a close associate of Rush, Franklin, and other campaigners for practical education, famously elevated the notion of "common sense" to a revolutionary doctrine with the publication in early 1776 of his inflammatory pamphlet of the same name—perhaps the single most influential text in the history of American letters.[59] Franklin, a talent spotter of the first order, had successfully encouraged Paine, a corset maker by trade, to emigrate from his native England two years earlier. Now, Paine's proffer of "nothing more than simple facts, plain arguments, and common sense" in support of his contention that America must now throw off British rule and create a representative government pushed public opinion toward outright independence at a time when many colonists were ambivalent about so drastic a course.

By eschewing the ponderous classical references that characterized the political language of the day, *Common Sense* spoke directly to the American people in unaccustomed ways, and to unprecedented effect.* Paine's essay also tapped

---

* Paine was not above invoking classical references in the adoption of his various pen names, such as Atlanticus, Humanus, or Vox Populi, but he otherwise broke with tradition and never relied on epigraphs or literary quotations in support of his arguments. See Alfred Owen Aldridge, "Thomas Paine and the Classics," *Eighteenth-Century Studies* I (4): 371, 378.

into the colonists' predominant religious idiom, that of Protestant dissent shared by such disparate communities as the Puritans and the Quakers, the German sectaries, and the New Light Calvinists of the Middle Colonies, as a way of undermining the legitimacy of both the British king and breaking with British notions of political liberty.[60]

For Paine, as for Franklin, Jefferson, Rush, and the other founders of the republic, the rights of the people rested on a self-evident foundation, validated not by any British or ancient authority but by common sense. Education in the new nation would need to help clear away the dead weight of tradition. In later writings, Paine argued that persistent reliance in the schools on Latin and Greek was calculated to advance the interests of a corrupt church and an illegitimate state.[61] By looking backward to antiquity for inspiration and channeling scientific and philosophical ideas through the medium of dead languages, the forces of reaction retained their grip on power.

"The human mind has a natural disposition to scientific knowledge, and the things connected with it," argued Paine in *The Age of Reason*, citing the inclination of even the youngest child to build toy bridges, play with paper boats, dam gutters, and otherwise imitate "the works of man." Only with the introduction of traditional schooling is such worthy behavior on the part of the child extinguished. "It afterwards goes to school, where its genius is killed by the barren study of a dead language, and the philosopher is lost in the linguist."[62]

Rush, who had first proposed the title *Common Sense* and helped Paine find a publisher for the seminal tract and then edited much of the text, further underscored the vital relationship between the new nation and a new system of education: "I consider it possible to convert men into republican machines. This must be done, if we expect them to perform their parts properly, in the great machine of the government of the state." He then went on to outline the ideal republican curriculum in an essay whose title sums up his heartfelt support for practical education: "Observations upon the Study of the Latin and Greek Languages, as a Branch of Liberal Education, with Hints of a Plan of Liberal Instruction, without Them, Accommodated to the Present State of Society, Manners and Government in the United States."

In short, the new country simply did not have time to waste and had to dedicate itself to the pursuit of science and other useful knowledge. "Here the opportunities of acquiring knowledge and advancing private and public

Benjamin Franklin Drawing Electricity from the Sky by Benjamin West, ca. 1816. Franklin's kite experiment demonstrated that electricity in the laboratory and lightning in the sky were one and the same, establishing a place in the world for American science. His subsequent invention of the lightning rod, with its promise of protection from often deadly strikes, made him a larger-than-life figure for many and helped further his personal, political, and diplomatic ambitions.

Interior of a London Coffee-house, ca. 1650–1750. London's coffeehouses captured the imagination of Franklin during his first visit to the imperial capital. These institutions provided the young printer with access to pamphlets and gazettes, the latest news, and seemingly endless discussion of the day's affairs, developments in science, and other intellectual pursuits. Years later, Franklin still recalled fondly the "very ingenious Acquaintance" he made in the city's cafes and taverns.

© THE TRUSTEES OF THE BRITISH MUSEUM/ART RESOURCE, NY

Benjamin Franklin wearing the uniform of the Union Fire Company, which he founded in Philadelphia in 1736. The pursuit of knowledge was, for Franklin, both social and socially useful. A debate within his secret club, the Junto, about the danger of fire in Philadelphia's narrow lanes led to the formation of volunteer fire companies across the city and later to the creation of America's first fire insurance scheme, with Franklin at its head. PRIVATE COLLECTION/PETER NEWARK AMERICAN PICTURES/THE BRIDGEMAN ART LIBRARY

Franklin published this cartoon in 1754—with a snake representing the American colonies, severed into their constituent parts—to accompany an editorial in his *Pennsylvania Gazette* on the importance of unity. Here was an early recognition that the only way forward for the colonies lay in some degree of coordinated legislation and executive administration. LIBRARY OF CONGRESS

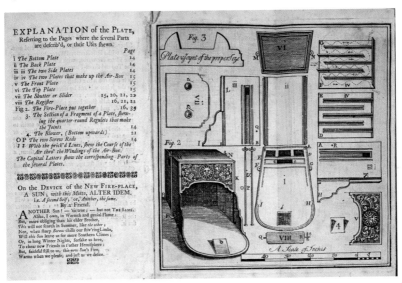

Original Benjamin Franklin stove design. In Franklin's world, useful knowledge was a collective pursuit. Even his most famous contributions to science and technology, including the lightning rod, were the products of teamwork and the free exchange of information, ideas, and observations. The more efficient Franklin stove first took shape after a debate within the Junto over how best to combat the persistent problem of smoky chimneys and to reduce the consumption of increasingly scarce firewood. PRIVATE COLLECTION/THE BRIDGEMAN ART LIBRARY

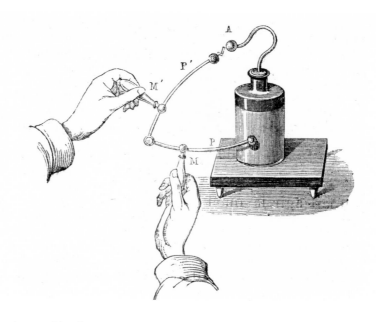

The Leyden jar, capable of storing electricity for later discharge, was crucial to experimentation in the mid-eighteenth century. It takes its name from the Dutch city where one of its co-inventors, Pieter van Musschenbroek, lived and worked. Franklin and his fellow Philadelphia electricians later linked a series of similar devices into a "battery," the first of its kind. ALBUM/ART RESOURCE, NY

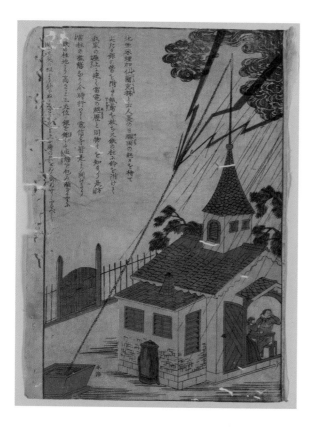

Furankurin to kaminari no zu: A Japanese woodcut, ca. 1868–1875. Franklin's experiments, both his famous electric kite and an earlier version using a soldier's sentry box to attract lightning and capture some of its power, were performed across the scientific world, from England, France, and the Netherlands to Russia and as far away as Japan.
BELLA C. LANDAUER COLLECTION AT THE LIBRARY OF CONGRESS

A detail view of a Rittenhouse orrery. The orrery, or mechanized planetarium, built by David Rittenhouse enthralled the European virtuosi and assured his fellow Americans that they were capable of attaining great heights in science and engineering. "The amazing mechanical representation of the solar system which you conceived and executed, has never been surpassed by any but the world of which it is a copy," wrote Thomas Jefferson in a letter to the inventor. Like his comrades, Jefferson saw the Rittenhouse orrery as a product of natural, American genius, untouched and untroubled by traditional learning.

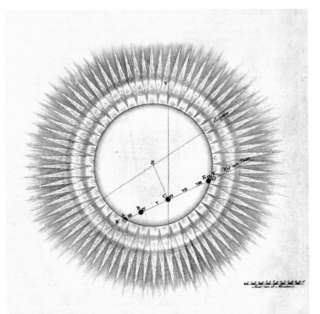

A drawing of the transit of Venus of 1761, by Nicholas Ypey. The transit of the planet Venus across the face of the sun gave eighteenth-century astronomers and mathematicians an opportunity to calculate the absolute size of the visible universe. A pair of transits, in 1761 and 1769, captured the imagination of both the European and American publics and served as a showcase for colonial scientific achievement.

David Rittenhouse by Charles Willson Peale, 1796. David Rittenhouse, an instrument maker and largely self-taught astronomer, was instrumental in the early work of the American Philosophical Society, in particular its work on the transit of Venus in 1769. Rittenhouse, who served in the revolutionary government in Pennsylvania, succeeded Franklin as president of the Philosophical Society.

Benjamin Rush by Thomas Sully, 1812. Benjamin Rush, the revolutionary physician and educator, was one of many scientifically inclined signatories to the Declaration of Independence. A protégé of Franklin, he was a tireless campaigner against the use of Greek and Latin in American classrooms.

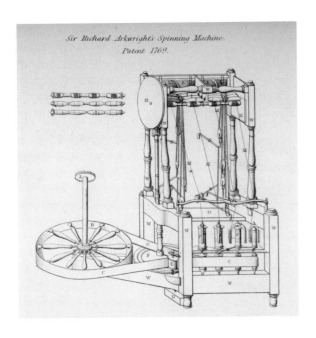

Drawing of Sir Richard Arkwright's spinning machine, patented in 1769, ca. 1830 by Joseph Wilson Lowry. The revolutionary textile technology of Richard Arkwright was a closely guarded secret in Great Britain, which then led the world in the production of finished cloth. His machines were the object of early American efforts at industrial espionage.

Tench Coxe by Jeremiah Paul, 1795. Tench Coxe, a fallen aristocrat and former Loyalist, narrowly avoided prosecution at the hands of the victorious patriots. He went on to carve out a career as a publicist and campaigner on behalf of a strong federal government and as America's leading advocate of the role of mechanized industry in the new republic.

View from the terrace of Monsieur Franklin at Passy of the first flight under the direction of Monsieur de Montgolfier, November 21, 1783. Franklin witnessed the first hydrogen balloon flight, in Paris in 1783, an event that fired his imagination to think of possible uses for this new technology. "This Experiment is by no means a trifling one," he reported to the head of the Royal Society of London. "It may be attended with important Consequences that no one can foresee." BIBLIOTHÈQUE NATIONALE, PARIS, FRANCE/THE BRIDGEMAN ART LIBRARY interest are so numerous, and the rewards of genius and industry so certain, that not a particle of time should be misspent or lost. . . . To spend four or five years learning two dead languages is to turn our backs on a goldmine in order to amuse ourselves catching butterflies."[63]

Chapter Seven

KNOWLEDGE AND REBELLION

A growing taste for useful knowledge is an important characteristic of the people of this new world.

—Rev. David M'Clure

FRANKLIN'S FOREIGN MISSIONS deprived America of its most visible advocate of useful knowledge for years at a time. Yet, the same social, economic, and political developments that accompanied the colonies' slow march toward independence worked in favor of the gradual resuscitation of his American Philosophical Society, as well as the formation of other organizations around the colonies to encourage scientific experimentation, practical learning, and innovation.

Just as the laws and practices of the new republic that emerged began to reflect profound American distrust of centralized power, intellectual elites, state-sponsored religion, and authoritarian institutions in general, so, too, did revolutionary-era science and technology begin to take an American turn. Here, New World belief in usefulness—to man, to society, to the newly independent states now freed from empire's heavy hand but also stripped of many of its advantages—trumped notions of theoretical purity and mathematical exactitude.

Shortly before the Revolution, one hundred of Virginia's leading figures created a knowledge association modeled directly along the lines of the societies taking shape in Philadelphia. Known as the Virginia Society for the Promotion of Useful Knowledge, its members included future presidents George Washington and Thomas Jefferson, as well as the prominent patriots George Mason and Arthur Lee. A philosophical society formed in 1774 in Charleston, South Carolina, garnered a flurry of international fame for its study of electric eels, a follow-on to Franklin's work with lightning and other aspects of electrical fire.

The immediate postwar years saw a proliferation of societies dedicated to useful knowledge, from the Philosophical Library in Salem, Massachusetts—whose collection began with the wartime seizure of learned books and papers on board a British merchant ship—to the Mississippi Society for the Acquirement and Dissemination of Useful Knowledge.[1] But before such organizations could take firm root in American soil, they would have to overcome their relative isolation and develop the collective enterprise of Enlightenment science in ways that could meet the high standards set by the Royal Society, the Académie des Sciences, and the other European associations. This meant mastering the techniques and idioms of experimental science before it could be turned in new directions befitting a new society.

The opportunity for America's would-be virtuosi to make their grand entrance into the world of Western science came, quite literally, from the heavens. England's Astronomer Royal Edmond Halley, of comet fame, died in 1742, one year before Franklin circulated his initial call for a colonial philosophical society, but Halley's appeal to posterity that "the curious strenuously . . . apply themselves" to observing a pair of celestial phenomena in June 1761, and again eight years later, did not go unheeded.[2] The astronomer's vision sparked an unprecedented global effort and helped goad America's nascent scientific community, then plagued by a general lack of purpose and personal squabbles, into its first significant collective action.

At stake, Halley pointed out to the Royal Society, was "the certain and adequate solution of the noblest, and otherwise most difficult problem" in astronomy, namely determining the absolute size of the visible universe.[3] Until the twentieth century, astronomers lacked sophisticated tools that could measure directly the distance between earth and the other planets. Instead, they generally were restricted to a system of angular measurements and relative distances that described any one of the celestial bodies only in terms of the others.

Over the centuries, the ancient Greeks, the Chinese, and the great medieval Muslim astronomers, among others, made ingenious attempts to measure the actual distance between celestial bodies, say from the earth to the sun; if this could be established, then all the other dimensions of the visible universe would fall neatly into place. Lacking this vital piece of information, the Newtonian revolution that had so excited the scientific and popular imagination at the beginning of the eighteenth century remained essentially unfinished.

Here was Halley's "noblest" of all problems, one whose best chance of solution, he suggested, lay with the recurrent astronomical phenomenon known as the transit of Venus, a partial eclipse of the sun by the intervening planet. Viewed from earth, Venus would appear as a small black disk sliding across the face of the sun, a phenomenon that would allow astronomers in distant locations to time its progress and then compare their findings. Discrepancies in the observed time of the transit, due to the apparent displacement of the sun when viewed from different points on earth—the so-called solar parallax—would in theory allow relatively accurate determination of the earth's distance from the sun.

The entire process, Halley assured his readers with startling understatement, would be easy. "From these differences, duly observed, the sun's parallax may be determined, even to a small part of a second of time, and that without any other instruments than telescopes and good common clocks, and without any other qualifications in the observer than fidelity and diligence, with a little skill in astronomy."[4] His proposed solution, much of it lifted from the Scottish mathematician James Gregory, had one other vital requirement—patience. Transits of Venus are predictable but rare events, generally occurring in eight-year pairs separated by intervals of more than a century. If the "curious" missed the next cycle in 1761 and 1769, their successors would have to wait until 1874 for another chance.*

As a result, preparations got under way in the scientific capitals of Europe years in advance. Expeditions were carefully planned to far-off lands, where the first of the two transits would be most visible. Halley's method, meanwhile, was refined considerably, in particular by the Frenchman Joseph-Nicolas Delisle, one-time astronomer to the Russian tsars. Delisle realized that the same result could be achieved by the simpler method of recording from different locales the exact time the transit either began or ended. This offered some protection against bad weather obscuring the entire event, and it opened up a much wider range of potential observation points by including those many portions of the globe where the sun would not be visible throughout the full transit.[5]

Interest in the British colonies was first piqued almost nine years in advance, after a letter from Delisle with instructions to a colleague in French-controlled

---

* The most recent pair of transits took place in June 2004 and June 2012, with the next cycle due in December 2117 and December 2125.

Quebec about an imminent transit of the planet Mercury fell into American hands in late 1752. This was essentially a dry run for the later observation of Venus, and a rough translation alerted Franklin and Colden, among a handful of others, to the importance of the upcoming event. Franklin, ever attuned to the growing American thirst for scientific findings, duly informed the readers of his *Poor Richard Improved*: "In the Year 1761, the Distance of all the Planets from the Sun will be determined to a great Degree of Exactness by Observations on a Transit of the Planet *Venus* over the Face of the Sun."[6]

The pending arrival of the 1761 transit sparked a concerted international effort. Scientific societies and interested governments across Europe dispatched dozens of observation teams, from the Indian Ocean to Siberia to the coast of Newfoundland, the only place in North America that both offered a clear view and was relatively accessible from existing settlements. Countless others were set up by interested members of the public, their imaginations fired by the Enlightenment vogue for experiential science.

The state of war between Europe's leading scientific powers—Britain and France—hindered a number of these expeditions, while the unanticipated difficulty of determining the transit's precise beginning, or point of contact with the sun, further complicated matters. Particularly vexing to eighteenth-century observers was the so-called black drop effect, an optical illusion that distorted Venus's round shape at the precise moment that it crossed the outlines of the sun. This made consistent and accurate measurement of the transit's duration almost impossible.

Moreover, the preferred method of recording either the beginning or the end of the transit required knowledge of the observer's exact location, something that still eluded contemporary science. Even the geographical coordinates of such established astronomical centers as Paris and Greenwich, England, remained imprecise. Bad weather in a number of important locales further undermined the success of the project.

Harvard mathematics professor John Winthrop, great-great-grandson of the founder of the Massachusetts Bay Colony, set off on a mission to Newfoundland aboard the provincial sloop *Boston* after the governor invoked the utilitarian prospects, as well as local prestige, in his appeal for financial support from the legislature. "You must know that this Phenomenon, (which has been observed but once before since the Creation of the World) will, in all Probability, settle some Questions in Astronomy which may ultimately be very serviceable to

Navigation. . . . We shall hereby serve the Cause of Science, and do Credit to the Province."[7]

Winthrop and his team, including two of his best students, endured "the infinite swarms of insects" that sought in vain to drive them from their hilltop encampment. Unlike some of the other observers, the Americans—armed with a telescope from Harvard and "an excellent pendulum Clock"—enjoyed fine weather for astronomical observation. "The morning of the 6th of June was serene and calm," Winthrop recorded in his account of the expedition.[8] His findings later proved to have been among the more accurate of any of the worldwide observations, coming in just about 6 percent short of today's accepted figure.* However, measurements from the different global teams varied so widely as to make the collated data essentially unusable. The virtuosi would have to do better in 1769.

Prospects for success during the second of the two eighteenth-century transits were greatly enhanced by the fact that it would be far more visible in both Europe and North America than the first one had been. That this second transit was just eight years away certainly helped as well, something the Royal Society noted with palpable relief: "In this uncertainty, the astronomers of the present age are peculiarly fortunate in being able so soon to have recourse to another transit of Venus in 1769."[9] Technology and methods of measurement had also improved considerably in the intervening years, feeding hopes that this time the virtuosi would be able to inform the world of the true size of the universe.

The American colonies experienced an upsurge in popular interest in astronomy, and in science in general. The flawed 1761 expeditions had been widely discussed in the press. Newspapers, magazines, and serial publications such as the almanacs produced by Franklin and his competitors continued to carry accounts of new scientific developments, challenges, and theories. Eager anticipation of the next transit ensured the mobilization of a number of organized and well-equipped observation teams, backed by educational institutions, scientific circles, or wealthy benefactors and spread out at different vantage points along the Eastern Seaboard.[10]

---

*   Today's astronomers, armed with telemetry data from space probes, have calculated the mean distance between the earth and the sun, known as the Astronomical Unit, at 92.955 million miles.

Much of this renewed American activity centered on the slowly expanding legions of the learned and the curious in Philadelphia. By 1768, almost all of the original members of the Leather Apron Club, or Junto, were dead, and their leader Franklin was back in England, on a second semiofficial diplomatic tour. But new groups and movements had begun to displace the Junto and the Library Company. Among the most successful of these associations was the so-called Young Junto, which modeled itself directly after Franklin's secret club and included the sons of three of the latter institution's original members.[11]

Like the society that inspired it, the Young Junto was composed primarily of Quakers, or those who generally shared the Friends' sensibilities toward knowledge, civic duty, and self-improvement. Most, too, were craftsmen—a hatter, an instrument maker, an ironmonger, among them—or directly connected to the small world of colonial science, such as the two sons of botanist John Bartram. The club's initial formation followed many of the precepts first laid down by Franklin, including that of secrecy to protect the interests of its membership.[12]

The activities of this Young Junto, however, were intermittent and lapsed altogether by 1762, before a rebirth several years later prompted by increasing, organized resistance among Americans angered at British management of colonial affairs. Charles Thomson, a vociferous champion of colonial rights who inspired the revival of the Young Junto, was adamant that useful knowledge in the fields of agriculture and manufactures could help protect Americans from the economic depredations of their colonial masters back in England.[13]

In the autumn of 1767, Thomson called for a systematic examination of America's resources and prospects for growth, which he noted were "likely to be opposed by increasing Obstacles from abroad."[14] Six months later, he proposed that the Young Junto shed its secrecy and mobilize the colonial forces of useful knowledge in order to resist British pressure. "In this Country, almost every man is fond of reading and seems to have a thirst for knowledge. . . . Nothing seems wanting but a public Society to encourage and direct Enquiries and experiments . . . and to unite the labors of many to attain one grand End, namely the Advancement of useful Knowledge and the Improvement of our Country."[15]

Under Thomson's leadership the Young Junto went public with its program and ideals, and significantly expanded its membership, both in the colonies and abroad. It also renamed itself the American Society held at Philadelphia for Promoting Useful Knowledge, and proclaimed the value of such knowledge in no uncertain terms. "Knowledge is of little use when confined to mere Speculation," read the group's manifesto, published in the *Pennsylvania Chronicle* of March 7, 1768. "But when speculative Truths are reduced to Practice, when Theories, grounded upon experiments, are applied to common Purposes of life, and when, by these Agriculture is improved, Trade enlarged, and the Arts of Living made more easy and comfortable, and of Course, the Increase and Happiness of Mankind promoted, Knowledge then becomes really useful."[16]

Separately, Thomas Bond, the physician in Franklin's original scheme for a learned society back in the mid-1740s, had also resolved to resurrect their philosophical circle. Soon Philadelphia found itself with two rival groups, each competing for high-profile members, international contacts, and the attention of the general public. They even published their findings and announcements in separate Pennsylvania newspapers; Thomson's American Society preferred the *Pennsylvania Chronicle*, while Bond's old-line Philosophical Society favored the *Pennsylvania Gazette*.

In keeping with the tenor of contemporary life in the province, the two associations were largely divided along political lines. The American Society generally aligned with Franklin and the pro-Quaker faction, while Bond's reborn Philosophical Society hewed predominantly to the proprietary party. Class and social position also played their part: at least half the membership of the American Society came from the artisan and small merchant classes—the leather aprons; participants in the Philosophical Society were drawn primarily from the political and commercial elites.[17]

Prominent figures in both camps soon realized they would ultimately have to combine their efforts whatever their differences. After a number of false starts and a year or so of wary negotiations, a treaty of union was formally concluded December 20, 1768, and ratified shortly thereafter. "Two Societies having formerly subsisted in Philadelphia, whose views and ends were the same, viz. '*the Advancement of useful Knowledge*,' it was judged that their Union would be of public advantage," proclaimed the new joint association. Henceforth, the new body would be formally known by an amalgamation of their respective names: the American Philosophical Society held at Philadelphia for Promoting Useful Knowledge.[18] Most simply referred to it as the American Philosophical Society, the name it retains to this day.

Prospects for the success of the new unified Society were enhanced by the symbolic election in absentia of Franklin as president, albeit with considerable reservations from the proprietary circle. Most prominent among Franklin's opponents, John Penn, a member of the proprietary family and the last governor of prerevolutionary Pennsylvania, angrily rebuffed the customary request that he serve as the Society's patron ex officio.

Thomas Bond, who had helped set the process of integration in motion, decried in a personal note to Franklin the inevitable politicking that surrounded the union and predicted that little good would come from the entire endeavor. "I long Meditated a Revival of our American Philosophical Society and at length I thought I saw my Way clear in doing it, but the Old party Leven split us for a Time," he wrote to his old colleague in London. "We are now united and with your Presence may make a Figure, but till that happy Event, I fear much will not be done."[19]

Several members of the Young Junto faction refused to join the united association, alleging the entire maneuver had been designed by the city's political and academic leadership to co-opt their earlier achievements. Before the union, the American Society had been busy presenting inventions by new members, including an automated "register" to control heat or fire and a power-driven pump to clear water from ships, and association members were keen to protect their intellectual property.[20] Prominent among the dissidents was the physician Cadwalader Evans, who denounced the joint society and explained his withdrawal in a letter of his own to Franklin. "It was my opinion then, that the eagerness the Professors of the College showed for a Junction of the two Societies was to avail themselves of the Labors of others and filch reputation from their knowledge. Several instances have occurred to confirm it."[21]

For the newly amalgamated American Philosophical Society, the 1769 transit of Venus, predicted for the afternoon of June 6, provided an ideal opportunity to rally around a scientific venture of global import. Its members were well aware that successful observations and the production of accurate data could secure for the Americans the respect of the skeptical European virtuosi. Closer to home, it would surely smooth over the hurt feelings created by the union and prove the doubters, defectors, and infighters wrong. Likewise, failure and the inevitable recriminations to follow could send the American Philosophical Society back into decline, perhaps permanently.

Franklin, of course, would have been the natural candidate to lead such a complex organizational and scientific endeavor. In his absence, the Philadelphians turned to another homegrown talent, the clockmaker and astronomer David Rittenhouse whose wondrous planetarium, or orrery, replicated the intricate movement of the planets and so captivated the American public. Rittenhouse and his colleagues got right to work determining the best observation points, procuring the necessary instruments, and lining up their observation teams.

From an early age it was clear that David Rittenhouse was a mechanical and mathematical prodigy, and he quite literally made the family farm his classroom. As a lad at work in the fields, David occupied his fertile mind with mathematical problems. His brother, Benjamin, recalled that when he fetched his older sibling from his chores "not only the fences at the head of many of the furrows, but even his plow and its handles, were covered over with chalked numerical figures."[22]

Manual labor, according to Rittenhouse's nephew and chronicler William Barton, provided an appropriate beginning for this budding genius. It also served as a badge of honor for the new breed of American natural philosophers. "To follow the plow is not a servile labor," Barton assured the readers of his *Memoirs of the Life of David Rittenhouse.* "It is an employment worthy of a freeman, and if the person, thus engaged, be a man of native talents, aided by some improvement of mind, scarcely any occupation can afford him greater scope for philosophic reflection."[23]

Rittenhouse was born in 1732 and spent his youth on the family's one hundred acres in Norriton, about twenty miles outside of Philadelphia. The adult Rittenhouse, recorded Barton, "was, in his stature, somewhat tall; in his person, slender and straight; and although his constitution was delicate, his bodily frame did not appear to have been, originally, weak; his gait was somewhat quick, and his movements in general were lively."[24]

Inspired by a set of carpenter's tools, some handwritten notes and scribbled calculations, and a few basic mathematical texts left behind after the death of an uncle, twelve-year-old David displayed an early fascination and an uncommon facility with geometry and arithmetic. The tool chest provided Rittenhouse "some means of exercising the bent of his genius toward mechanism."[25] Soon he had convinced his reluctant father to allow him to set up shop on the farm as a maker of clocks. In time, he became known for designing and crafting scientific instruments of increasing sophistication, unquestioned utility, and real beauty.

Rittenhouse made his living primarily as a clockmaker from around 1750 until the outbreak of the Revolution. In the evenings, he pored over astronomical and mathematical texts, including a copy of Newton's *Principia* provided by his biographer's father, Thomas Barton, a teacher at the Philadelphia academy who later married Rittenhouse's elder sister. "This occupation, connected with that of a mathematical instrument maker, is such as may be well supposed to have presented itself to his youthful ingenuity; being in accordance with the philosophical bent of his genius in his early years, while yet untutored in science and unknown to the world," wrote the ever-enthusiastic Barton.[26]

As seen by his contemporaries and memorialized shortly after his death, Rittenhouse fully embodied the new virtues of the new republic: he was self-directed and largely self-taught; he applied ingenious technical approaches to practical problems; his interests could not be contained within the restrictive confines of pure science; and he was not above putting down his clockmaker's tools or his astronomy books and getting his hands dirty, whether working the fields, running surveyors' lines along disputed provincial boundaries, or supervising the wartime production of gunpowder and cannon, or the design of fortifications.

Moreover, he had a propensity to think big. Not content to spin out well-fashioned clocks and the odd surveying instrument, Rittenhouse strained to outdo all others in his field. He designed the first-known portable metal thermometer and also produced fine telescopes and other astronomical instruments, balance scales, mercury barometers, and eyeglasses.[27] Most spectacular of all was the design and construction of his extravagantly ambitious mechanical planetarium, which combined a sophisticated understanding of celestial motion with the highest order of mechanical skill and workmanship.

Like the public electricity demonstrations of Franklin and Kinnersley, such planetaria brought the latest in science into the salon and the lecture hall, part of the experiential approach to natural philosophy that characterized the times. The particular device that Rittenhouse had in mind—accurately mimicking the planets as they orbited the sun—took its name from the Fourth Earl of Orrery, for whom one of the first of its kind had been constructed sixty years earlier. The appeal of the orrery no doubt lay in its mechanical representation of a harmonious and constant natural world, reliably ticking along like clockwork in keeping with the vogue for the new Newtonian physics.

Yet, Rittenhouse had no intention of producing just any mechanical plane-tarium. "I did not design a machine which should give the ignorant in astronomy a just view of the Solar System: but would rather astonish the skilful and curious examiner, by a most accurate correspondence between the situations and motions of our little representatives of the heavenly bodies, and the situations and motions of those bodies, themselves," he informed Thomas Barton in a letter of January 28, 1767. "I would have my Orrery really useful, by making it capable of informing us, truly, of the astronomical phenomena for any particular point of time; which, I do not find that any Orrery yet made, can do."[28]

According to Rittenhouse's detailed specifications, this revolutionary plan-etarium would for the first time reproduce the elliptical orbits of the planets in place of the conventional and far simpler, but less accurate, circular ones. Each of these orbits would revolve at fluctuating speed and in its own plane relative to the earth. A miniature telescope placed on the model of the earth and then used to sight a planet would generate its accurate celestial coordinates.

The device would track the movement of Jupiter and its multiple moons, Saturn and its rings, as well as the exact time and nature of all lunar eclipses. The entire machine, run by "a strong pendulum clock" or operated independ-ently by a winch, was designed to display accurate astronomical data for a period of five thousand years in either direction. "It must be understood that all these motions are to correspond exactly with the celestial motions, and not to differ to some *Degrees* from the truth, as is common in orreries."[29] It would also play music.

Rittenhouse's outsized ambitions for his orrery—some of which he was forced to jettison as impractical—created a sensation in the colonial press and touched off a bidding war between the Pennsylvania virtuosi, led chiefly by Provost William Smith, and their rivals at the College of New Jersey, who swooped in with a cash deal to secure the rights to the as-yet-unfinished device. Rittenhouse only managed to placate his Philadelphia supporters by producing a second such orrery, even grander and more complex than the first.

Excitement over the orreries established Rittenhouse as the province's preeminent instrument maker and gradually drew him away from the peaceful surroundings of his Norriton farm. He spent more and more time in nearby Philadelphia, in the hopes of expanding the clientele for his instrument busi-ness and securing patronage for his scientific projects from among the provin-cial authorities and the city's wealthy and powerful.[30]

With some reluctance, Rittenhouse entered fully into Philadelphia's politicized intellectual life. He had already been elected a member of Charles Thomson's American Society, and he now began work on the upcoming transit of Venus on behalf of the joint philosophical association. The feverish pace of these preparations forced Rittenhouse to put a temporary halt to work on his orreries. It also undermined his fragile health, which was plagued from his youth by what may have been a chronic duodenal ulcer. He was later rewarded for these efforts with his election as one of three secretaries of the American Philosophical Society—and, after Franklin's death, as its second president.

With past divisions largely behind it, the Philosophical Society was able to secure public funds for its transit project from the Pennsylvania Assembly and private support from the Library Company. Franklin, meanwhile, commissioned a prominent London firm to produce a state-of-the-art reflecting telescope for the Society's use, paid for by Thomas Penn and later housed at the University of Pennsylvania. A number of citizens agreed to underwrite observation posts.

Almost two dozen independent teams, from Canada to Virginia, supplemented the more organized efforts of the knowledge associations and the universities, many of them funneling their data through the American Philosophical Society for verification, collation, and dissemination. Britain's royal astronomer published a forty-four-page instructional pamphlet to guide the worldwide effort. John Winthrop, the Harvard mathematics professor, now too infirm to repeat his exploits in Newfoundland eight years earlier, delivered a series of popular lectures on the importance of the transit.[31] He later carefully reworked data collected from numerous teams in a concerted and largely successful effort to smooth out many of the inevitable observational errors.

Mounting public interest in the transit of 1769 further enhanced the role of science in colonial life, and with it the status of the American Philosophical Society. Local newspapers provided detailed accounts of the individual observation teams, while wealthy amateurs vied with one another to acquire the most up-to-date astronomical apparatus. Each post required, at the bare minimum, a telescope and an accurate means of telling time, but other instruments were often deployed as well. These included quadrants, sextants, barometers, and thermometers.[32]

In Providence, Rhode Island, members of the general public helped a private observation party, directed by self-taught mathematician Benjamin West and financed by a local businessman, to set their clocks by the position of the sun. "That our observations might be as useful as possible," West later recounted, "notice was given beforehand to the people (whose curiosity was excited by the preparations) that on the day before the transit, when the Sun came on the meridian, a cannon would be fired, which being done, most of the inhabitants marked meridian lines on their windows, or on their floors" to help synchronize their clocks and watches.[33]

The American Philosophical Society focused its primary efforts on two well-equipped observation points, one at the State House in central Philadelphia and the other at Rittenhouse's farm in Norriton. A more ambitious plan that would have sent an expedition into upstate New York to observe the transit and then stay on to explore the Hudson River valley was rejected.[34] A third observation point was established at Cape Henlopen, on Delaware Bay, but the Norriton post under Rittenhouse's immediate direction received the most attention and resources from the Society. Assisting Rittenhouse in the observations and timekeeping were William Smith, provost of the College of Pennsylvania; the province's chief surveyor; a member of the Pennsylvania Assembly; and several assistants to record the time and other data.

This lead observation team was equipped with three optical telescopes, including the largest refractor telescope in America, its lenses purpose-built in London. According to Smith's account, other devices on hand included "an excellent clock; a transit telescope, nicely moving in the plane of the meridian; and a very accurate equal altitude instrument, supported in the observatory on a stone pedestal," all built by Rittenhouse himself.[35] Rittenhouse had also constructed a temporary observatory platform at his farm, and his team worked out an elaborate series of hand signals that would allow the three observers to inform the timekeepers of their sightings of the start and end of the transit without distracting the others or prejudicing their observations.

By the morning of the transit, Rittenhouse was clearly exhausted. He had already spent many months, often outside in the cold late at night, taking careful astronomical readings in preparation for the big event. His clock had to be regularly adjusted, the micrometer attached to one of the telescopes needed periodic testing and recalibration, and the exact coordinates of the observatory had to be determined, checked, and checked again. He even had to install the new British-made refractor lenses himself. Rittenhouse was also acutely aware that he would get no second chance to record and measure a major astronomical phenomenon that could unlock one of the mysteries of the known universe: its actual size. The next transit was not due for another 105 years.

The observations at Norriton began smoothly enough, with each team member buried in his own assigned task, but the tightly wound Rittenhouse was soon overcome with emotion. "In pensive silence and trembling anxiety, they waited for the predicted moment of observation," recalled Benjamin Rush years later in a public eulogy for his old friend. "It came and . . . in our philosopher, it excited in the instant of one of the contacts of the planet with the sun an emotion of delight so exquisite and powerful as to induce fainting."[36]

William Smith and the others kept working and Rittenhouse recovered sufficiently to observe the rest of the transit. He never personally referred to his fainting spell, which could have dashed all his hopes, although he did acknowledge the powerful spiritual effect of watching the transit unfold. Somehow, the Norriton team still managed to collect some of the most accurate and useful data from among the more than seventy-five observation posts worldwide. A later analysis of the Norriton figures suggested a mean distance between the earth and the sun of around 93 million miles, not far off today's accepted value of 92.955 million miles.

The efforts by the Philosophical Society to observe and record the transit helped seal its position as America's premier knowledge association, with the scientifically inclined from across the colonies eagerly lining up for membership. Energized by the experience, members of the Society took another large step toward integration into the global scientific community, with the publication in 1771 of the first volume of their official *Transactions*. Almost the entire first section of the new journal was devoted to the colonials' reports on the transit of Venus, or related problems, and it won the American Philosophical Society considerable attention and even praise from Europe.

Nevil Maskelyne, the Astronomer Royal, lauded the Americans in a letter to proprietor Thomas Penn, who had passed along the Society's data: "I thank you for the account of the Pennsylvania Observations which seem *excellent* and *complete*, and do Honor to the Gentlemen who made them."[37] From Stockholm came predictions that great things lay ahead for colonial science. "I have been agreeably surprised to observe the rapid progress of your American Society," wrote Carl Magnus Wrangel, who later became one of the Society's earliest overseas members. "Your accurate Observations of the Transit of Venus have given infinite satisfaction to our astronomers; as will the rest of your *Transactions*, to the literary world, when they come to be further known."[38]

*   *   *

Until the late 1760s, Benjamin Franklin remained a sincere, if at times frustrated, supporter of what he recalled with residual fondness "that fine and noble China Vase the British Empire."[39] After all, the primary aim of his second political mission to London, in late 1764, was to curry support for removing the proprietary Penn family from power and placing the province under the direct control of the Crown—perhaps with Franklin himself as royal governor.

He felt considerable disquiet over the rowdy protests then gripping the colonies against British tax and trade policies. Not even the passage of the Stamp Act of 1765, which so outraged the Americans and threatened to ruin Franklin's fellow printers, including his reliable business partner David Hall, could sway him at first. Franklin went so far as to nominate an associate back home as a collector for the new taxes, a move that immediately exposed his friend's life and property to mob violence.

This apparent lack of enthusiasm for the American point of view saw Franklin's public standing back in Pennsylvania plummet. Benjamin Rush, the revolutionary physician whom Franklin had assisted years earlier, broke temporarily with his mentor: "O Franklin, Franklin, thou curse to PA and America, may the most accumulated vengeance burst speedily in thy guilty head."[40] Cut off in London from the fast pace of political and social developments in the colonies and frustrated in his attempts to carve out a place of his own in British society, Franklin found himself alienated from both England and his native America.

Still, he could not easily shake his long-held conviction that the economic and political interests of both America and Great Britain were one and the same. "I am not much alarmed about your Schemes of raising Money on us," Franklin wrote to a sympathetic British parliamentarian, shortly before the firestorm over the Stamp Act broke out in the colonies. "You will take care for your own sakes not to lay greater Burdens on us than we can bear; for you cannot hurt us without hurting yourselves."[41] His serious miscalculation over the reaction at home to aggressive efforts by Britain to levy new taxes and to reassert its absolute authority over the colonies was only the most acute symptom of his increasing isolation.

By late 1768, the strain had begun to show. "I do not find that I have gained any point in either country, except that of rendering myself suspected by my impartiality, in England of being too much an American, and in America of being too much an Englishman."[42] Seeking to restore his name and political fortunes back home, Franklin reversed himself on the Stamp Act and testified before Parliament for its repeal. Soon enough, his zeal for independence was ignited—perhaps burning all the brighter for his earlier reticence and for his ill-treatment by the ruling elite of a nation he had deeply admired ever since his first visit as an aspiring young printer more than forty years earlier. There would be, he had realized, no royal appointment after all.[43]

His London mission in shambles, Franklin returned to Philadelphia in the spring of 1775. He immediately threw himself into American politics, taking a seat in the Second Continental Congress, designing a new colonial currency, and helping to edit Jefferson's draft of the Declaration of Independence. He used his newspaper and his pen to great effect in support of the rebellion, taking a more forthright public position on outright independence than many other colonial politicians. Franklin's private views toward the British, however, were more complex, and he did his best to maintain cordial relations through-out the conflict in discreet correspondence with many of his former friends and associates back in London.

The general ineffectiveness of political and economic resistance that preceded the Revolution had already revealed many of the structural weak-nesses of late colonial America. These included a minute manufacturing base, overreliance on single crops in the agricultural southlands, the inability to access foreign markets, an unstable currency regime and a lack of capital, lingering opposition among the provinces to greater integration, and an acute shortage of scientific and technical skills. Moreover, Britain's powerful navy controlled the Atlantic shipping lanes and, with them, communications to Europe and among the more distant colonies themselves. The start of armed rebellion against the Crown would transform these practical difficulties into outright threats to the entire project of American independence.

Franklin had already devoted much of his middle years in Philadelphia to redressing a number of these problems with ambitious plans for civic improve-ments. His chief prerevolutionary efforts, such as the creation of the Junto, the Library Company, the American Philosophical Society, and the Philadelphia academy, the drafting of the Albany Plan of Union, improvements to the colonial postal system, and the campaign on behalf of paper currency, had all come in response to the immediate demands of a specific time and place. None of these schemes were undertaken in anticipation of American independence, or to hasten its arrival. They were simply a recognition on Franklin's part that the needs of a maturing community had outgrown its old institutions.

Even his startling prediction, published in 1755, that the American population would within a century outpace that of Great Britain could not help, Franklin confidently proclaimed at the time, but redound to the greater glory of the mother country: "What an Accession of Power to the British Empire by Sea as well as Land! What Increase of Trade and Navigation! What Numbers of Ships and Seamen!"[44] Yet, each of Franklin's projects was to prove invaluable on the path first to colonial independence and then to the success of the new federated United States.

Well to the south, in a world away from the urban ferment of prerevolutionary Boston and Philadelphia, the structural weaknesses of the American economy and its vulnerability to British pressure were also being driven home to the grandees of Virginia's rich tobacco country. The region's almost exclusive focus on the production of tobacco meant that the plantations and their large populations of slaves were at the mercy of British-controlled trade just to meet basic needs for food, supplies, tools, and even clothing. Like Benjamin Rush and Charles Thomson, a number of Virginia planters—including the future rebel George Washington—began to draw a direct connection between the encouragement of American science and technology and greater freedom from imperial domination, if not outright independence.

Since the late seventeenth century, the leading planters relied almost exclusively on the so-called consignment system, whereby British merchants acted as agents for the transport and marketing of their sweet Tidewater tobacco and credited the growers' accounts upon final sale on the English and Continental markets. These same firms also controlled the supply of British-made goods to the growers, whether luxuries for the family home or basic implements and foodstuffs for the plantations, charging the costs against current or future earnings.[45] One list of English suppliers to Washington's plantation at Mount Vernon included an apothecary, a toolmaker, a milliner, a stationer, a platemaker, and a rope maker, as well as purveyors of pickles, wine, and ale.[46]

As early as the 1720s, the local assembly, the House of Burgesses, had sought ways to reduce Virginia's dependence on tobacco. Other proposals followed

that would have restricted imports of the slaves needed to work the leaf plantations or set strict production quotas, but opposition at the English court, led
by merchants eager to protect their transatlantic interests, helped block such
moves.[47] Decades later, one anonymous writer noted in the *Virginia Gazette*, little
had changed. "The tobacco trade cannot so properly be called the trade of this
colony as of Great Britain, in as much as the merchants concerned therein
mostly reside there, where the profits center."[48]

What had changed, however, was a new urgency to the problem of colonial
economic dependence, exemplified in the eyes of Washington and his Virginia
colleagues by overreliance on tobacco cultivation and the growing recognition
of the threat this posed to their aspirations for life, liberty, and the pursuit of
happiness. Significant weakness in world tobacco prices throughout much of
the 1760s only added to the pressure on the growers, as did a number of simul-
taneous British measures designed to tighten control over the colonies and to
raise additional revenue above and beyond the huge economic value inherent to
the mercantilist system.

These included the Sugar Act, which promised stricter enforcement of
duties on sugar, molasses, and other items; the Currency Act, which required
the costly retirement of local paper currency, already in very short supply; and,
perhaps most incendiary of all, the short-lived Stamp Act, with its taxes on
such everyday items as newsprint, legal documents, and even playing cards. The
Townshend Acts, which followed repeal of the Stamp Act, imposed fresh
duties on tea, glass, paint pigment, and other items as well as punitive measures
against colonial dissenters, and only served to exacerbate transatlantic enmity.
So, too, did a separate Declaratory Act, by which Parliament asserted its absolute authority over the colonies.

In response, the colonists began to adopt a number of strategies against
what were in effect backhanded attempts to impose new taxes, under the guise
of duties and related measures, without their consent, in violation of the
implied British social contract between ruler and ruled. Here was the origin of
the rallying cry, "Taxation without Representation." In addition to formal
protests pursued by the local assemblies, and amplified by colonial agents at the
royal court, such as Franklin, individual communities rallied around nonimportation campaigns. These were designed both to reduce colonial dependence
on Britain's exports and to pressure British merchants to lobby for repeal of the
new duties as injurious to their own long-term economic interests.

"The Eyes of our People (already beginning to open) will perceive, that many of the Luxuries which we have heretofore lavished our Substance to Great Britain for can well be dispensed with whilst the Necessaries of Life are to be procured (for the most part) within ourselves," Washington, by now a leader in Virginia's campaign against imports, warned his tobacco merchants, Robert Cary and Co. "This consequently will introduce frugality, and be a necessary stimulation to Industry. Great Britain may then load her Exports with as Heavy Taxes as She pleases but where will the consumption be?"[49]

Up and down the colonies, inventors, entrepreneurs, and visionaries of various stripes turned their attention to the production of goods traditionally imported from the mother country, or otherwise subject to imperial trade restrictions. Isaac Bartram, son of the Pennsylvania botanist, experimented with the brewing of spirits from homegrown persimmons as a substitute for heavily taxed imported molasses, used to make rum. The *Boston Gazette* proudly reported in 1770 that the entire graduating class at Harvard appeared that year at commencement in American-made clothes. The industrious folk at Germantown, meanwhile, were said by one English visitor to be capable of turning out thousands of high-quality stockings per year.[50] These efforts were backed by voluntary nonimportation campaigns throughout much of the 1760s and 1770s, organized either by local authorities or extralegal citizens' committees and carried out by sympathetic merchants.

✳ ✳ ✳

The more prescient colonists, Washington among them, recognized that simply doing without imported British goods was not much of a strategy for the long term. Over time, many of these boycotts ran out of steam, although not without inflicting some financial hardship on their intended targets. Still, the colonies would have to restructure their economies, diversify their agricultural production, develop their own manufacturing industries, and modernize their currency regimes and credit systems. This, in turn, required a far greater understanding of colonial resources, as well as the useful knowledge and technological expertise to exploit them to full advantage. It would also entail a direct challenge to British economic and political authority over every aspect of colonial life.

Washington informed Robert Cary and Co. that he had begun to explore the substitution of industrial crops, such as hemp and flax, for his customary tobacco, and he even placed an order in an enclosed invoice for specialty tools needed for this new venture: "I Set of (Haynes's) best Heckles for Flax [and] I Ditto . . . for Hemp."[51] He later experimented with sowing wheat at Mount Vernon, developed a thriving fisheries operation nearby, and attempted large-scale production of textiles to supply the day-to-day needs of his plantations.

Meanwhile, the Virginian Arthur Lee, at the time studying medicine in Edinburgh, suggested to friends and family back home that the local authorities offer premiums to encourage the development of domestic industry, a practice he would have encountered firsthand among the improvement societies then gaining popularity in England and Scotland. He also proposed the recruitment of skilled British workers, to be carried out in secret so as to evade "that jealous eye, with which Britain will ever view the rise & progress of Arts & Manufactures in America."[52]

Agrarian Virginia, like its southern neighbors, found itself hard-pressed to mount an effective nonimportation regime, for it lacked a strong urban merchant class to enforce such a boycott. Attention, instead, turned to the political arena and the elected House of Burgesses, now increasingly at odds with the colony's royal governor. The burgesses took up a proposal to create a nonimportation association, drafted by George Mason and backed enthusiastically by Washington, who personally carried the text to Williamsburg for consideration by the assembled delegates.

In addition to proposing a sharp reduction in British imports, Mason, a staunch defender of colonial rights whose ideas later helped shape Jefferson's Declaration of Independence, floated a more radical plan to overhaul the colony's tobacco-based economy in favor of industrial development. "If we were to desist purchasing Slaves, and making Tobacco, we should have a Number of Spare Hands to employ in Manufactures, and other Improvements; every private Family would soon be able to make whatever they wanted, for their own Use," Mason argued in the *Virginia Gazette*, writing under the pen name Atticus. "Many of the Manufactures of *Great-Britain*, finding no longer the usual Encouragement at Home, would remove hither for Employment, a general Spirit of Frugality and Industry would prevail, and our Difficulties daily decrease."[53]

On return from his studies in Scotland, Arthur Lee pressed for an organized boycott of British goods and a concomitant focus on the creation of domestic industry to be accompanied by petitions for relief to the Crown. "Let us . . . by our frugality and industry in manufacturing for ourselves convince our adversaries of their mistake in one grand point, that we are under a necessity of using the manufactures of *Britain*," Lee wrote in the first of a series of ten polemical letters published in the *Virginia Gazette* in 1768.

Underscoring the degree to which cultivating and harnessing the know-how necessary for industrial development had now converged with the push for colonial self-determination, Lee added, "Let *the people of every county instruct their members to petition, and let associations be formed to promote manufactures,* that we may manifest to all the world, how unanimously we are determined, both with hand and heart, to maintain our freedom, and frustrate the designs of those, who, by *dividing,* would *enslave us.*"[54]

The rebellious burgesses, forced to meet in the Apollo Room at the Raleigh Tavern after their formal suspension by the royal governor in 1769, approved a limited nonimportation drive—cheap clothing for the colony's large slave population was excepted—but balked at any halt to tobacco exports.[55] Over the succeeding years, however, the assembly took a number of steps to promote domestic industry and to widen the colony's agricultural base.

Bounties were offered for the production of hemp, in high demand for ships' rigging, as well as for the establishment of Virginia's first vineyards and, with notably less success, the cultivation of olives and the raising of silkworms. Tellingly, the same meeting of the Virginia Convention in late March 1775 that voted to make George Washington part of the colony's delegation to the second Continental Congress in Philadelphia appointed him a member of a special committee to "prepare a plan for the encouragement of Arts and Manufactures in this Colony."[56]

The push for modernization of the colonial economy that accompanied the growing differences with Great Britain further piqued the general public's interest in scientific and technical matters, a trend to which predominantly pastoral Virginia was not immune. The *Virginia Gazette* did its best to address this growing market, particularly on medical topics such as the ever-worrisome threat of smallpox.[57] Other articles covered the latest reports of wonders from the Royal Society and the Académie des Sciences. The international effort, spearheaded by the French and British societies and taken up by colonial enthusiasts, to track the transit of Venus across the face of the sun in 1769, prompted the *Gazette* to carry a number of items on the science of the stars. One year later, the newspaper published details of the revolutionary device to pump water automatically from leaky ships proposed by a member of Charles Thomson's American Society.

The growing social campaign for greater self-sufficiency, resting on practical and applied learning, culminated in the autumn of 1772 with the creation of the Virginia Society for the Promotion of Useful Knowledge, an explicit effort to copy the earlier example of Philadelphia. There had already been several failed attempts in Virginia to form a lasting scientific association, along the lines of the European societies. William Small, a celebrated professor at William and Mary and an inspiration to the young Thomas Jefferson, founded a circle in 1759 to inquire into medicinal plants and other problems in the natural world, but it faded away after Small's return to England. This time, however, prominent members of Virginia society rallied to the idea, and one local newspaper account later noted that the new society now consisted of one hundred members and was under the patronage of the provincial governor.[58]

A separate public notice in the press explained the group's aims: "The Object of their Hopes is to direct the Attention of their Countrymen to the Study of Nature, with a View to multiplying the Advantages that may result from this Source of Improvement." Such study promised to unlock the colony's untapped potential. "Virginia furnishes a Field both spacious and almost untrodden," said the anonymous author. "Who can tell what may accrue the Inhabitants from an Acquaintance with the Nature and Effects of the Climates and Soils?"[59]

A "Friend in Virginia," meanwhile, pointed out to readers of the *Gazette* that New York, Rhode Island, and other colonies to the north were all flourishing, despite their lack of the natural riches enjoyed by Virginia, on account of the more advanced state of their transportation links, commercial infrastructure, and diversified economies. "Pennsylvania, that is much nearer to us, abounds in towns, villages and a city—indeed, a city (though but of yesterday as to us) that may vie with many in Europe."[60]

One month later, the essayist "Academicus" repeated the notion that Virginia offered untold natural riches that needed to be explored and studied.* The writer suggested that by bringing together the colony's resident "Geniuses for their Investigation," the new Society for the Promotion of Useful Knowledge might provide "that Intercourse and Association which is necessary to the

---

* Guessing the identity—or identities—of the pseudonymous author has become something of an academic parlor game. Among those proposed as the source of at least one of these contributions to the *Virginia Gazette* is Thomas Jefferson. It is likely that multiple authors adopted the popular literary persona of Academicus.

Perfection of every Power of Man" and that had been so far sorely lacking in sparsely populated Virginia.[61] This same lack of anything resembling an urban center in the colony also dictated that the Society's regular meetings be held to coincide with the scheduled sessions of the legislature in the capital Williamsburg—the only sure way to gather Virginia's best-educated and most influential figures in the same place.

As befitted his pen name, Academicus was clearly steeped in the ideas of Francis Bacon, intellectual patron saint of the Royal Society, and he provided his readers with a brief tour of contemporary Western learning to show how the basic sciences supported the more accessible public arts and benefited society as a whole. He was almost certainly familiar with Franklin's original proposal for the American Philosophical Society, by now experiencing its rebirth in Philadelphia, for he repeated many of its arguments in favor of useful knowledge.

And, like the theoreticians of the Royal Society, Academicus touted the valuable contributions to the sciences that may be made by the nonspecialist. "Here then is a Line of Business which private Gentlemen can have no Excuse to decline; for though many may not be Proficients in Natural Philosophy and Mathematics, yet all may make Experiments in Agriculture, without Detriment to the usual Course of their Business."[62]

Over the next several years, the Virginia Society held regular meetings, collected meteorological data and medical accounts of the treatment of victims of lightning strikes, and awarded a gold medal to John Hobday for his revolutionary and economical new threshing machine—the first such American prize for invention. It also forged links with the American Philosophical Society and inducted several of Philadelphia's virtuosi, including Franklin, as members.

But like most of the other local knowledge associations that sprouted up in the late 1760s and early 1770s, it could not weather the approaching conflict with the British, which disrupted all aspects of colonial life. An announcement in the *Virginia Gazette* in May 1777 marked the Society's formal demise after a hiatus of two years, although it suggested, optimistically as it turned out, that a committee of nine members would from time to time collect scientific papers for future publication.[63]

The brief tenure of associations such as the Virginia Society and the acute teething problems of the more successful American Philosophical Society belie their broader importance to the colonial movement for useful knowledge. Born of a combination of scientific curiosity and mounting economic and political necessity, these early societies brought together many of the figures who would play such decisive parts in the independence campaign, the Revolutionary War, and the subsequent creation of the United States.

At the same time, the early societies demonstrated the importance and power of the new colonial knowledge networks that increasingly linked what had once been thirteen disparate settlements into a recognizable whole. Two decades after the defeat of Franklin's proposed Albany Plan of Union, which sought to give concrete expression to the need for collective action, the American colonies were now far more aware of their common interests. But just in case, or so legend tells us, the author of the Albany Plan reminded the other signatories to the Declaration of Independence in 1776 just how much things had changed since then: "We must, indeed, all hang together, or most assuredly we will all hang separately."*

---

* This quotation and its attribution to Franklin remain uncertain. Similar words were expressed in a range of eighteenth-century texts, under quite different circumstances. Yet the notion that it issued from Franklin's mouth at the signing of the Declaration refuses to die. This version can be found in Jared Sparks, ed., *The Works of Benjamin Franklin* (Chicago: Townsend MacCoun, 1882 I: 408.

Chapter Eight

THE MECHANICS OF REVOLUTION

By establishing manufactories among us, we erect an additional barrier against the encroachments of tyranny. A people who are entirely dependent upon foreigners for food or clothes, must always be subject to them.

—Benjamin Rush

BY THE MID-EIGHTEENTH century, most of Europe's virtuosi no longer had the inclination or the technical skills to construct the increasingly sophisticated instruments that their investigations demanded, and the fabrication of bespoke apparatus emerged as a distinct, and somewhat less prestigious, vocation.[1] Such was decidedly not the case in colonial-era America, which lacked the industrial and intellectual base, as well as the Old World class rigidities, to abet such a division of labor.

Unlike their transatlantic brethren, the Americans built their own instruments, trudged through uncharted wilds in search of their own specimens, designed their own fireplaces, and tended their own fields and vineyards, gathering what information they required as they went along. Even Jefferson, one of the great theoreticians of the American republic, preferred to direct his genius toward practical problems: he applied his love for Newton's mathematical innovations to the improvement of the common plow and rigged his own calendrical clock in the foyer of his stately home at Monticello, cutting a hole in the floorboards to allow the apparatus enough range of motion to display all seven days of the week.

Praise from abroad for the recent work surrounding the transit of Venus by Rittenhouse and his colleagues in the Philosophical Society celebrated the Americans as both artisans and scientists, as both practitioners and theoreticians. "There is not another Society in the world," wrote Rev. William Ludlam, an astronomer at Cambridge University, "that can boast of a member such as

Mr. RITTENHOUSE: theorist enough to encounter the problems of determining (from a few Observations) the Orbit of a Comet; and also mechanic enough to make, with his own hands, an Equal-Altitude Instrument, a Transit-Telescope, and a Timepiece. I wish I was near enough to see his mechanical apparatus. I find he is engaged in making a curious Orrery."[2]

In the wake of the colonists' break with Europe, sealed by the War of Independence, this unity of theory and practice evolved into something of a national principle, one that emphasized the practical demands of the work-shop, the powder mill, the battlefield, and the naval yard over the disciplined requirements of the classroom, or the unbending demands of scientific theory. Underpinning this shift was an approach to useful knowledge grounded in the immediate needs of nation building; it prized expediency, utilitarian value, common sense, and human experience over formalized book learning. This new outlook secured for Franklin and the instrument maker Rittenhouse, along with botanist John Bartram, hallowed places in what one intellectual historian has called "an American triumvirate of natural genius."[3]

In their time of extreme peril, the rebellious colonists turned to the mechanic, the artisan, and the skilled professional—in short, to the leather aprons—for practical solutions to pressing military, financial, and political challenges that must surely have seemed overwhelming.* Franklin, that autodidact supreme, now saw his own star rise precipitously. He had recovered much of his reputa-tion among the Americans by deftly reversing himself on the Stamp Act, campaigning against it in the British press and before Parliament, and even winning considerable credit for its eventual repeal. Yet, he had found that he was not wholly welcome on his return to Philadelphia. He remained, it seems, "too much an Englishman."

Many of his old political allies and intellectual associates were dead, and a new generation of civic and business leaders were in the ascendant. Franklin, radicalized by his experiences in London, found himself out of step with the generally conciliatory opinion that initially prevailed in the province. John Dickinson, the chairman of the Pennsylvania delegation to the Continental Congress, of which Franklin was a member, was an antagonist of long

---

* John Bartram was already in declining health when the war broke out. He died at the age of seventy-eight, on September 22, 1777, four days before British troops began their occupa-tion of Philadelphia.

standing—one who refused to affix one of his rival's protective lightning rods to his house purely out of spite.[4]

The crisis that followed the opening of outright hostilities suddenly made Franklin, eager as ever to make his mark on events, invaluable. Familiar with the ways of the European courts and a darling of the overseas virtuosi, he was dispatched to France in October 1776 as the closest thing America had to an old diplomatic hand. Once there, he carefully banked on his image as Dr. Franklin, the simple homespun scholar. He adopted as his sartorial trademarks a rough fur hat and bifocals, an invention of his own that the French lovingly mistook for a pair of cracked spectacles that the famously frugal American was loath to replace.[5] Franklin's public diplomacy proved highly effective. He first won the backing of the French political and social elite and then that of the more cautious King Louis XVI.

John Adams, newly arrived in Paris to join the diplomatic mission and already fearful that his own contributions to American independence would be overlooked by posterity, later whined to an old friend: "The History of our Revolution will be one continued Lie from one end to the other. The essence of the whole will be *that Dr. Franklin's electrical Rod smote the earth and out sprang General Washington. That Franklin electrified him with his rod, and thenceforward these two conducted all the Policy, Negotiations, Legislatures, and War.*"[6]

The frenetic Adams was particularly miffed that his fellow diplomat seemed to do little more than attend long lunches and elaborate soirees with the leading lights of Parisian society. What he had failed to apprehend was the extent to which European adulation for Franklin's scientific reputation, in particular his "taming" of the frightful danger of lightning strikes, made his entreaties for French financial assistance and political support hard to resist. Franklin the colonial scientist made Franklin the colonial diplomat a formidable and successful figure. He was welcomed warmly by the Parisian intellectuals, capped with the great Enlightenment icon Voltaire personally blessing the American's grandson.

Franklin's every move was fawned over by the French press and his likeness was re-created in marble and captured on canvas, silk, and porcelain. He understood instinctively that it was enough to serve as a living representation of the French ideal of republican America—plainspoken, practical, and modest— and then wait for the court to catch up with the general public's enthusiasm for the revolutionary cause.

Whenever possible, Franklin used his years in Paris, amid the press of diplomatic duties and the temptations of the city's social whirl, to limit damage from the war to the cooperative, global pursuit of useful knowledge. Throughout his time in France, from 1776 to 1785, he scrupulously maintained his correspondence with an impressive roster of British and other European scientific figures. Parties on both sides of the conflict generally sought to keep political differences out of their exchanges, but passions at times ran high and old relationships frayed. He even took the extraordinary step of renouncing one of his dearest British colleagues in public only to keep up a friendly, if at times bland, correspondence in private.

Early on, Franklin offered to route the botanist John Bartram's regular shipments of seeds and plants to England, now interdicted by war, through his own hands in Paris.[7] And in a grand gesture that did not go unnoticed in the halls of the Royal Society of London, he used his ministerial powers in March 1779 to call on American warships and privateers to grant safe passage to "that most celebrated Navigator and Discoverer Captain [James] Cook," now due back in England from his third voyage to the Pacific aboard HMS *Resolution*.*

Taking a page from his 1743 manifesto on useful knowledge, Franklin sent a directive reminding "all Captains & Commanders of armed Ships acting by Commission from the Congress of the United States of America" that "the Increase of Geographical Knowledge facilitates the Communication between distant Nations, in the Exchange of useful Products and Manufactures, and the Extension of Arts, whereby the common Enjoyments of human Life are multiplied and augmented, and Science of other kinds increased to the Benefit of Mankind in general." They were to "treat the said Captain Cook and his People with all Civility and Kindness, affording them as common Friends to Mankind, all the Assistance in your Power which they may happen to stand in need of."[8]

Franklin's "passport" for the Pacific expedition elicited a letter of thanks from Joseph Banks, a veteran of Cook's first mission that had included observation of the 1769 transit of Venus from the southern vantage point of Tahiti. Banks was now president of the Royal Society, and soon the pair began a steady correspondence that extended into the postwar period.

*   *   *

---

* Unbeknownst to Franklin, and to the rest of the scientific world, Cook had been killed one month earlier in a dispute with Hawaiian islanders.

Franklin's diplomatic post in Paris, while essential to the long-term success of the Americans, was for now a sideshow to the Revolution. Closer to home, few proponents of the useful knowledge movement loomed as large as David Rittenhouse. In a sign of the growing interconnectedness of American science, Virginia's Society for the Promotion of Useful Knowledge had recently added Rittenhouse, along with Franklin, Rush, and other Philadelphia luminaries, to its rolls.[9] Soon plans were afoot to secure for Rittenhouse a government appointment as Pennsylvania's first public astronomical observer, but the long, drawn-out affair was ultimately abandoned in the face of war with the British.

Despite his considerable scientific achievement and growing reputation, Rittenhouse—like Franklin—continued throughout his lifetime to identify himself as an artisan or mechanic, albeit one who labored at the intersection of engineering and science. One of his favorite sources of information was the *General Magazine of Arts and Sciences*, published by a London instrument maker and directed at a general audience. Rittenhouse was also an avid reader of the colonial press, which regularly featured reports of scientific discoveries, medical advances, and other technical breakthroughs. It was telling, then, that Rittenhouse signed a detailed letter to the *Pennsylvania Gazette* about Newton and Archimedes simply "A Mechanic."[10]

Rittenhouse was drawn into revolutionary activism through his membership in Pennsylvania's militant Mechanics Association, which held a mass protest against the British at the State House in June 1774. The association, originally formed as part of a colonies-wide movement of patriotic artisans and craftsmen, named the celebrated instrument maker to a special committee to work with fraternal societies along the Eastern Seaboard in opposition to the British and to their Royalist allies among the rich and powerful. The association also passed a resolution in support of a Continental Congress to address the growing crisis.[11]

A similar organization in New York City, the General Committee of Mechanics, also backed the Congress and soon demanded outright independence from Great Britain.[12] To the north, in Boston, perhaps the most famous hero of the early days of the Revolution, Paul Revere, was himself a mechanic and, later, an industrialist, entrepreneur, and innovator in the working of copper and other metals. Many members of Revere's immediate family were also artisans, including carpenters, metalsmiths, and shipwrights.

Additional sources of the growing influence of mechanics and other leather aprons in colonial affairs included the provincial militia movement, the fire companies, and the Masonic lodges—all beneficiaries of Franklin's earlier exertions—as well as specific craft associations such as the Tailors Company and the Carpenters' Company. These institutions were backed by the master printers and the presses they controlled, and by the prestige of the American Philosophical Society, which counted many leading mechanics and artisans among its ranks.[13]

The mechanics, often supported by the small farmers, were particularly powerful in Pennsylvania, where Franklin, Rittenhouse, and others crafted a provincial constitution that gave full voice to their interests at the expense of the local elite. After all, argued one of their own in the *Pennsylvania Evening Post*, they represented the true voice of the new republic. "Do not mechanics and farmers constitute ninety-nine of a hundred of the people of America? . . . Is not half the property in the city of Philadelphia owned by men who wear LEATHERN APRONS? Does not the other half belong to men whose fathers or grandfathers wore LEATHERN APRONS?"[14]

Throughout the revolutionary period, the leather aprons were steadfast in their support for key elements of grassroots democracy, including secret ballot, direct election, and limited tenure in public office, all of which were enshrined in the new Pennsylvania constitution. They also supported strong centralized powers for the federal government—first to combat the British and, after independence, to construct a new, postwar economy based on expanded domestic production and overseas trade.[15]

Armed conflict with Britain began in earnest in April 1775. Cut off by the British navy from trade with the outside world, and short of everything from gunpowder and ammunition to provisions, uniforms, blankets, and cannon, the rebellious colonies were impelled toward greater self-sufficiency. To help address the acute lack of war materiel, Pennsylvania's Committee of Safety, created to oversee the local military effort, turned to some of the province's leading mechanics. These included Rittenhouse and his fellow watchmaker and astronomer Owen Biddle.

Both were members of the American Philosophical Society, and they had been instrumental in the association's observations of the transit of Venus in 1769, when Biddle led the observation team at Cape Henlopen. The inclusion of Biddle and Rittenhouse on the Committee of Safety, the latter as chief engineer, reflected Americans' faith in the practical utility of both scientists and scientific knowledge. Mechanics and other artisans had already taken the lead in many of the urban campaigns for nonimportation of British goods, and now they assumed prominent positions in the war effort itself.[16]

The chief engineer's new duties included surveying defensive fortifications, inspecting prototype naval vessels, and overseeing the production of munitions. "Rittenhouse is a mechanic; a mathematician, a philosopher, and an astronomer. Biddle is said to be a great mathematician," Adams, who joined the two men on a tour of ten new Pennsylvania warships, noted in his diary. "Rittenhouse is a tall slender man, plain, soft, modest, no remarkable depth or thoughtfulness in his face, yet cool, attentive, and clear."[17]

Six months later, Adams won the approval of the Continental Congress for a resolution that local authorities "take the earliest measures for erecting and establishing, in each and every colony a society for the improvement of agriculture, arts, manufactures, and commerce, and to maintain a correspondence between such societies, that the rich and numerous natural advantages of this country, for supporting its inhabitants, may not be neglected." The Congress then called for specific steps to introduce or improve production of canvas, sailcloth, and steel in preparation for war.[18]

At Rittenhouse's recommendation, the Pennsylvania Committee contracted with a local ironmonger for new artillery, although his suggestion, based on his own experiments, that the cannon barrels be rifled to improve their accuracy proved beyond the capabilities of the province's modest industry.[19] Other government-backed projects sought to increase the output of such strategic commodities as iron and paper. Meanwhile, Franklin was conspiring with the French military in Paris to secretly provide "skilled engineers, not exceeding four" to aid the American cause.[20]

War has always provided a spur to technological innovation, and American experimenters stepped forward with a number of ingenious ideas for new or improved weapons to deploy against superior British firepower. Among the most ambitious was David Bushnell's miniature submarine, powered by hand and designed to slip silently alongside an enemy ship and attach an explosive, on a timed fuse, to the hull. Bushnell received financial support for his scheme, immediately dubbed Bushnell's Turtle, from the Connecticut legislature, but his several attempts against the British fleet in New York harbor were thwarted by his inability to affix the bomb to its target.

Hampered by a lack of experience and of anything resembling an industrial base, efforts by the rebels to stimulate wartime production made little real progress. Even when victory was in sight, General Washington recognized that America's army would long remain dependent on European expertise. "A Peace Establishment is now under consideration, in which it is recommended that Congress should form Military Academies & Manufactories as part of this Establishment," he wrote in 1783 to a senior French officer, Brigadier General Louis Lebègue Duportail, then the Continental Army's commandant of engineers. Washington went on to suggest that the services of the French engineering corps be retained for this purpose after the war. The French declined but Duportail provided a list of ideas for such an institution, a number of which the Americans would later adopt.[21]

As short as the rebels were of warships and cannon, they were in greatest need of gunpowder. At the outbreak of fighting, the colonies had only limited, aging supplies on hand, most dating back to the Seven Years' War. According to one estimate, the Americans entered the fray with just eighty thousand pounds of black powder, half of which had already been frittered away by the ill-disciplined troops by the time Washington formally assumed command of the Continental Army in July 1775.[22] "Our want of powder is inconceivable. A daily waste and no supply administers a gloomy prospect," Washington reported from his headquarters at Cambridge, Massachusetts, on Christmas Day.[23] To keep the British in the dark about the dwindling supply of powder, the Americans periodically lobbed a lone cannonball in the enemy's general direction from a hilltop outside Boston.

Officials in Philadelphia put Rittenhouse in charge of securing potassium nitrate, commonly known as saltpeter and the central ingredient in gunpowder. Across the colonies, the authorities sought to promote the mining and collection of the precious substance. The Second Continental Congress distributed recipes for homemade powder to the various colonies and offered substantial bounties to spur large-scale production. Efforts were made to forage for potassium nitrate residue from farmyards, the floors of tobacco warehouses, stables, cellars, and dovecotes.

Rittenhouse threw himself into the subject, consulting the scientific and military literature and sounding out his more learned friends and associates on the subject, yet the drive for domestic production fell far short of expectations. By far the bulk of the black powder used by the Americans, particularly in the early years of the war, was smuggled from France, by way of the West Indies.[24] Rittenhouse had better luck with the thankless task of juggling Pennsylvania's disastrous finances as its treasurer from 1777 to 1789, invoking sleight of hand accounting as well as his undoubted arithmetic skills to somehow keep the debt-ridden state afloat.

British troops overran Philadelphia in late September 1777, forcing the dispersal of the Second Continental Congress as well as Pennsylvania's government. What little scientific activity that had survived the early war years now came to a halt. Like many of the other colonial educational institutions, the grounds of the academy were given over to the billeting of soldiers and treatment of the wounded. However, Provost Smith, no enthusiast for American independence, successfully prevailed upon the British commander to safeguard the school's prized Rittenhouse orrery throughout the occupation.[25]

The British withdrawal from the city nine months later opened the way for a gradual resuscitation of intellectual life, grouped around the American Philosophical Society and the College of Philadelphia. Rittenhouse and Jefferson, who was then in Williamsburg, Virginia, even managed to exchange letters on their respective attempts to observe a major eclipse on June 28, 1778, and the latter chided his friend for failing to complete construction of a timepiece that would have greatly aided the effort. Jefferson could not refrain from worrying about the demands of Rittenhouse's government posts when he might better spend his time in pursuit of more useful matters. "You should consider that the world has but one Rittenhouse, and that it never had one before."[26]

*   *   *

The gradual winding down of the war after the British defeat at Yorktown allowed Rittenhouse to turn his attention back to the American Philosophical Society, and he was elected to the organization's newly formed governing council in 1783, in the company of Jefferson and other veterans of the independence effort. Recent events had been hard on the Society, whose internal divisions had been exacerbated by what Francis Hopkinson, son of one of Franklin's original "electricians" and an inaugural graduate of the Philadelphia academy, called the "dreary tempest of war."

With independence, Hopkinson warned his colleagues, America risked disappointing the Europeans, who were now turning to the new nation not so much for political inspiration as for future intellectual leadership. "They look towards us as a country that may be a great nursery of arts and sciences, as a country affording an extensive field of improvement in agriculture, natural history, and other branches of useful knowledge."[27] In order to justify these hopes and realize the full benefits of sovereignty, America had to redouble its efforts in scientific study, experimentation, and invention.

This meant realizing the promise of earlier Puritan and Quaker attitudes toward learning and overthrowing the established economy of knowledge. "The door to knowledge seems to be wider open than it ever was. . . . It is now perceived, that it is not absolutely *necessary* that a man should be what is called *learned* in order to be a [natural] philosopher," argued Hopkinson. "A judicious and careful examination of the phenomena of nature, and experiments, simple and easily made, may, and often do, lead the attentive enquirer to most important discoveries, even without any knowledge of what are called the learned languages."[28]

Accompanying this intellectual opening to the leather aprons, most of whom lacked much in the way of traditional education, was an equally inviting political one: the opportunity for the independent artisan to take meaningful part in postwar affairs. One result was the branching out of the useful knowledge societies to encompass activities specifically aimed at improving the art of manufacturing. Others specifically addressed improvements in agriculture. Inventors, amateur scientists, and the curious all flocked to the new associations, frequently joining more than one at a time.[29]

The United Company of Philadelphia for Promoting American Manufactures formed in 1775, and similar societies were soon active in Boston, Baltimore, and New York. Smaller communities, including Richmond, Virginia; Wilmington, Delaware; Morristown and Newark, New Jersey; and Elkton, Maryland, followed in their footsteps.[30] The United Company combined the established institution of the workhouse with the new enthusiasm for the outright development of American technology and industry. Unlike traditional schemes to address poverty and idleness, it also set out to enhance productivity and to make a profit, relying on advances in automation and power, and the expansion of the workforce to include women and young children to operate the machines.

The United Company gave way after the war to the Pennsylvania Society for the Encouragement of Manufactures and the Useful Arts, essentially a commercial enterprise without its predecessor's charitable or other social functions.[31] This and other such associations mostly served as clearinghouses for new ideas and as sources of prizes and other financial incentives for technological innovation.[32] Little was actually added in the way of manufacturing capacity by such early efforts, but they nonetheless helped lay the political, social, and intellectual foundations for the coming industrialization of the new republic.

This was particularly striking not so much in the creation of large-scale enterprises, which generally failed to take root before the turn of the century, as in the immediate strengthening of the role of artisans, mechanics, and craftsmen in the less-visible reaches of the national economy and their associated entry into the political arena. Some farsighted merchants supported these efforts and even invested their capital in manufacturing, but most were more concerned with returning to lucrative prewar trade patterns in which they acted as passive middlemen rather than as entrepreneurs. As a result of agitation mostly by the leather aprons, the notions of patriotism, practical invention, and industrial development began to converge.[33]

Pennsylvania, with its Quaker traditions of craftsmanship and respect for labor, proved particularly receptive to the efforts of the mechanics, whose presence on the political and economic scene was already greater there than in the other colonies. For decades, Franklin and his fellow artisans had carved out significant influence in the affairs of the province, promoting everything from practical education to expanded civic amenities and the useful knowledge movement.

In an early sign of this influence, Philadelphia artisans under the leadership of Franklin acolyte Charles Thomson thwarted efforts to hold the First Continental Congress in September 1774 at the official State House, where they feared it could fall under the sway of the provincial establishment. Instead, the sessions were held in Carpenters' Hall, a mechanics stronghold that also played host to the Library Company of Philadelphia, the American Philosophical Society, and like-minded groups. Three leading members of the artisan class, Franklin foremost among them, signed the Declaration of Independence.*

After the war, the mechanics and their allies emerged as major supporters of a strong federal government to protect their economic interests as manufacturers, as well as their recent social and political gains. On July 4, 1788, the mechanics' associations of Boston, Philadelphia, and New York took leading

---

* The others were Roger Sherman, a New England shoemaker, and George Walton, trained as a carpenter in Georgia. Both later went on to successful careers in law and politics.

roles in celebratory parades to mark the ratification of the federal Constitution and the introduction of a centralized government to replace the old Confederation. Fourteen hundred marchers, representing forty separate crafts, took part in Boston. Another two thousand gathered in New York, and around five thousand in Philadelphia.[34]

Elaborate floats, pulled by teams of horses, celebrated the new federal government and the individual craft associations, while banners hoisted by the marchers expressed the artisans' support for government intervention in the economy on behalf of both traditional crafts and the new mechanized industry. A pale blue carriage, "in the shape of a bald eagle" and carrying the newly ratified Constitution, led the Philadelphia procession. The Manufacturing Society float featured a wool carding machine, a spinning machine with eighty spindles, and other machinery, under the motto: MAY THE UNION GOVERNMENT PROTECT THE MANUFACTURES OF AMERICA.

In New York, the shipwrights proclaimed, "The federal ship will commerce revive, And merchants and shipwrights and joiners shall thrive."[35] Delivering the ceremonial oration at the Philadelphia parade, the nation's largest, James Wilson, a signatory to the Declaration of Independence and later a Supreme Court justice, paid the required homage to America's agricultural roots, before adding, "The *industrious village*, the *busy city*, the *crowded port*—all these are the gifts of liberty; and without a good government, *liberty* cannot exist."[36]

*   *   *

Upon his return from Paris in the autumn of 1785, Franklin displaced Rittenhouse as the nation's most famous mechanic. This set off an immediate scramble among the main factions and personalities of the American Philosophical Society for his support. But it also helped reinvigorate the organization, and experimental work in general. Hopkinson, Franklin, and Rittenhouse set aside one evening a week for what the latter described as "a little, pleasing philosophical Party." This prompted a jealous rebuke from his absent friend Jefferson, still on diplomatic duty in Paris. Meanwhile, the long-delayed second volume of the Society's *Transactions* finally appeared in print.[37]

Plans, proposals, and new inventions and designs began to pour into the American Philosophical Society, which found itself, like its forerunner the Royal Society of London, pressed to arbitrate among competing claims of intellectual property, feasibility, and practical utility. "We have abundance of projectors and pretenders to new Discoveries, and many applications to the

Legislature for exclusive privileges, some of them ridiculous enough," a bemused Rittenhouse wrote to Jefferson. "The self-moving boat, the Mechanical Miller, the improved Ring Dial for finding the Variations of the Needle. The Surveying Compass to serve 20 other purposes, and a project for finding the Longitude by the Variation of the Magnetical Needle."[38]

Ever the intellectual entrepreneur, the eighty-one-year-old Franklin created his last study circle in February 1787, this time dedicated to the improvement of a branch of useful knowledge that he had so far largely ignored. The inaugural meeting of the Society for Political Inquiries was held at Philadelphia's City Tavern, although the fortnightly sessions—suspended during the oppressive heat of the mid-Atlantic summer—soon shifted to Franklin's home, in deference to his declining health.[39] The American Philosophical Society likewise moved its regular gatherings to the Franklin residence, which had recently been expanded to accommodate such sessions and to make room for his "very considerable" library.[40]

"The moral character and happiness of mankind, are so interwoven with the operations of government, and the progress of the arts and sciences, is so dependent on the nature of our political institutions, that it is essential to the advancement of civilized society to give ample discussion to these topics," declared the opening lines of the new group's constitution, written by the revolutionary publicist Thomas Paine. This was all the more the case with the American republic, which by necessity had "grafted on an infant commonwealth the manners of ancient and corrupted monarchies."[41]

In addition to Paine, founders of the new political society included such longtime Franklin stalwarts as Rittenhouse, Rush, the printer William Bradford, and Franklin's grandson and personal secretary William Temple Franklin. The fathers of six of the participants had taken part in Franklin's earlier ventures, the Library Company and the Union Fire Company; twenty-two members were on the rolls of the American Philosophical Society, of which he remained president; and nine, led by Franklin himself, were delegates to the Constitutional Convention, which met in Philadelphia over the summer of 1787.[42]

Franklin and his fellow leather aprons brought the same attitudes, ideas, and approaches to the study of politics that they had earlier applied to other branches of useful knowledge, those of collective discussion, social action, and experimentation. Shortly before the creation of the Society for Political Inquiries, Franklin wrote to a sympathetic English bishop of the Americans' steady progress toward the drafting of the Constitution: "You seem desirous of knowing what Progress we make here in improving our Governments. We are, I think, in the right Road of Improvement, for we are making Experiments."[43]

Also finding a home in the Society for Political Inquiries was the unlikely figure of Tench Coxe, a notorious speculator and former Royalist who only narrowly avoided prosecution for treason at the hands of the patriots. Coxe had spent much of the immediate postwar period churning out polemics in support of a strong federal Constitution, a talent that drew the attentions of such leading revolutionaries as Jefferson, Rush, Hamilton, and James Madison, and kept him one step ahead of the law. A good word to the court from Pennsylvania's chief justice, an old friend of the Coxe family, no doubt helped as well. The charges were dropped, though never forgotten.

Such were Coxe's exertions as a publicist that he served at various times as virtual coeditor of three Philadelphia newspapers, and by his own count authored thirty articles in support of the proposed federal Constitution, designed to replace the wartime Articles of Confederation.[44] He also took an oath of loyalty to the new nation, whose independence he had once opposed. Ever the optimist, Coxe summed up his hopes of rehabilitation in a letter to his brother John, written in 1778 as British forces were withdrawing from his native Philadelphia: "I am (*if* permitted) likely to become a good American."[45]

Coxe likewise benefited from long-standing personal ties to Franklin. Their two families cooperated in speculative land deals, and Franklin had nominated Coxe's father, William, as collector of the ill-fated Stamp Tax for the province of New Jersey. In 1786, Franklin used his influence as formal head of Pennsylvania's government to appoint Coxe to represent the state at preliminary talks on the future of the confederation, held at Annapolis, Maryland. Franklin, Coxe, and Rush also served together in the leadership of the state abolitionist movement.[46]

Yet Coxe was never fully trusted, due to his past Tory sympathies and his ill-concealed aristocratic airs. The public repeatedly denied him elected office, while many among his newfound friends in the revolutionary generation eventually tired of his naked careerism. Jefferson, an aristocrat of a slightly different order, later grouped Coxe among those "cormorants hungry for office," while Hamilton, with whom he often collaborated, dismissed him as "too cunning to be wise." To John Quincy Adams, Coxe was a "wily, winding, subtle, and insidious character."[47]

This did not keep most of them from relying heavily on Coxe, whose expertise, boundless energy, and vigorous rhetorical support they valued, and his views certainly would have merited close attention from Franklin's Society for Political Inquiries. Coxe soon found himself one of the few major figures of the day able to cross the divide that was beginning to open between the Federalists around Hamilton and the Jeffersonian Republicans, for he somehow managed to juggle support for the fiscal policies of the former and the commercial policies of the latter.[48]

Among the questions debated by the Society for Political Inquiries were the limits to press freedom in a constitutional system; the efficacy of public punishment for criminals; the fairest system of taxation; and the utility, if any, of the study of Greek and Latin. One matter before the circle was particularly dear to Coxe's heart: "How far may the interposition of government be advantageously directed to the regulation of agriculture, manufactures, and commerce?" The group considered this last issue so vital that it established a prize in the form of an inscribed gold plate for the best essay on the subject.[49]

Coxe had already arrived at his own answer. A more recent convert to the American cause than others in this illustrious cohort, he nonetheless used an early meeting of the Society for Political Inquiries as a sounding board for what was perhaps the most revolutionary and prescient vision to date of the new nation's future. He then published an expanded version in a pamphlet, *An Enquiry into the Principles on which a Commercial System for the United States Should be Founded*, dedicating the slim volume to the delegates to the Constitutional Convention and effectively placing his far-reaching prescriptions before the public at large.[50] He also sent a personal copy to Franklin, who had actively assisted in its publication.

For Coxe, the wholehearted embrace of technology, including the improved steam engine recently developed by Scottish inventor James Watt, was vital. "Factories, which can be carried on by watermills, windmills, fire, horses and machines ingeniously contrived, are not burdened with any heavy expense of boarding, lodging, clothing and paying workmen, and they multiply the force of hands to a great extent without taking our people from agriculture," he argued in a keynote address in the summer of 1787 to the new Pennsylvania Society for the Encouragement of Manufactures and the Useful Arts, a number of whose members also took part in the Society for Political Inquiries.[51]

"In short," Coxe concluded, "combinations of machines with fire and water have already accomplished much more than was expected from them by the most visionary enthusiast."[52] New labor-saving devices, assisted by inevitable technological innovation, would effectively inoculate America against the very social ills that Jefferson and many others feared—the creation of a large laboring underclass, dangerous and unhealthy conditions in the factories, and the diversion of manpower and other resources directed toward agriculture. Prudent deployment of technology would allow America to reap the full potential of its rich natural resources without endangering the republican vision Coxe had belatedly embraced.

Others were floating similar ideas, including the Boston financier James Swan. Another outspoken advocate of industry was Rittenhouse's nephew and biographer William Barton, who invoked Franklin's predictions that the American population would double every twenty-five years. "What, then, is to become of this vast increase of the inhabitants of our towns? They cannot be all laborers; and but a small part can engage in husbandry, the learned professions, or merchandize: consequently, the greater part must apply to trades and manufactures, or starve," wrote Barton, now chairman of the Pennsylvania Society for the Encouragement of Manufactures and the Useful Arts.[53] The Irish immigrant printer Matthew Carey, another in a long line of Franklin protégés, used the pages of his *American Museum* magazine to advance the cause of manufactures as fundamental to national independence.

But it was Tench Coxe in particular who brought together these different strands and forged what the critic Leo Marx has called a "prophetic vision of machine technology as the fulcrum of national power."[54] Unlike his warring patrons—Hamilton, who wanted to imitate and eventually challenge Great Britain, and Jefferson, who sought to withdraw for as long as possible into the deep pastoral recesses of the continent—Coxe saw that America was uniquely suited to the wholesale introduction of the machine. By the early years of the fast-approaching nineteenth century, such an idea would become as commonplace as it is today.

*   *   *

Coxe's own education at the College of Philadelphia had been cut short by the war, but his approach to knowledge was fully compatible with that of Franklin, Rittenhouse, Rush, and other American virtuosi. The son of a wealthy merchant family with roots among the early settlers, young Coxe had enjoyed easy access to a range of books. As an adult his library overflowed with works on philosophy, history, grammar, and agronomy. But he was far more interested in the useful and practical than the theoretical or speculative, and his true métier lay with the comforting order provided by rows and columns of financial ledgers, industrial facts and figures, tables of agricultural production, customs forms, and the like. "To him what was useful was good, and what was good could best be described by incontrovertible statistical data," concludes the only modern study of the man.[55]

In order to unleash America's enormous potential, Coxe advocated a strong, centralized government; protections from unfair foreign competition, particularly British dumping of cheap goods on the postwar market; settlement of the outstanding wartime debt to support a national currency and a workable credit regime; and the encouragement of cotton cultivation in the South and textile manufactures in the North. Most of all, he called for the unabashed application to industrial production of power technologies—steam, water, draft animals, or fire—and machines.

Residual doubts surrounding Coxe's political loyalties complicated his role as a spokesman for the manufacturing lobby, at a time when the real debate was not so much about specific policies as it was about two competing futures for America. Yet he was able to assert his views through his collaboration with Hamilton on the Treasury Department's Report on Manufactures, sent to Congress in December 1791. Many of the arguments in the report bear the distinctive hallmark of Coxe, who by then was serving as Hamilton's chief deputy. However, the document's outright refusal to acknowledge the concerns of the Jeffersonian Republicans, even rhetorically, and its assertion that manufacturing powers were in all ways superior to agrarian states were surely the work of the more pugnacious Hamilton.[56]

This American struggle over the proper place of manufactures was caught up in the wider "problem" of luxury, which has long troubled social thinkers. "Is not the Hope of one day being able to purchase and enjoy Luxuries a great Spur to Labor and Industry?" Franklin wondered in 1784, sounding much like his old coffeehouse interlocutor, the "facetious" Bernard Mandeville, who had scandalized Europe with its assertion that private vices fueled public benefits. "May not Luxury therefore produce more than it consumes," asked Franklin, "if without such a Spur People would be as they are naturally enough inclined to be, lazy and indolent?"[57]

Over the years, Franklin had gradually shed his opposition to American manufactures. As tensions mounted with the Crown in the late 1760s and early 1770s, he had begun to advocate the inalienable right of Americans to produce finished goods on a large scale, even those that competed directly with British industrial products, such as glass, china, and nails.[58] Inspired by the nonimportation movements, Franklin asked why his countrymen should support the opulent lifestyles of British businessmen grown fat on exports of "flimsy manufactures." Rather, he wrote from London in 1769, "we should disdain the thralldom we have so long been held in by this mischievous commerce, reject it forever, and seek our resources where God and Nature have placed them WITHIN OUR SELVES."[59]

This represented a direct challenge to the entire British colonial system, not unlike Franklin's earlier assault on the economy of knowledge whereby Europe's virtuosi created "science" from American raw materials provided by the likes of John Bartram, Alexander Garden, and John Clayton. It was also an important step toward political and economic autonomy, and it explains Franklin's later interest in Tench Coxe, the apostle of American manufacturing and technological innovation.

The activist Hamilton, intent on the swiftest possible transformation of the new, untested federal structure into a permanent edifice of government, sought to direct the creative powers of the mechanics, inventors, and entrepreneurs toward this goal. "There is, at the present juncture, a certain fermentation of mind, a certain activity of speculation and enterprise which, if properly directed, may be made subservient to useful purposes," Hamilton argued before Congress. Success in such a venture was, he assured his skeptical audience, a matter of national security, particularly in the event of war, and would ultimately guarantee the nation's true independence.[60]

As others had done before him, Hamilton turned to the indefatigable Coxe for assistance. So intent were the two men on their shared vision that they were seemingly prepared to beg, borrow, or steal their way to this industrial promised land. Coxe had already launched a private campaign of industrial espionage against the British, in an attempt to join private gain with public benefit. Likewise, Hamilton began to enrich his closest political cronies and business partners, if not himself, through shady land deals and other questionable transactions in support of private industry and the banks. And together, Hamilton and Coxe hatched a secret plan to create a "national manufactory" from scratch in what was then the wilds of New Jersey—a scheme, they reckoned, that would set America on course for rapid and irreversible industrialization and generate considerable profits for them and their fellow insiders.*

Coxe formed a discreet partnership in 1787 with Andrew Mitchell, an expatriate Englishman, who agreed to return home, purchase or steal models and patterns of England's best industrial technology, and then smuggle them back to America in violation of strict British export controls. As a side venture, Mitchell would make a stopover to sell a copy of the plans to French textile interests, just as eager as the Americans to undermine British industrial superiority.[61] According to a contract between Coxe and Mitchell, the scheme was "to procure for their joint and equal benefit and profit, and for the good of the United States, models and patterns of a number of machines and engines now used in the Kingdom of Great Britain . . . for manufacturing cotton."[62]

However, Mitchell may well have swindled his American partner. He later informed Coxe that the British authorities had prevented his departure with the pirated materials after he had spent considerable amounts of his American partner's money to obtain them. A suitcase full of models that Mitchell claimed to have left behind for safekeeping was never found. Similar plans were clearly afoot as early as 1783, when a pair of British sympathizers in Philadelphia, including one of the early proponents of the American Philosophical Society, snapped up a British spinning machine that had been smuggled out of the country and returned it safely to England.[63]

Coxe and Hamilton also arranged for bounties to be paid to skilled British workmen, ideally plant foremen or other supervisors, who brought with them the secrets of modern textile technology, in particular the closely guarded designs of the engineer and inventor Richard Arkwright. In one such case, Coxe collaborated successfully with George Parkinson, an English weaver now living in Philadelphia, to introduce the latest British methods of spinning flax, hemp, and wool to the American market.

Even Jefferson, whose office of secretary of state then oversaw U.S. patents, set aside his general disapproval of manufactures and granted the assignment of intellectual property rights to Parkinson in 1791 for what was clearly a

---

* Given Coxe's personal ambitions and his natural inclination to hedge his bets, it is not surprising that he shared the secret with Hamilton's archrival Jefferson, for whom Coxe later drafted a number of economic reports and policy papers.

purloined version of Arkwright's latest spinning machine.[64] Meanwhile, an Arkwright employee, Samuel Slater, emigrated to Rhode Island, where he helped set up a successful enterprise using his former boss's system, known as the water frame, for harnessing moving water to power textile mills.

For Hamilton and Coxe, industrial piracy was only a stopgap measure. They were confident that in the long run America's technological advances could best be addressed by homegrown inventors such as Rittenhouse, master of the mechanical planetarium and other useful devices, rather than through outright theft. "On the subject of mechanism America may justly pride herself," crowed Coxe. "Every combination of machinery may be expected from a country, a NATIVE SON of which, reaching this inestimable object at its highest point, has epitomized the motions of the spheres, that roll throughout the universe."[65]

*   *   *

Coxe's utilitarian cast of mind, combined with his overweening ambition and ardent desire to restore the family fortune, impelled him to cut corners in pursuit of his political and personal goals. In this way, he represented the perfect partner for the equally striving figure of Hamilton, for whom the failure of his economic vision was unimaginable. "As to whatever may depend on enterprise, we need not fear to be outdone by any people on earth," Hamilton later declared in defense of his policies. "It may almost be said that enterprise is our element."[66] Working together at the Treasury Department, Hamilton and Coxe pooled their organizational skills, business connections, and rhetorical talents to create what was in effect a test bed for their radical notions of state-backed industrialization and technological development.

The sheer ambition of the complex, to be known as the Society for Establishing Useful Manufactures, or SUM, was breathtaking. The project boasted an authorized capital of one million dollars, almost certainly greater than the total of all investment at the time in America's joint stock manufacturing enterprises and equivalent to around 2 percent of the nation's public debt.[67] The Society would deploy some of the latest technology to power textile machines, sawmills, printing presses, and other industrial applications, including the dubious Parkinson patent and the water frame drive mechanism "borrowed" from Arkwright's original design. Hamilton even contracted with Pierre L'Enfant, the original architect of the new federal city under construction in Washington, to create a glorious national capital of industry.

Financial and political considerations dictated that the SUM be located near both Philadelphia, still the seat of the federal government, and New York, already a major center of commerce and finance. Hamilton was certain that he knew just the spot. In July 1778, as General Washington's aide-de-camp, he had enjoyed a brief respite from the war during a picnic on the banks of New Jersey's Passaic River in the company of his commander and other staff. The military men lunched on cold ham, tongue, and biscuits, washed down by "some excellent grog." A fresh-water spring bubbled underfoot, and the air was bathed in the cool mists thrown up by the nearby Great Falls, which sent plumes of water crashing over a rocky lip and into a basin carved into the basalt more than seventy feet below.[68]

Thirteen years later, Hamilton chose these same flowing waters to drive his monumental experiment in the early mechanization of America. This new city was to be named Paterson, after New Jersey governor William Paterson, in return for crucial support for the project, including tax abatements, an exemption for military service for SUM employees, and the legal authority to create an incorporated company town essentially outside state jurisdiction.

A carefully calibrated public relations campaign accompanied the unveiling of the SUM. Hamilton provided the first public hints of the forthcoming project in his 1791 Report on Manufactures. "It may be announced that a Society is forming, . . . in behalf of which measures are already in train for the prosecution on a large scale of making and printing of Cotton Goods," he informed the Congress.[69] Meanwhile, Hamilton and Coxe circulated among potential investors a formal three-page prospectus—drafted by Hamilton personally—that touted the advantages that the Society for the Establishing Useful Manufactures would realize from federal backing and an effective monopoly on large-scale cotton textile production.[70]

Finally, the pair used their extensive contacts in the American press to secure favorable coverage of their plans in leading newspapers. The *National Gazette*, for example, ignored early criticism of the SUM and instead trumpeted the project's financial prospects, citing the abundance of nearby raw materials and easy access to the power of the Great Falls: "These advantages, together with its contingency to, and easy communication with one of the first cities of the United States, makes it unquestionably one of the most eligible and desirable situations in the world for the permanent establishment of manufactures."[71]

Spurred by glowing newspaper accounts, public excitement about the project ran high and the demand among the well heeled and the well connected for shares in the new corporation proved robust. However, the enterprise faced enormous challenges from the outset, many of which were exacerbated by poor judgment on the part of Hamilton in doling out key managerial positions to loyal but unscrupulous business associates. Facing ruin after provoking America's first financial scare, the panic of 1792, SUM chairman and former Hamilton aide William Duer absconded with Society funds in a failed attempt to stave off personal bankruptcy and a stint in debtors' prison. Other board members were also implicated in Duer's financial wrongdoings, which caused a run on the fragile American banking system and forced the intervention of the federal government.

Meanwhile, the SUM's planned investment of fifty thousand dollars in textile machinery apparently vanished into the hands of a perfidious corporate agent. Even honest investors found it difficult in the immediate aftermath of the panic to make good their pledges of funds for the Society's shares, further slowing the construction of the planned canals, the reservoir, and the raceway needed to capture the power of the falls for industrial use. The lack of real manufacturing experience on the part of the directors, almost all of whom were well-connected professional speculators, and the high cost of importing skilled European labor only added to the Society's start-up woes.

By 1794, the SUM nonetheless succeeded in setting up limited operations. The new construction manager Peter Colt, who replaced the ill-disciplined, free-spending L'Enfant, managed to complete a four-story, water-powered spinning mill, driving 768 spindles—then the largest such complex in America.[72] An initial scheme that relied on oxen to drive the spinning of cotton, at the so-called Bull Mill, gave way in the summer to the full use of water-power—a technological breakthrough marked by a grand parade and a renewed, if short-lived, rush of enthusiasm for the entire project. Some months earlier, a hotel and tavern had opened on the site, further sweetening the public mood.

An advertisement for goods for sale at the complex in December 1795 included such items as "Candlewick, both common and Superfine"; "All kinds of white or printed cotton goods"; and "All kinds of Stocking-Yarns, for needle or frame, either grey or bleached." According to one estimate, the new industrial town of Paterson featured around five hundred residents, of whom one quarter were directly affiliated with the Society.[73]

However, the whiff of financial scandal that surrounded the early years of the Society for Establishing Useful Manufactures clung to Hamilton, his associates at the treasury, and his private circle of financial and political backers. The treasury secretary himself had played an extraordinary, hands-on role in what was essentially a private business project, supervising the construction of machinery for the SUM, dictating its exact site, tussling with the board over every detail, and even issuing questionable guarantees for a last-minute bank loan needed to launch the venture and backing tariffs that would protect the Society's nascent cotton industry from foreign competition.[74]

The early difficulties faced by the scheme delighted Hamilton's domestic critics and seemed to justify widespread skepticism among British commentators and politicians toward the notion of a technologically advanced America. Many at home were alarmed from the outset at governmental support for industry, in particular the use of special legal powers and tax holidays and the granting of monopolies that threatened smaller, more traditional enterprises. Public anger also broke out over the use of state lotteries to help finance the SUM to the benefit of its shareholders, rather than the public at large.

Jefferson and his allies were outraged at this government-backed assault on their ideal of a yeoman republic, and the SUM came in for repeated political attack as a powerful symbol of the secretary's broader ambitions. "If it has been imputed to others as criminal to incorporate a company of merchants, engaged in a particular trade, or a company of manufacturers engaged in the fabrication of particular goods, or a company of gamblers to fleece the people by lotteries," asked "An Observer" in the *Philadelphia Advertiser* as early as January 1792, "what must we think of this institution who have united all these political crimes in one act?"[75] The financial panic only exacerbated the nation's anxieties over Hamilton's aggressive fiscal and banking policies, in particular the heavy reliance on debt.

After just two years, the persistent cost overruns and general mismanagement of the initial construction forced a radical change in the direction of the Society for Establishing Useful Manufactures. Plans spelled out for the production of hats; the spinning of flax, wool, and hemp; the making of shoes; and the cultivation of silkworms, all promised in the prospectus, had come to naught, while the Society's printing operations had essentially collapsed. A revamped board of directors quietly voted to cease direct manufacturing in 1796, and the SUM steadily transformed itself into an industrial developer, selling or leasing factory space and providing power to entrepreneurs, inventors, and engineers of various stripes.

Significantly, the SUM's many shortcomings did not stem from any failure of technical innovation, creative energies, or industrial vigor on the part of the Americans, and the complex steadily took on a life of its own, animated by the same impulses of "mechanism" that began to drive economic development and industrialization elsewhere in the country. With the basic infrastructure in place, Paterson emerged in the nineteenth century as a manufacturing power-house and became, for a time, one of the largest and fastest-growing cities in America.

Along the way, the SUM went through cycles of boom and bust in the face of rapid technological change. The working of cotton textiles gave way, first to small-scale manufacturing, then to the casting of iron and the fabrication of heavy machinery, and subsequently to the production of fine silk. Paterson's signature industry, representing more than 125 firms in 1891, earned it the nickname Silk City.[76] The advent of the airplane industry provided one final burst of activity. The Society itself held on, more or less intact, until 1945 when it was absorbed by the city it had created.

While volatile economic conditions played their part, each distinct phase in Paterson's industrial history was primarily driven by innovation, the transfer-ence of skills and ideas from old industries to new ones, and the subsequent development of novel techniques, applications, and systems. At the forefront stood some of America's leading inventors—mechanics, artisans, and other heirs to the traditions of useful knowledge and practical experimentation dating back to Franklin's original Leather Apron Club—rather than scientists or other academically trained experts.

These included textile worker Samuel Colt, who developed some of his first revolvers, the Colt Paterson, at the SUM, beginning in 1835; Thomas Rogers, a journeyman carpenter who directed his early experience with Paterson's cotton machines into a successful venture building steam locomotives; Thomas Edison, the telegraph-operator-turned-inventor who oversaw the replacement of the SUM's hundred-year-old system of waterpower with a hydroelectric plant in 1914; and the Wright brothers, former bicycle mechanics whose Wright Aeronautical Corporation took over a former SUM textile mill to build the engine that powered Charles Lindbergh's solo flight across the Atlantic in 1927 and later to outfit U.S. aircraft during World War II.

Had Hamilton not been killed in his infamous duel with Vice President Aaron Burr in the summer of 1804, the former treasury secretary might well have looked back at the Society for Establishing Useful Manufactures and reminded critics of his prediction at its birth: "The establishment of manufactures in the United States when maturely considered will be found to be of the highest importance to their prosperity. ... Communities which can most completely supply their own wants are in a stage of the highest political perfection."[77]

EPILOGUE: MANUFACTURING AMERICA

Say it! No ideas but in things—
nothing but the blank faces of the houses
and cylindrical trees
bent, forked by preconception and accident
split, furrowed, creased, mottled, stained
secret—into the body of the light—
These are the ideas, savage and tender
somewhat of the music, et cetera
of Paterson, that great philosopher—
              —William Carlos Williams,
                         Paterson (1927)

BENJAMIN FRANKLIN DIED quietly in his bed on April 17, 1790, at the age of eighty-four. His public funeral four days later was one of the most extraordinary processions of humanity in American history, with a crowd of mourners, marchers, and onlookers estimated at roughly twenty thousand—or two thirds of Philadelphia's total population. A phalanx of local printers, practitioners of Franklin's beloved craft, walked behind the coffin to the Christ Church cemetery, followed by members of the American Philosophical Society, physicians from the medical college, the clergy, and delegates from the various artisans' associations. The House of Representatives and its French counterpart, the National Assembly, each observed one month of official mourning.

Provost William Smith, Franklin's one-time nemesis in educational and political affairs, delivered a gracious eulogy before the American Philosophical Society and both houses of Congress. "His original and universal genius was capable of the *greatest* things, but disdained not the *smallest*, provided they were useful," intoned Smith, who then elevated Franklin above the world's great philosophers and lawgivers "by uniting the talents of both, in the Practical philosophy of doing good."[1] Franklin, it is fair to say, had fulfilled the supreme ambition he expressed to his mother, Abiah Folger, forty years earlier: "The last will come, when I would rather have it said, *He lived usefully*, than, *He died rich.*"[2]

Franklin bequeathed his personal telescope to Rittenhouse, the lone mechanic among his six pallbearers. In effect, he also handed over to Rittenhouse stewardship of the movement for useful knowledge and its flagship institution, the American Philosophical Society. With Rittenhouse installed as its leader, America's preeminent knowledge society retained its focus on the useful and the practical. The new president himself addressed large-scale engineering projects, chiefly the construction of roads, canals, and other improvements to river transportation, all designed to serve the commercial needs of a young and growing nation.

Among the many practical challenges facing the country were the creation of a trusted system of coinage and the establishment of reliable standards of weights and measures. As they had done with many of the most trying problems during the war, the leaders of the republic turned to the day's foremost scientific practitioners for help. Soon Rittenhouse found himself drafted to head up the new U.S. Mint, where his reputation for learning, experimental skills, and intellectual integrity would be a great help with the development, production, and safeguarding of a new American currency.

Rittenhouse, whose health was never very strong, at first begged off the assignment, but he was cajoled into accepting by his old friend Jefferson, who as secretary of state was responsible for the Mint, and by a direct appeal from President Washington. Despite his growing infirmity, such a project must have held considerable appeal for Rittenhouse, for it drew on his considerable practical skills—as a surveyor, an instrument maker, an engineer, and general problem solver. Among the challenges facing the new director were the refining of silver for the production of coins and the regulation of the exact amount of the precious metal that should go into each one.

"He directed the construction of the machinery; [and] made arrangements for providing the necessary apparatus," records his nephew Barton. "And, in daily visits to the Mint, whenever his health permitted, personally superintended, with the most sedulous fidelity, not only the general economy of the institution, but its operations in the various departments—duties, which his love of systems and order, his extensive knowledge, and his practical skill in mechanics, eminently qualified him to perform with peculiar correctness."[3]

Here, Rittenhouse was following in the footsteps of Isaac Newton, who was made warden of Britain's Royal Mint in 1696, in recognition of his own great scientific achievements. Yet, Rittenhouse never deviated from his true vocation, the practice of mechanics. Where Newton was ultimately a mathematician, Franklin, Rittenhouse, Jefferson, and the other American virtuosi were decidedly engineers, content to find workable solutions to specific problems and leave theoretical nicety, and even mathematical exactitude, to others.

Rittenhouse's published study of the workings of the pendulum, undertaken at Jefferson's request as part of an effort to create the world's first metric system, exhibits throughout the sensibilities of the mechanic, rather than those of the formally trained scientist or mathematician.* "His mathematical paper revealed the manner in which practical clock construction, physics, and mathematics were related in his life," writes his modern biographer, of the work on the pendulum. "He remained a mechanic to whom practice was the only consideration in certain projects."[4] Rittenhouse ended his tenure at the Mint on the grounds of poor health in June 1795 and died one year later.

Summing up his life before an audience that included President Washington, the Congress, state officials, foreign dignitaries, and the membership of the American Philosophical Society, Benjamin Rush publically enshrined Rittenhouse as a natural genius for the new American epoch: self-taught, yet able to rival the greatest mathematical minds of the Old World; heroic to the point of sacrificing his fragile health for his useful endeavors; republican from birth; and sensate to the "natural connection between a knowledge of the works of nature and just ideas of the divine perfections."[5]

Most important of all, Rush informed the assembled mourners packed into Philadelphia's sumptuous new First Presbyterian Church, Rittenhouse remained untainted by the institutional remnants of an educational system "adopted in Europe in the sixteenth century" that would only have quashed his spirit and extinguished his innately *American* talents. As a result, the self-taught Rittenhouse, who had once solved mathematical problems in his head while plowing the family fields, was free to pursue useful knowledge wherever it took him, to the true benefit of society.

---

* Jefferson's idea was to base the proposed new measure, the meter, on the length of a pendulum that would oscillate exactly one second in each direction, at a latitude of 45°. His Plan for Establishing Uniformity in the Coinage, Weights, and Measures of the United States was submitted to Congress July 13, 1790, but never implemented.

"I am disposed to believe that his extensive knowledge and splendid character are to be ascribed chiefly to his having escaped the pernicious influence of
monkish learning upon his mind in early life," said Rush, by now a well-established, if caustic, campaigner against classical instruction in the schools.
Otherwise, "Rittenhouse the philosopher, one of the luminaries of the eighteenth century, might have spent his hours of study in composing syllogism, or
in measuring the feet of Greek and Latin poetry."[6]

*   *   *

Traditional assessments tend to view America's technological triumphs as the
natural, logical outgrowth of the nation's political system and its dedication to
free enterprise. Popular icons invoked in support of this notion invariably
include the lone inventors, the industrial systematizers, and the ingenious
marketers whose technological prowess has been confirmed by great commercial success and accompanying celebrity—the Wrights, Edison, Frederick
Winslow Taylor, Henry Ford, Steve Jobs, among many others. This is, however,
to look at the problem backward, to write a history of the present.

In fact, the colonial movement for useful knowledge, dating back at least to
the Junto of the late 1720s, preceded and then made possible the Revolution
and the subsequent rise of America's characteristic political and economic
systems. This movement, which produced such figures as Ebenezer Kinnersley,
David Rittenhouse, Benjamin Rush, and of course Franklin, firmly embedded
the values of the mechanic, the artisan, the engineer, and the inventor in
American society. In their hands, earlier European notions of practical learning
and the idea of science took on a revolutionary cast, one that anticipated the
coming political resistance against the British.

Long before the Boston Tea Party or other overt acts of defiance to imperial
rule, the leather aprons and the institutions they introduced or adopted successfully challenged the social, political, and intellectual order of the day. The
accompanying knowledge revolution, epitomized by Franklin and his fellow
Philadelphia electricians in the 1740s and early 1750s, freed the colonists of
constraints imported and imposed from Europe and laid the necessary ground-
work for American independence.

In the ensuing decades, proponents of this movement, notably the mechanics and craftsmen in the colonial urban centers, steadily enhanced their political
influence and economic well-being through the creation of subscription libraries, lecture and study circles, voluntary fire brigades, cooperative insurance

schemes, and local militias. Improvements in printing technology and communications—Franklin was, after all, a successful publisher, an innovative postmaster, and a master intellectual networker—spread their ideas far and wide.

The close affinities between the leading lights of the colonial movement for
useful knowledge and the revolutionary generation of American political leaders ensured that the values and attitudes of the knowledge societies would be
institutionalized in the new republic. The two groups often overlapped directly,
sometimes at the very highest level: Franklin served for three years as
Pennsylvania's chief executive; Jefferson headed the American Philosophical
Society for eighteen years; and John Adams directed Boston's American
Academy of Arts and Sciences for more than two decades. Washington and
Hamilton stand out among the Philosophical Society's many politically promi-
nent members of the period.

These figures, their colleagues, and associates all placed a premium on the
utility of knowledge and tended to value the inventor, the experimenter, and
the mechanic over the theoretician, the metaphysician, or other learned authority. Once in power, they wasted little time enshrining this notion and rewarding
its practitioners under American law. Article One of the U.S. Constitution
explicitly calls on Congress "to promote the Progress of Science and useful
Arts." Among the earliest items to come before America's new legislative body
were the granting of patents and the issuing of copyrights, areas where the
influence of Tench Coxe's ideas was considerable.[7] Washington's so-called
Farewell Address, delivered in 1796, linked the diffusion of knowledge to the
long-term survival of American democracy.

In a sure sign of the intellectual and economic ferment at work, knowledge
associations, in emulation of the American Philosophical Society, proliferated
throughout the period, from New England south to New Orleans and west-
ward to Cincinnati, Nashville, and St. Louis. Each society was at the outset
local in nature, designed to allow for the personal exchange of ideas and shared
interests that still characterized the practice of Enlightenment science. In
general, they were open to different walks of life and less reliant than their
European counterparts on the social or economic elite. This ensured an
approach to knowledge that appealed equally to the farmer, the artisan, the
merchant, or the "curious" gentleman.[8]

Over time, a degree of specialization began to appear within the broader
movement for useful knowledge. At first, this mostly took the form of small,

localized professional associations, for example uniting physicians in Boston or Philadelphia. More significant was the branching out of the knowledge societies to address agricultural improvement, the development of manufactures, or other specific questions in applied science. They frequently offered prizes or cash premiums for solutions to problems in industry or farming, encouraged the exchange of information and ideas among members and with other, likeminded associations, and increasingly distributed public funds in support of these efforts.

Franklin's Society for Political Inquiries served as an effective incubator for both the industrial vision of Tench Coxe and the ideal of practical education championed by Benjamin Rush. There were even societies devoted to specific technological challenges. The Rumsean Society, created by Franklin in 1787, was formed to support the work of steamboat designer James Rumsey, who carried on a seemingly endless patent fight with rival inventor John Fitch that also drew in Jefferson, Rush, Washington, and other leading political and scientific figures. Other groups included the Society for the Improvement of Inland Navigation, in Philadelphia, and the Boston Mechanic Association, one of the first societies to address the interests of artisans and engineers alike.[9]

Among the most important were the manufacturing associations, which united the aspirations of the mechanics with broader notions of economic development, political independence, and patriotism. New organizations such as Philadelphia's Franklin Institute of the State of Pennsylvania for the Promotion of the Mechanic Arts and New York's Society for the Promotion of the Useful Arts drew on the older, general-knowledge societies for members. Like their predecessors, they attracted a diverse range of skills, occupations, and social groups: craftsmen, merchants and financiers, accountants, lawyers, instrument makers, and the slowly growing pool of academic scientists.[10]

So powerful was the promise of the movement for useful knowledge that there was little real chance of slowing or deflecting America's coming technological and industrial revolution, despite deep divisions among the Founding Fathers—and in society at large—over the future place of manufactures. Just as colonial notions of practical utility anticipated the final break with Great Britain, so, too, did these ideas operate largely outside the control of the postwar political factions.

Alexander Hamilton's blueprint for a manufacturing utopia collapsed under the weight of unsavory dealings, managerial malfeasance, and technical incompetence. Nonetheless, his Society for Establishing Useful Manufactures ultimately produced the industrial colossus that once was Paterson, New Jersey. Jefferson, meanwhile, found that imagining a republican idyll was one thing but realizing such a state in a world of international trade, diplomacy, and war was quite another. To protect itself, the young republic would have to turn away, at least in part, from its agricultural vocation. "Our enemy has indeed the consolation of Satan on removing our first parents from Paradise," Jefferson conceded to a friend during the War of 1812 against the British. "From a peaceable and agricultural nation, he makes us a military and manufacturing one."[11]

✳   ✳   ✳

Having escaped the dangerous terrain of his youthful "metaphysical Reasonings," Benjamin Franklin never looked back. His faith in the pursuit of useful knowledge—and in the social networks that made that pursuit possible—survived the setbacks, professional rivalries, and political upheavals that punctuated his long and eventful life. Not even rebellion against the British could shake the intellectual ties that Franklin had carefully cultivated ever since his early days in the coffeehouses, taverns, and salons of London.

With the end of the war, he sought where possible to resume his scientific correspondence with former friends and associates in the Royal Society. While he could not resist chiding the British for not "spending those Millions in doing Good which in the last War have been spent in doing Mischief," Franklin nonetheless struck clear notes of optimism and even wonder as he looked toward a world of scientific advances and technological change that he could never hope to see.

"The rapid Progress *true* Science now makes, occasions my Regretting sometimes that I was born so soon," wrote Franklin ten years before his death. "It is impossible to imagine the Height to which may be carried in a 1000 Years the Power of Man over Matter. We may perhaps learn to deprive large Masses of their Gravity & give them absolute Levity, for the sake of easy Transport. Agriculture may diminish its Labor & double its Produce."[12] Franklin was prescient in his predictions, if not in the timing. Had he somehow managed to live just another century, he would certainly have been among the early adopters of new technologies. One can readily imagine a joyful Franklin reveling in train travel, or behind the wheel of an early automobile.

Already, the lighter-than-air balloon, or aerostat, had become the latest vogue in France, and it fired Franklin's imagination to think of possible uses.

"This Experiment is by no means a trifling one," he reported to Joseph Banks, head of the Royal Society, whom he strongly encouraged to pursue similar experiments. "It may be attended with important Consequences that no one can foresee."[13] Yet, the overall direction of America's scientific and technological development would not have come as a surprise.

Nor would Franklin have been particularly distressed, as are some modern students of the period, by the general absence of significant theoretical breakthroughs on the part of Americans.[14] On the contrary, the great milestones of nineteenth-century America were overwhelmingly the products of fields that Franklin, Rush, Rittenhouse, Coxe, and their associates would have recognized and encouraged as natural outgrowths of the movement for useful knowledge—applied science, practical invention, mechanics, and engineering.

These included the steam locomotive, the typewriter, the sewing machine, the reaper, and the revolver, among other icons of America's accelerating industrialization. The Civil War, an incubator of terrible innovation, produced ironclad ships, more accurate naval artillery, mass production of uniforms and shoes, modern ammunition, and the machine gun.[15] And, just as Tench Coxe had predicted, all were products of the machine applied to the American landscape, with its rich natural resources and its enormous, sparsely populated expanses ripe for reinvention, reinterpretation, and redevelopment by the mechanic, the engineer, and the inventor. In the face of such rapid developments, the struggle between the Federalists and the Republicans over the place of industry in immediate postrevolutionary American life would soon seem little more than a quaint fairy tale from long ago.

Writing in the influential *North American Review* in 1831, Timothy Walker, a recent graduate of one of the country's leading universities, expressed the view of many among the new educated generation that American technology and industrialization had simply realized the latent promise of the movement for useful knowledge, present at least since the 1720s and Franklin's Leather Apron Club: "Where she [nature] denied us rivers, Mechanism has supplied them. Where she left our planet uncomfortably rough, Mechanism has applied the roller. Where her mountains have been found in the way, Mechanism has boldly leveled or cut through them."[16]

ACKNOWLEDGMENTS

Benjamin Franklin placed the social element at the very center of his conception of useful knowledge, so I am particularly delighted to note that the knowledge production on these pages represents something of a cooperative effort. Like Franklin, I, too, benefited from the opportunity to try out my ideas on a diverse group of talented friends, associates, and colleagues.

Foremost, I want to thank Michelle Johnson for her steady hand as reader, adviser, and companion throughout this journey. Cecile Baril, Evelyn Lyons, and Bryce Johnson read early iterations of the manuscript and provided helpful comments along the way. Kevin Cross shared many pleasant hours over mussels and beer discussing theoretical and practical aspects of useful knowledge. Lewis Lapham contributed helpful leads and provided welcome enthusiasm for the project from the outset.

Also, I want to thank my longtime agent, Will Lippincott, for once again helping me realize the promise hidden in the original conception, as well as my editors at Bloomsbury Press, Peter Ginna and Pete Beatty, for the support, advice, and close reading of the manuscript needed to see this project through to fruition. Needless to say, the final results and any errors of omission or commission remain firmly my own doing.

NOTES

A Note on Sources:
Where possible I have relied on original sources in order to allow the leading figures in America's early movement for useful knowledge to tell their story, in their words.

Of invaluable help to this project has been the work of scholars at Yale University to collect and edit the papers of Benjamin Franklin. To date, forty volumes have been published, with more in progress. Franklin's correspondence, unless otherwise noted, is drawn from these volumes and indicated by date and recipient.

Below is a list of abbreviations, used in the notes that follow, from the most commonly cited works:

ABF   Benjamin Franklin, *The Autobiography of Benjamin Franklin*, 2nd edition, ed. Leonard W. Labaree and others (New Haven: Yale University Press, 2003).

CLON   *Selection of the Correspondence of Linnaeus, and Other Naturalists*, ed. James Edward Smith (London: Longman, 1821).

LPCC   Cadwallader Colden, *The Letters and Papers of Cadwallader Colden* (New York: New York Historical Society, 1918–37).

MDR   William Barton, *Memoirs of the Life of David Rittenhouse* (Philadelphia: Edward Parker, 1813).

MJB   John Bartram, *Memorials of John Bartram and Humphrey Marshall* [1849], ed. William Darlington (New York: Hafner, 1967).

PAH   Alexander Hamilton, *The Papers of Alexander Hamilton*, ed. Harold C. Syrett and others (New York: Columbia University Press, 1961–1987).

PBF   Benjamin Franklin, *The Papers of Benjamin Franklin*, ed. Leonard W. Labaree and others (New Haven: Yale University Press, 1959–).

PTJ   Thomas Jefferson, *The Papers of Thomas Jefferson*, ed. Julian P. Boyd and others (Princeton: Princeton University Press, 1950–).

PG   *Pennsylvania Gazette*

PGW   George Washington, *The Papers of George Washington*, Colonial Series, ed. W. W. Abbot, Dorothy Twohig, and others (Charlottesville, VA: University Press of Virginia, 1983–1995).

PMHB   *Pennsylvania Magazine of History and Biography*
VG   *Virginia Gazette*
WBF   Benjamin Franklin, *The Works of Benjamin Franklin*, ed. John Bigelow (New York: G. P. Putnam's, 1904).

Notes to Chapter One: The Age of Franklin

1 BF, "Information To Those Who Would Remove to America," *WBF*, 9: 435–436.

2 BF to Mary Stevenson, November 1760.

3 BF to unknown recipient, June 14, 1883, *WBF*, 10: 126.

4 BF to John Lining, March 18, 1755.

5 George Washington, Farewell Address, September 19, 1796, available at http://gwpapers. virginia.edu/documents/farewell/transcript.html#p14. Last accessed November 29, 2012.

6 BF, "Proposal for Promoting Useful Knowledge among the British Plantations in America," *PBF*, 2: 380–81.

7 Ibid., 2: 383.

8 James D. Watkinson, "Useful Knowledge? Concepts, Values, and Access in American Education, 1776–1840," *History of Education Quarterly* 30 (3): 351.

9 John Adams to Abigail Adams, August 4, 1776, in *The Book of Abigail and John: Selected Letters of the Adams Family, 1762–1784*, ed. Lyman H. Butterfield and others (Boston: Northeastern University, 2002), 149.

10 Charter of Incorporation, *American Academy of Arts and Sciences*, available at http://www. amacad.org/about/charter.aspx. Last accessed March 27, 2012.

11 A. Hunter Dupree, "The National Pattern of American Learned Societies, 1769–1863," in *The Pursuit of Knowledge in the Early American Republic*, ed. Alexandra Oleson and Sanborn C. Brown (Baltimore: Johns Hopkins University Press, 1976), 22–23.

12 Meyer Reinhold, "The Quest for 'Useful Knowledge' in Eighteenth-Century America," *Proceedings of the American Philosophical Society* 119 (2): 121.

13 Whitfield J. Bell, Jr., "As Others Saw Us: Notes on the Reputation of the American Philosophical Society," *Proceedings of the American Philosophical Society* 116 (3): 271. Sydney Forman, "The United States Military Philosophical Society, 1802–1813: *Scientia in Bello Pax*," *William and Mary Quarterly*, Third Series 2 (3): 273–74.

14 Quoted in Reinhold, 119.

15 Roland Van Zandt, *The Metaphysical Foundations of American History* (The Hague: Mouton, 1959), 43–50.

16 Thomas Jefferson to Angelica Church, February 17, 1788, *PTJ*, 12: 601.

17 Van Zandt, 44.

18 Alexander Garden to John Ellis, November 19, 1764, quoted in Lee Alan Dugatkin, *Mr. Jefferson and the Giant Moose: Natural History in Early America* (Chicago: University of Chicago Press, 2009), 3.

19 William Darlington, "Progress of Botany in North America," *MJB*, 17–18.

20 Jefferson fashioned the original in 1781 as written responses to questions about America submitted by a French diplomat. An expanded text was first published in Paris in 1785, and later in America.

21 Thomas Jefferson, *Notes on the State of Virginia* [1787] (Boston: Lilly and Wait, 1832), 68–69.

22 William Bradford, *Of Plymouth Plantation, 1620–1647*, ed. Samuel Eliot Morison. (New York: Random House), 1952, 62, cited in Leo Marx, *The Machine in the Garden: Technology and the Pastoral Ideal in America* (New York: Oxford University Press, 2000), 41.

23 Alan Heimart, "Puritanism, the Wilderness, and the Frontier," *New England Quarterly* 26 (3): 361–62.

24 John Winthrop, *Life and Letters of John Winthrop*, ed. Robert C. Winthrop (Boston: Ticknor and Fields, 1867), 43, quoted in Heimart, 362.

25 L. Marx, 43–44. See also Perry Miller, *The New England Mind: The Seventeenth Century* (Cambridge, MA: Harvard University Press, 1954), 393–96.

26 Richard Foster Jones, *Ancients and Moderns: A Study in the Rise of the Scientific Movement in Seventeenth-Century England* (St. Louis: Washington University Press, 1961), 272.

27 Quoted in Reinhold, 110.

28 William Penn, *Passages from the Life and Writings of William Penn*, ed. Thomas Pym Cope (Philadelphia: Friends' Bookstore, 1882), 259.

29 Hugh Jones, *The Present State of Virginia* [1724], ed. Richard L. Morton (Chapel Hill: University of North Carolina Press, 1956), 44.

30 *Pennsylvania Gazette*, December 24, 1728. Cited in C. Lennart Carlson, "Samuel Keimer: A Study in the Transit of English Culture to Colonial Pennsylvania," *PMHB* 61 (4): 357–86.

31 William Penn, *Fruits of Solitude* [1695] (Philadelphia: Longstreth, 1877), 7.

32 BF to John Bartram, July 9, 1769.

33 Carl Bridenbaugh, *The Colonial Craftsman* (New York: Dover, 1990), 155.

34 BF, "To Those Who Would Remove to America," *WBF*, 9: 442.

35 Ibid.

36 Leonard W. Labaree and others, "Introduction," *ABF*, 22–24.

37 Ibid., 18.

38 Carla Mulford, "Figuring Benjamin Franklin in American Cultural Memory," *New England Quarterly* 72 (3): 420.

39 Max Weber, *The Protestant Ethic and the "Spirit" of Capitalism*, ed. and trans. Peter Baehr and Gordon C. Wells (New York: Penguin, 2002), 9–26.

40 Carl Van Doren, *Benjamin Franklin* (New York: Viking Press, 1938), v.

41 Ibid., 782.

42 Herman Melville, *Israel Potter: His Fifty Years of Exile* (New York: G. P. Putnam, 1844), 81. A useful study of the Franklin image in American letters through the 1890s can be found in Mulford, 415–43. For more recent examples, see Peter Bastian, "'Let's Do Lunch': Benjamin Franklin and the American Character," *Australasian Journal of American Studies* 24 (1): 82–88.

43 Mark Twain, "The Late Benjamin Franklin," in *Sketches New and Old* (Hartford, CT: American Publishing, 1901), 211–15.

44 D. H. Lawrence, *Studies in Classic American Literature* [1924] (London: Penguin, 1971), 19, 16–17.

45 Carl Becker, "Benjamin Franklin," *Dictionary of American Biography* (New York: Scribner's, 1931).

46 Thomas Jefferson to David Rittenhouse, July 19, 1778, *PTJ*, 2: 203.

47 Thomas Jefferson to John Adams, August 1, 1816, *The Works of John Adams*, ed. Charles F. Adams (Boston: Little Brown, 1856), 10: 223.

Notes to Chapter Two: Breaking the Chain

1 BF, "Journal of Occurrences in My Voyage to Philadelphia on Board the Berkshire," *PBF*, 1: 73.

2 Ibid., 1: 72.

3 Ibid., 1: 79.

4 Alfred Owen Aldridge, *Benjamin Franklin: Philosopher & Man* (Philadelphia: Lippincott, 1965), 376.

5 BF, "Journal of Occurrences," *PBF*, 1: 86–87.

6 Ibid., 1: 94.

7 Ibid., 1: 94.

8 *ABF*, 54–55.

9 Ibid.

10 Esmond Wright, *Franklin of Philadelphia* (Cambridge, MA: Belknap Press, 1986), 14.

11 *ABF*, 52–53.

12 Ezra Stiles, *The Literary Diary of Ezra Stiles* (New York: Scribner's, 1901), 2: 376.

13 *ABF*, 53.

14 *PBF*, 8: 454.

15 *ABF*, 57.

16 Bernard Faÿ, *Franklin, The Apostle of Modern Times* (Boston: Little, Brown, 1929), 29.

17 BF, *To Those Who Would Remove to America*, *WBF*, 9: 443.

18 BF, "Epitaph Written in 1728," *PBF*, 1: 111. Slight variants exist in a number of extant texts, including some in Franklin's own hand.

19 *ABF*, 99–100.

20 *ABF*, 96.

21 John Houghton, "A Discourse of Coffee," *Philosophical Transactions* 21: 311–17.

22 Mr. Town [Pseudonym], *Connoisseur* 1 (London: Baldwin, 1754), 2.

23 Wright, 114–15.

24 *ABF*, 113–14.

25 David Hume to BF, May 10, 1762, *The Letters of David Hume*, ed. J. Y. T. Greig (Oxford: Oxford University Press, 1932), 1: 192.

26 Edwin Wolf and Kevin J. Hayes, *The Library of Benjamin Franklin* (Philadelphia: American Philosophical Society, 2006), 7.

27 *ABF*, 85.

28 BF, *A Dissertation on Liberty and Necessity, PBF*, I: 58.

29 *ABF*, 96.

30 BF, *A Dissertation, PBF*, I: 71.

31 *ABF*, 97.

32 Bernard Mandeville, *The Fable of the Bees: Or, Private Vices, Publick Benefits*, 3rd edition (London: J. Tonson, 1724), 476.

33 Harold J. Cook, "Bernard Mandeville," in *A Companion to Early Modern Philosophy*, ed. Steven Nadler (Oxford: Blackwell, 2002), 460–70.

34 *ABF*, 97.

35 *ABF*, 98.

36 BF to Hans Sloane, June 2, 1725.

37 Quoted in Charles Richard Weld, *A History of the Royal Society* [1848] (New York: Arno Press, 1975), I: 146.

38 Martha Ornstein, *The Role of Scientific Societies in the Seventeenth Century*, 3rd edition (New York: Arno Press, 1975), 91–92.

39 Thomas Sprat, *History of the Royal Society* [1667], ed. Jackson I. Cope and Harold Whitmore Jones (St. Louis: Washington University, 1958), 71–72.

40 Royal Society of London, *Philosophical Transactions* 2: 402–06.

41 Sprat, 72–73.

42 *ABF*, 268.

43 BF to Vaughan, November 9, 1779.

44 *ABF*, 70–129.

45 BF to [Thomas Hopkinson?], October 16, 1746.

46 James Campbell, "The Pragmatist in Franklin," in *The Cambridge Companion to Benjamin Franklin*, ed. Carla Mulford (New York: Cambridge University Press, 2008), 107; Joyce E. Chaplin, *The First Scientific American: Benjamin Franklin and the Pursuit of Genius* (New York: Basic Books, 2006), 3.

47 Chaplin, "Benjamin Franklin's Natural Philosophy," in *The Cambridge Companion to Benjamin Franklin*, ed. Carla Mulford (New York: Cambridge University Press, 2008), 69.

48 Douglas Anderson, *The Radical Enlightenments of Benjamin Franklin* (Baltimore: Johns Hopkins University Press, 1997), 33.

49 *ABF*, 104.

50 *ABF*, 104.

51 *ABF*, 105.

52 *ABF*, 114.

53 H. B. Van Wesep, *Seven Sages: The Story of American Philosophy* (New York: Longmans, Green, 1960), 53.

54 *ABF*, 106.

Notes to Chapter Three: The Leather Apron Men

1 William Penn, "Instructions to the Commissioners," September 30, 1681, *The Papers of William Penn*, ed. Richard S. Dunn and Mary Maples Dunn (Philadelphia: University of Pennsylvania Press, 1987), 2: 121.

2 Richard Hofstadter, *America at 1750: A Social Portrait* (New York: Knopf, 1971), 5.

3 J. Hector St. John de Crèvecoeur, *Letters from an American Farmer* [1782] (New York: Fox Duffield, 1904), 75–76.

4 Alexander Hamilton, *Gentleman's Progress: The Itinerarium of Dr. Alexander Hamilton, 1744*, ed. Carl Bridenbaugh (Pittsburgh: University of Pittsburgh Press, 1992), 18.

5 Ibid., 21.

6 Gottlieb Mittelberger, *Journey to Pennsylvania* [1754], trans. and ed. Oscar Handlin and John Clive (Cambridge, MA: Belknap Press, 1960), 36.

7 Carl Bridenbaugh, *Cities in Revolt: Urban Life in America, 1743–1776* (New York: Knopf, 1955), 39.

8 William Black and R. Alonzo Brock, "Journal of William Black," *PMHB* I (4) (Philadelphia: Historical Society of Pennsylvania), 405.

9 Quoted in Wright, *Franklin of Philadelphia*, 32.

10 Hamilton, *Itinerarium*, 22–23.

11 Ibid., 23.

12 Ibid., 191.

13 Francis Daniel Pastorius, *The Bee Hive*, Mss. Am. I, Special Collections, I Van Pelt Library, University of Pennsylvania, quoted in Hofstadter, 19.

14 Hofstadter, 19; Carl Bridenbaugh and Jessica Bridenbaugh, *Rebels and Gentlemen: Philadelphia in the Age of Franklin* (New York: Oxford University Press, 1962), 4.

15 Merle Curti, *The Growth of American Thought*, 3rd edition (New Brunswick, NJ: Transaction Books, 1982), 35.

16 Wright, 32.

17 Bridenbaugh, *Cites in Revolt*, 43–44.

18 Gordon S. Wood, *The Americanization of Benjamin Franklin* (New York: Penguin Press, 2004), 41.

19 William Penn, *No Cross No Crown: A Discourse Shewing the Nature and Discipline of the Holy Cross of Christ* (London: Mary Hinde, 1771), 65.

20 Curti, 16.

21 Hamilton, *Itinerarium*, 22.

22 John Ray, *The Wisdom of God Manifested in the Works of the Creation* [1691] (London: William & John Innys, 1722), 164.

23 Anderson, *Radical Enlightenments*, 129.

24 BF, "Opinions and Conjectures," *PBF*, 4: 17.

25 Isaac Norris to unknown correspondent, April 30, 1725, quoted in Thomas Wendel, "The Keith-Lloyd Alliance: Factional and Coalition Politics in Colonial Pennsylvania," *PMHB* 92 (3): 299.

26 *ABF*, 117.

27 *ABF*, 116–17.

28 BF, "Proposals and Queries to Be Asked the Junto," *PBF*, I: 259.

29 BF, "Rules for a Club, Formerly Established in Philadelphia," in *Political, Miscellaneous, and Philosophical Pieces*, ed. Benjamin Vaughan (London: J. Johnson, 1779), 533–36.

30 Benjamin Rush, *A Memorial Containing Travels Through Life or Sundry Incidents in the Life of Dr. Benjamin Rush, Written by Himself* (Lanoraie, PA: Louis Alexander Biddle, 1905), 141.

31 Wendel, 296–97.

32 BF, *A Modest Enquiry into the Nature and Necessity of a Paper-Currency*, *PBF*, I: 144.

33 Ibid., I: 157.

34 *ABF*, 124.

35 Junto Minute Book, January 18, 1760, quoted in James Delbourgo, *A Most Amazing Scene of Wonders: Electricity and Enlightenment in Early America* (Cambridge, MA: Harvard University Press, 2006), 68–69.

36 *Poor Richard Improved: Being an Almanack and Ephemeris . . . for the Year of our Lord 1753*, *PBF*, 4: 408.

37 *ABF*, 163–64.

38 *ABF*, 165.

39 Curti, 69.

40 BF to Peter Collinson, May 21, 1751.

41 Ibid.

42 Edwin Wolf, "Franklin and His Friends Choose Their Books," *PMHB* 80 (1): 15–20.

43 Leman Thomas Rede, *Biblotheca Americana* (London: J. Debbett, 1789), 9, 18.

44 Carl Bridenbaugh and Jessica Bridenbaugh, *Rebels and Gentlemen: Philadelphia in the Age of Franklin* (New York: Oxford University Press, 1962), 87–88.

45 Ibid.

46 Raymond Phineas Stearns, *Science in the British Colonies of America* (Chicago: University of Illinois Press, 1970), 503–4.

47 George Champlin Mason, *Annals of the Redwood Library and Athenaeum* (Newport, RI: Redwood Library, 1891), 31.

48 Wolf, 15, 24–30.

49 Thomas Penn to Library Co., May 16 [?], 1733.

50 BF to Peter Collinson, March 28, 1747.

51 BF to Peter Collinson, May 25, 1747.

52 BF to Cadwallader Colden, September 29, 1748.

53 BF, "Promoting Useful Knowledge," *PBF*, 2: 381–82.

54 Ibid., 380.

Notes to Chapter Four: Useful Knowledge

1 Quoted in Weld, *History*, 2: 30.

2 Francis Bacon, *The Philosophical Works of Francis Bacon*, ed. John M. Robertson (London: Routledge, 1905), 262.

3 Ibid., 262, 250.

4 Jones, *Ancients and Moderns*, 30–40.

5 Bacon, *Philosophical Works*, 76.

6 Francis Bacon, *Novum Organum*, quoted in Margery Purver, *The Royal Society: Concept and Creation* (Cambridge, MA: MIT Press, 1967), 35.

7 Bacon, *Philosophical Works*, 79.

8 Sprat, *Royal Society*, 35–36.

9 Ibid., 62.

10 Ralph S. Bates, *Scientific Societies in the United States*, 3rd edition (Cambridge, MA: MIT Press, 1965), 1–2.

11 Ornstein, *Scientific Societies*, 4, 12.

12 A full text of the first charter is available at http://royalsociety.org/uploadedFiles/Royal_Society_Content/about-us/history/Charter 1_English.pdf. Last accessed November 29, 2012.

13 Quoted in Weld, 1: 137, 146. For a discussion of the Royal Society's early utilitarian leanings, see Stearns, *Science in the British Colonies*, 90–93.

14 George Fox, *The Journal of George Fox*, 7th edition (London: W. and F. G. Cash, 1852), 1: 53.

15 William Penn, *The Witness of William Penn*, ed. Frederick B. Tolles and E. Gordon Alderfer (New York: Macmillan, 1957), 42–43, quoted in Greaves, 43.

16 Penn, *Passages*, 259.

17 Purver, *Royal Society*, 63.

18 Joseph Glanvill, *Plus Ultra, or the Progress and Advancement of Knowledge Since the Days of Aristotle* (London: James Collins, 1668), 65.

19 Robert Hooke, *Micrographia, or, Some Physiological Descriptions of Minute Bodies Made by Magnifying Glasses* [1665] (Mineola, NY: Dover, 2003), xlii, cited in Ornstein, 117, n75.

20 John Locke, *An Essay Concerning Humane Understanding* [1690] (London: T. Tegg, 1836), ix.

21 William Petty, "The Advice of W. P. to Mr. Samuel Hartlib, for the Advancement of Some Particular Parts of Learning" [1648], in *Harleian Miscellany* (London: Robert Dutton, 1810), 6: 156.

22 William Walwyn, *The Compassionate Samaritane* (London: NP, 1644), 36–37, quoted in Greaves, 42.

23 Henry Oldenburg to John Winthrop the Younger, quoted in Stearns, 150, n66.

24 Stearns, 120–25.

25 John Winthrop the Younger to Henry Oldenburg, November 12, 1668, in *Correspondence of Hartlib, Haak, Oldenburg and Others of the Royal Society with Governor Winthrop of Connecticut, 1661–1672*, ed. Robert C. Winthrop (Boston: John Wilson, 1878), 34–35.

26 de Crèvecoeur, *Letters*, 265.

27 William Bartram, *Travels, and Other Writings* [1773–1777] (New York: Library of America, 1996), 577.

28 Ernest Earnest, *John and William Bartram: Botanists and Explorers* (Philadelphia: University of Pennsylvania, 1940), 22–23.

29 Ibid., 24.

30 *PG*, March 17, 1742.

31 Silvio A. Bedini, *At the Sign of the Compass and Quadrant: The Life and Times of Anthony Lamb* (Philadelphia: American Philosophical Society, 1984), 41–42. Godfrey later received the credit that was due him.

32 John Bartram to Peter Collinson, November 3, 1754, *MJB*, 196.

33 John Fothergill, "Memoirs of Peter Collinson," *London* 45: 5.

34 Peter Collinson to John Bartram, January 20, 1734, *MJB*, 62.

35 Peter Collinson to John Bartram, January 24, 1735, *MJB*, 63.

36 Nancy E. Hoffman and John C. Van Horne, eds., *America's Curious Botanist: A Tercentennial Reappraisal of John Bartram, 1699–1777* (Philadelphia: American Philosophical Society, 2004), xii, n1.

37 Peter Collinson to William Bartram, February 16, 1768, *MJB*, 296.

38 Alexander Garden to John Ellis, July 15, 1765, *CLON*, I: 538.

39 Peter Collinson to John Bartram, February 17, 1737, *MJB*, 89.

40 Peter Collinson to John Bartram, September 20, 1736, *MJB*, 81–82.

41 John Bartram to Peter Collinson, December 18, 1742, *MJB*, 161.

42 John Bartram to Peter Collinson, May (?) 1738, *MJB*, 119.

43 Earnest, 75–77.

44 Peter Collinson to Cadwallader Colden, March 7, 1741, *Selections from the Scientific Correspondence of Cadwallader Colden*, ed. Asa Gray (New Haven: Hamlen, 1843), 31–32.

45 Peter Collinson to John Bartram, January 24, 1735, *MJB*, 65.

46 Quoted in Lawrence Hetrick, "The Origins, Goals, and Outcomes of John Bartram's Journey on the St. John's River, 1765–1766," in Hoffman and Van Horne, eds., 131.

47 Peter Collinson to John Bartram, April 21, 1736, *MJB*, 75. Emphasis added.

48 Peter Collinson to John Bartram, March 14, 1736, *MJB*, 94.

49 Peter Collinson to John Bartram, July 10, 1739, *MJB*, 132.

50 Brooke Hindle, *The Pursuit of Science in Revolutionary America, 1735–1789* (New York: W. W. Norton & Co, 1974), 67.

51 BF to Cadwallader Colden, April 5, 1744.

52 Hindle, *Pursuit of Science*, 72–73.

53 BF to Cadwallader Colden, August 15, 1745.

54 John Bartram to Cadwallader Colden, October 4, 1745, *LPCC*, 3: 160.

55 Dupree, *National Pattern*, 21–24.

Notes to Chapter Five: Sense and Sensibility

1 Peter Collinson to Cadwallader Colden, August 23, 1744, *LPCC*, 3: 69.

2 Peter Collinson to Cadwallader Colden, March 30, 1745, *LPCC*, 3: 109–10.

3 BF to Peter Collinson, March 28, 1747.

4 BF, "Opinions and Conjectures," *PBF*, 4: 17.

5 Lorraine Daston and Katherine Park, *Wonders and the Order of Nature, 1150–1750* (New York: Zone Books, 1998), 336.

6 Quoted in ibid., 342.

7 John Neale, *Directions for Gentlemen Who Have Electrical Machines, How to Proceed in Making Their Experiments* (London: NP, 1747), 3, 26.

8 Ibid., 28.

9 BF to Peter Collinson, February 4, 1750.

10 Delbourgo, *Amazing Scene*, 56.

11 *ABF*, 241.

12 Quoted in J. A. Leo Lemay, *Ebenezer Kinnersley: Franklin's Friend* (Philadelphia: University of Pennsylvania Press, 1964), 20.

13 *PG*, April 11, 1751.

14 Lemay, *Kinnersley*, 65.

15 BF to Peter Collinson, May 25, 1747.

16 BF to Peter Collinson, August 14, 1747.

17 BF to Peter Collinson, April 29, 1749.

18 *PG*, June 21, 1753.

19 BF to John Lining, March 18, 1755. This letter includes excerpts from Franklin's original research notes, dated November 7, 1749.

20 Ibid.

21 BF, "Opinions and Conjectures," *PBF*, 4: 17.

22 *PG*, April 11, 1751.

23 BF to Deborah Franklin, June 10, 1758.

24 Delbourgo, 72.

25 Wright, *Franklin of Philadelphia*, 97.

26 Weld, *History*, 2: 101.

27 Earl of Macclesfield, "Speech Awarding the Copley Medal," *PBF*, 5: 130.

28 *AFB*, 242.

29 I. Bernard Cohen, *Franklin and Newton: An Inquiry into Speculative Newtonian Experimental Science and Franklin's Work in Electricity as an Example Thereof* (Philadelphia: American Philosophical Society, 1956), 75–77.

30 Hindle, *Pursuit of Science*, 77.

31 J. L. Heilbron, *Electricity in the 17th and 18th Centuries: A Study of Early Modern Physics* (Berkeley: University of California, 1979), 330–33.

32 Ibid., 317–18.

33 Delbourgo, 279–83.

34 Ibid., 281.

35 Ibid., 38–39.

36 I. Bernard Cohen, *Science and the Founding Fathers* (New York: W. W. Norton, 1995), 139–40.

37 Ebenezer Kinnersley to BF, March 12, 1761.

38 Cohen, *Science and the Founding Fathers*, 186.

39 Hindle, *Pursuit of Science*, 78–79; I. Bernard Cohen, *Benjamin Franklin's Science* (Cambridge, MA: Harvard University Press, 1990), 6.

40 Miller, *New England Mind*, 67, 90.

41 John Norton, *The Orthodox Evangelist* [1654] (New York: AMS Press, 1983), "Epistle Dedicatory," np, quoted in Miller, 67.

42 John Cotton, *Christ, The Fountain of Life* [1651] (New York: Arno Press, 1972), 145.

43 Curti, *American Thought*, 5.

44 Cadwallader Colden to Peter Collinson, May 1742, Colden, *Selections from the Scientific Correspondence of Cadwallader Colden*, ed. Asa Gray (New Haven: Hamlen, 1843), 36.

45 Johann David Schoepf, *Travels in the Confederation, 1783–1784*, trans. and ed. Alfred J. Morrison (Philadelphia: William J. Campbell, 1911), 2: 172.

46 Joseph I. Waring, *A History of Medicine in South Carolina, 1670–1825* (Charleston [?]: South Carolina Medical Association, 1964), 65–67.

47 Alexander Garden to John Ellis, November 19, 1764, *CLON*, 519.

48 Alexander Garden to John Ellis, January 1761, *CLON*, 502.

49 Alexander Garden to Linnaeus, April 12, 1761, *CLON*, 304.

50 Konstantin Dierks, "Letter Writing, Masculinity, and American Men of Science, 1750–1800," *Pennsylvania History* 65 167–68.

51 Alexander Garden to John Ellis, March 25, 1755, *CLON*, 343.

52 Alexander Garden to John Ellis, March 25, 1755, *CLON*, 343, 345, quoted in Dierks, 170.

53 *ABF*, 210.

54 BF, "The Albany Plan of Union," *PBF*, 5: 387–92.

55 Ibid.

Notes to Chapter Six: Dead and Useless Languages

1 *ABF*, 181.

2 Wright, *Franklin of Philadelphia*, 77–79.

3 Thomas Penn to Richard Peters, June 4, 1748, quoted in J. A. Leo Lemay, *The Life of Benjamin Franklin, Volume 3: Soldier, Scientist, and Politician, 1748–1757* (Philadelphia: University of Pennsylvania Press, 2009), 49.

4 Ronald Schultz, *The Republic of Labor: Philadelphia Artisans and the Politics of Class, 1720–1830* (New York: Oxford University Press, 1993), 28; Bridenbaugh, *Colonial Craftsman*, 174.

5 *ABF*, 269.

6 BF, Silence Dogood, No. 4, *New England Courant*, May 14, 1722.

7 BF, *Proposals Relating to the Education of Youth in Pennsylvania*, *PBF*, 3: 397–98.

8 BF, *Education of Youth in Pennsylvania*, *PBF*, 3: 418–19.

9 Ibid.

10 Ibid.

11 BF, *Idea of the English School*, *PBF*, 4: 107.

12 Quoted in James Pyle Wickersham, *A History of Education in Pennsylvania* (Lancaster, PA: Inquirer Publishing, 1866), 39.

13 BF, *Idea of the English School*, *PBF*, 4: 108.

14 Edward Potts Cheyney, *History of the University of Pennsylvania, 1740–1940* (Philadelphia: University of Pennsylvania Press, 1940), 32–33.

15 Hofstadter, *America at 1750*, 217, 265; Thomas Harrison Montgomery, *A History of the University of Pennsylvania: From Its Foundation to A.D. 1770* (Philadelphia: George W. Jacobs, 1900), 110.

16 *ABF*, 145–46.

17 BF to Josiah and Abiah Franklin, April 13, 1738.

18 *ABF*, 146.

19 *ABF*, 147.

20 BF to unnamed recipient, December 13, 1757.

21 BF, *Poor Richard Improved*, 1751, *PBF*, 4: 96.

22 J. A. Leo Lemay, *The Life of Benjamin Franklin, Volume 2: Printer and Publisher, 1730–1747* (Philadelphia: University of Pennsylvania Press, 2006), 420.

23 *ABF*, 175, 180.

24 *ABF*, 177.

25 Hofstadter, 271–72.

26 Jonathan Edwards, "Thoughts on the Revival," in *The Works of Jonathan Edwards* (London: William Ball, 1839), I: 391.

27 BF, "Paper on the Academy," July 31, 1750, available at http://www.archives.upenn.edu/histy/features/1700s/bfacadpaper1750.html. Last accessed November 29, 2012.

28 *ABF*, 176.

29 Cheyney, 22–24.

30 *ABF*, 195.

31 BF, *Observations Relative to the Intentions of the Original Founders of the Academy in Philadelphia*, *WBF*, 12: 85.

32 Extensive biographies of the founding trustees can be found in Montgomery, 53–108.

33 Samuel Johnson to BF, November 1750.

34 Quoted in Montgomery, 134–35.

35 Cheyney, 30; Montgomery, 138.

36 Edward M. Griffin, "Introduction," in William Smith, *A General Idea of the College of Mirania* [1753] (New York: Johnson Reprint, 1969), vi–vii.

37 Smith, 11, 10.

38 Ibid., 14–15.

39 Ibid., 15–16.

40 Montgomery, 234–35.

41 Cheyney, 83.

42 William Smith, "Account of the College, Academy and Charitable School of Philadelphia, in Pennsylvania," in *The Works of William Smith* (Philadelphia: Maxwell & Fry, 1803), I: 242.

43 Smith, "Sermon XVII," in *Works*, 2: 343.

44 Quoted in Montgomery, 288.

45 Cheyney, 82.

46 BF to Ebenezer Kinnersley, July 28, 1759.

47 BF, *Observations Relative to the Intentions, WBF*, 12: 75.

48 Ibid., 101.

49 Cheyney, 173–75; Montgomery, 255–58.

50 7 U.S.C. § 304, available at http://www.law.cornell.edu/uscode/text/7/304. Last accessed November 27, 2012.

51 Rush, *A Memorial*, 14.

52 Alyn Brodsky, *Benjamin Rush: Patriot and Physician* (New York: St. Martin's Press, 2004), 19–20.

53 Benjamin Rush, *The Autobiography of Benjamin Rush* (Princeton, NJ: Princeton University Press, 1948), 36.

54 Rush, *A Memorial*, 24.

55 Ibid., 36, 39–41.

56 Ibid., 26.

57 Lyman H. Butterfield, "Benjamin Rush as a Promoter of Useful Knowledge," *Proceedings of the American Philosophical Society* 92 (1): 33.

58 David Ramsay, *The History of the American Revolution* (Philadelphia: R. Aitken, 1789), 2: 316.

59 Harvey J. Kaye, *Thomas Paine and the Promise of America* (New York: Hill and Wang, 2005), 43; Howard Zinn, *A People's History of the United States* (New York: HarperCollins, 1980), 69.

60 Anthony J. Di Lorenzo, "Dissenting Protestantism as a Language of Revolution in Thomas Paine's *Common Sense*," *Eighteenth-Century Thought* 4 (4): 236, 250–79.

61 Alfred Owen Aldridge, "Thomas Paine and the Classics," *Eighteenth-Century Studies* 1 (4): 375–76.

62 Thomas Paine, *The Age of Reason: Being an Investigation into True Fabulous Theology* (Boston: Josiah Mendum, 1852), 43.

63 Benjamin Rush, *Essays, Literary, Moral and Philosophical* (Philadelphia: Bradford, 1806), 39.

Notes to Chapter Seven: Knowledge and Rebellion

1 Bell, "As Others Saw Us," 271.

2 Edmond Halley, "A New Method of Determining the Parallax of the Sun, or His Distance to the Earth," *Philosophical Transactions of the Royal Society of London*, 4: 246.

3 Ibid.

4 Ibid., 4: 245.

5 Harry Woolf, *The Transits of Venus: A Study of Eighteenth-Century Science* (Princeton, NJ: Princeton University Press, 1959), 34.

6 BF, *Poor Richard Improved*, facsimile in *Benjamin Franklin: Representative Selections, with Introduction, Bibliography, and Notes*, ed. Frank Luther Mott and Chester E. Jorgenson (New York: American Book, 1936), 233.

7 John Winthrop, *Relation of a Voyage from Boston to Newfoundland, for Observation of the Transit of Venus, June 6, 1761* (Boston: Edes and Gill, 1761), 23.

8 Ibid., 9–10.

9   Thomas Hornsby, "On the Transit of Venus in 1769," *Philosophical Transactions* 55: 265, quoted in Woolf, 161.

10 Woolf, 148–49.

11 American Philosophical Society, *An Historical Account of the Origin and Formation of the American Philosophical Society* [1841] (Philadelphia: American Philosophical Association, 1914), 88.

12 Hindle, *Pursuit of Science*, 121–24.

13 Ibid., 123–24. The history of the Young Junto and its ultimate transformation into the American Philosophical Society is a long and complex one, with a number of important points so far lost in obscurity. For the American Philosophical Society's official account, including a dissenting opinion on several important aspects, see American Philosophical Society, *An Historical Account of the Origin and Formation of the American Philosophical Society* [1841] (Philadelphia: American Philosophical Association, 1914).

14 Quoted in Whitfield J. Bell, *Patriot-Improvers: Biographical Sketches of Members of the American Philosophical Society*, vol. 1 (Philadelphia: American Philosophical Society, 1997), 189.

15 Ibid.

16 *Pennsylvania Chronicle*, March 7, 1768.

17 Hindle, *Pursuit of Science*, 127–32.

18 "Laws & Regulations," *Transactions of the American Philosophical Society, held at Philadelphia, for Promoting useful knowledge* I (Old Series): v.

19 Thomas Bond to BF, June 7, 1769.

20 Hindle, *Pursuit of Science*, 133.

21 Cadwalader Evans to BF, June 11, 1769.

22 Quoted in *MDR*, 97.

23 *MDR*, 95, n17.

24 *MDR*, 453.

25 *MDR*, 106–7.

26 *MDR*, 122, 142.

27 Brooke Hindle, *David Rittenhouse* (Princeton, NJ: Princeton University Press, 1964), 25, 84.

28 David Rittenhouse to Thomas Barton, January 28, 1767, *MDR*, 194.

29 "Description of a New Orrery," *Transactions of the American Philosophical Society* I: 1–3.

30 Hindle, *Rittenhouse*, 82.

31 Albert E. Lownes, "The 1769 Transit of Venus and Its Relation to Early American Astronomy," *Sky and Telescope* 2 (6): 4.

32 Ibid.

33 Benjamin West, *An Account of the Observation of Venus upon the Sun, the Third Day of June, 1769, at Providence, in New-England. With Some Account of the Use of those Observations* (Providence: J. Carter, 1769), 14–15.

34 Woolf, 174.

35 William Smith and others, "Account of the Transit of Venus Over the Sun's Disk, as Observed at Norriton; in the County of Philadelphia, and Province of Pennsylvania, June 3, 1769," *Philosophical Transactions* (59): 293.

36 Benjamin Rush, *An Eulogium Intended to Perpetuate the Memory of David Rittenhouse, Late President of the American Philosophical Society* (Philadelphia: Ormond & Conrad, 1796), 12–13.

37 Nevil Maskelyne to Thomas Penn, August 2, 1769, *Early Proceedings of the American Philosophical Society for the Promotion of Useful Knowledge* (Philadelphia: McCalla & Stavely, 1884), 46.

38 Charles Magnus Wrangel to William Smith, October 18, 1871, *MDR*, 182.

39 BF to Lord Howe, July 20, 1776.

40 Benjamin Rush to Ebenezer Hazard, November 5, 1765, *Letters of Benjamin Rush*, ed. Lyman H. Butterfield (Princeton, NJ: Princeton University Press, 1951), I: 18.

41 BF to Richard Jackson, January 16, 1764.

42 BF to unknown recipient, November 28, 1768.

43 Wood, *Americanization of Benjamin Franklin*, 138–39; Wright, *Franklin of Philadelphia*, 190.

44 BF, *Observations Concerning the Increase of Mankind*, *PBF*, 4: 225.

45 Bruce A. Ragsdale, "George Washington, the British Tobacco Trade, and Economic Opportunity in Prerevolutionary Virginia," *Virginia Magazine of History and Biography* 97 (2): 136.

46 Invoice from Robert Cary & Co., April 13, 1763, *PGW*: 7: 191–98, cited in Ron Chernow, *George Washington: A Life* (New York: Penguin Press, 2010), 140.

47 Ragsdale, *A Planters' Republic: The Search for Economic Independence in Revolutionary Virginia* (Madison: Madison House, 1996), 44, 68.

48 *VG* (Purdie & Dixon), March 22, 1770. The *Virginia Gazette*, based in Williamsburg, enjoyed a colorful history in early America, complicated by political, economic, and family rivalries that saw three separate publications appear under the same name and, for a spell, at the same time. I have followed the traditional convention in the endnotes of identifying each edition in question by its respective publisher.

49 George Washington to Robert Cary & Co., September 20, 1765, *PGW*, 7: 401.

50 Hindle, *Pursuit of Science*, 197, 204.

51 George Washington to Robert Cary & Co., September 20, 1765, *PGW*, 7: 403.

52 Arthur Lee to Richard Henry Lee, January 13, 1765, *Lee Family Papers*, (UVA microfilm), quoted in Ragsdale, *Planters' Republic*, 56.

53 Atticus, *VG* (Purdie & Dixon), May 11, 1769.

54 Lee's letters, published between February and April of 1778 in the *Virginia Gazette* (Rind), constituted a local response to John Dickinson's popular "Letters from a Farmer," which helped crystallize opposition to the new taxes and duties across the colonies. For a full text of both series, see John Dickinson, *The Farmer's and Monitor's Letters to the Inhabitants of the British Colonies* [1769] (Williamsburg, VA: Virginia Independence Bicentennial Commission, 1969). The quoted text can be found on pages 62–63.

55 Ragsdale, *Planters' Republic*, 78–80.

56 "Delegates to the Continental Congress elected by ballot, Committee to prepare a plan for the encouragement of Manufactures in the Colony, March 25, 1775," in *American Archives* Series 4, 2: 170, available at http://lincoln.lib.niu.edu/cgi-bin/amarch/getdoc.pl?/var/lib/philologic/databases/amarch/.2183. Last accessed March 26, 2012.

57 Richard A. Overfield, *Science in the* Virginia Gazette, *1736–1780* (Emporia, KS: Kansas State Teachers College, 1968), 9.

58 *VG* (Purdie & Dixon), May 13, 1773.

59 *VG* (Purdie & Dixon), July 22, 1773.

60 A Friend in Virginia, *VG* (Rind), June 14, 1770.

61 Academicus, *VG* (Purdie & Dixon), August 5, 1773.

62 Ibid.

63 Overfield, 51; Hindle, *Pursuit of Science*, 214–15.

Notes to Chapter Eight: The Mechanics of Revolution

1 E. Morton Grosser, "David Rittenhouse and European Astronomy," *Publications of the Astronomical Society of the Pacific* 72: 382–83.

2 Rev. William Ludlam to the American Philosophical Society, January 25, 1772, *MDR*, 181, n7.

3 Delbourgo, *Amazing Scene*, 143–44.

4 Wright, *Franklin of Philadelphia*, 235.

5 Robert Middlekauff, *Benjamin Franklin and His Enemies* (Berkeley: University of California Press, 1996), 145–46; Wood, *Americanization of Benjamin Franklin*, 174–75.

6 John Adams to Benjamin Rush, April 4, 1790, *Old Family Letters*, ed. Andrew Biddle (Philadelphia: Lippincott, 1892), 55.

7 BF to John Bartram, May 27, 1777.

8 BF, "To All Captains and Commanders of American Armed Ships," *WBF*, 7: 449–50.

9 Hindle, *David Rittenhouse*, 100–01.

10 *MDR*, 154. Hindle; *David Rittenhouse*, 33–35.

11 Hindle, *David Rittenhouse*, 123–24.

12 Staughton Lynd, "The Mechanics in New York Politics, 1774–1788," *Labor History* 5 (3): 244.

13 Bridenbaugh, *Colonial Craftsman*, 174–75.

14 *Pennsylvania Evening Post*, March 14, 1776.

15 Lynd, 245; Lawrence A. Peskin, *Manufacturing Revolution: The Intellectual Origins of Early American Industry* (Baltimore: Johns Hopkins University Press, 2003), 30.

16 Hindle, *David Rittenhouse*, 125; Peskin, 41–45.

17 John Adams, Diary, September 28, 1775, *The Works of John Adams*, ed. Charles F. Adams (Boston: Little, Brown, 1865), 2: 429.

18 *Journals of Continental Congress* (Washington: Government Printing Office, 1906), 4: 224.

19 Hindle, *David Rittenhouse*, 126.

20 Elizabeth S. Kite, *Brigadier-General Louis Lebègue Duportail: Commandant of Engineers in the Continental Army, 1777–1783* (Baltimore: Johns Hopkins Press, 1933), 2.

21 Kite, 257.

22 Orlando W. Stephenson, "The Supply of Gunpowder in 1776," *American Historical Review* 30 (2): 271–73.

23 George Washington to Joseph Reed, December 25, 1775, *PGW*, Revolutionary War Series, ed. Philander D. Chase (Charlottesville, VA: University Press of Virginia, 1985): 2: 607.

24 Stephenson, 274–79; Hindle, *David Rittenhouse*, 125–26.

25 *MDR*, 274.

26 Thomas Jefferson to David Rittenhouse, July 19, 1778, *PTJ*, 2: 203.

27 Francis Hopkinson, "An Address to the American Philosophical Society," *The Miscellaneous Essays and Occasional Writings of Francis Hopkinson* (Philadelphia: T. Dobson, 1792), I: 361–62.

28 Ibid., 364.

29 Peskin, 101–102.

30 Ibid., 98, n28.

31 Jennifer Ann Moon, "The Best Poor Man's Industry: Politics and the Political Economy of Poor Relief in Revolutionary Philadelphia," Ph.D. diss., University of Virginia, 1995, 153–58.

32 Joseph S. Davis, *Essays in the Earlier History of American Corporations* (Cambridge, MA: Harvard University Press, 1917), I: 258.

33 Charles S. Olton, *Artisans for Independence: Philadelphia Mechanics and the American Revolution* (Syracuse: Syracuse University Press, 1975), 27–32.

34 Peskin, 87.

35 Ibid., 88.

36 Quoted in Francis Hopkinson, *Account of the Grand Federal Procession, Philadelphia, July 4, 1788: To Which Is Added a Letter on the Same Subject* (Philadelphia: M. Carey, 1788), 16.

37 Hindle, *David Rittenhouse*, 271–75.

38 David Rittenhouse to Thomas Jefferson, April 4, 1787, *PTJ*, 11: 293.

39 "Minutes of the Society for Political Inquiries," in *Hazard's Register of Pennsylvania*, ed. Samuel Hazard (Philadelphia: W. F. Geddes, 1832), 8: 125.

40 BF to Alexander Small, February 17, 1789.

41 *Rules and Regulations of the Society for Political Enquiries: Established at Philadelphia, 9th February, 1787* (Philadelphia: Robert Aitken, 1787), I.

42 Alan Houston, *Benjamin Franklin and the Politics of Improvement* (New Haven: Yale University Press, 2008), 217–18.

43 BF to Jonathan Shipley, February 24, 1786, *WBF*, 10: 250.

44 Jacob E. Cooke, *Tench Coxe and the Early Republic* (Chapel Hill: University of North Carolina Press, 1978), 110–11, xi.

45 Tench Coxe to John Coxe, June 10, 1778, quoted in Cooke, *Tench Coxe*, 44.

46 Cooke, *Tench Coxe*, 11–12, 93; John Thomas Scharf and Thompson Westcott, *History of Philadelphia, 1609–1884* (Philadelphia: L. H. Everts, 1884), I: 445.

47 Cooke, *Tench Coxe*, xii; L. Marx, *Machine in the Garden*, 151.

48 Cooke, *Tench Coxe*, x.

49 *Hazard's Register*, 8: 126.

50 Michael Vinson, "The Society for Political Inquiries: The Limits of Republican Discourse in Philadelphia on the Eve of the Constitutional Convention," *PMHB* 113 (2): 203.

51 Cooke, *Tench Coxe*, 102. In addition to Coxe, members in both groups included Rush, Rittenhouse, Thomas Mifflin, and George Fox. Vinson, 203.

52 Tench Coxe, *An Address to an Assembly of the Friends of American Manufactures* (Philadelphia: R. Aitken, 1787), 8.

53 William Barton, "Essay on the Promotion of American Manufactures," *American Museum* 2: 258–59, cited in Drew R. McCoy, *The Elusive Republic: Political Economy in Jeffersonian America* (Chapel Hill: University of North Carolina Press, 1980), 115.

54 L. Marx, 155.

55 Cooke, *Tench Coxe*, 201.

56 McCoy, 147–49. Based on his review of the Coxe family papers, which were previously unavailable to scholars, Jacob E. Cooke concludes that Coxe provided "the most decisive" influence on the text of the report, but that Hamilton augmented his recommendations with "a philosophical argument for the indispensability of American manufactures to an essentially agricultural and underdeveloped nation." See Jacob E. Cooke, "Tench Coxe, Alexander Hamilton, and the Encouragement of American Manufactures," *William and Mary Quarterly*, Third Series, 32 (3): 370–92.

57 BF to Benjamin Vaughan, July 26, 1784, *WBF*, 3: 275.

58 Peskin, 32.

59 BF to Timothy Folger, September 29, 1769.

60 Alexander Hamilton, "Report on Manufactures," *PAH*, 6: 296. Washington strongly supported Hamilton's views on the relationship between domestic industry and national security.

61 Anthony F. C. Wallace and David J. Jeremy, "William Pollard and the Arkwright Patents," *William and Mary Quarterly*, Third Series, 34 (3): 410.

62 Hugh Henry Brackenridge to Tench Coxe, March 18, 1790, quoted in Cooke, *Tench Coxe*, 107.

63 Joanne Loewe Neel, *Phineas Bond. A Study in Anglo-American Relations, 1786–1812* (Philadelphia: University of Pennsylvania Press, 1968), 55–60.

64 Doron Ben-Atar, "Alexander Hamilton's Alternative: Technology Piracy and the Report on Manufactures," *William and Mary Quarterly*, Third Series, 52 (3): 389.

65 Coxe, *Address to an Assembly*, 11.

66 *PAH*, 19: 196.

67 Davis, 1: 369. Christopher Norwood, *About Paterson: The Making and Unmaking of an American City* (New York: E. P. Dutton, 1974), 35.

68 Bernard C. Steiner, *The Life and Correspondence of James McHenry* (Cleveland: Burrows Brothers, 1907), 22.

69 *PAH*, 3: 216.

70 William Nelson, *The Founding of Paterson as the Manufacturing Metropolis of the United States* (Newark, NJ: Advertiser Printing House, 1887), 9–14.

71 *National Gazette*, July 14, 1792, quoted in Davis, 1: 472.

72 Nelson, 16.

73 Davis, I: 494.

74 Davis, I: 419, 470–84.

75 *Philadelphia Advertiser*, January 7, 1792, quoted in Davis, I: 430–31.

76 William Nelson and Charles A. Shriner, *History of Paterson and Its Environs* (New York: Lewis Historical Publishing, 1920), 348–50. Paterson was also the site, in 1913, of a crippling labor dispute between workers and mill owners over wages, hours, and working conditions. The strike, which garnered international attention, ended with the silk workers' defeat after five months.

77 "Prospectus of the Society for Establishing Useful Manufactures," *PAH*, 9: 144.

Notes to Epilogue: Manufacturing America

1 William Smith, "Being an Eulogium on Dr. Benjamin Franklin," *The Works of William Smith* (Philadelphia: Hugh Maxwell and William Fry, 1803), I: 50–51.

2 BF to Abiah Folger, April 12, 1750.

3 *MDR*, 388.

4 Hindle, *David Rittenhouse*, 329.

5 Benjamin Rush, *Eulogium*, 26–27.

6 Ibid., 23–24.

7 Cooke, *Tench Coxe*, 149–51.

8 Dupree, "National Pattern," 21–23. Bates, *Scientific Societies*, 28.

9 Bates, 26.

10 John C. Greene, "Science, Learning and Utility: Patterns of Organization in the Early American Republic," in *The Pursuit of Knowledge in the Early American Republic*, ed. Alexandra Oleson and Sanborn C. Brown (Baltimore: Johns Hopkins University Press, 1976), 6–7.

11 Thomas Jefferson to William Short, November 28, 1814, *PTJ*, 15: 108.

12 BF to Joseph Priestly, February 8, 1780, *WBF*, 8: 10.

13 BF to Joseph Banks, November 21, 1783, *WBF*, 10: 208.

14 For a prominent example, see I. Bernard Cohen, "Some Reflections on the State of Science in America during the Nineteenth Century," *Proceedings of the National Academy of Sciences of the United States of America* 45 (5): 666–77. Like many of his colleagues, Cohen views the events of the past exclusively through the lens of modern science. From this perspective, those endeavors and discoveries that demonstrably led to the practice of science as we know it today, or to theoretical breakthroughs that remain important now, are seen in a positive light. Everything else is, essentially, misguided or a waste of time and rarely given serious attention. Thus, Cohen uses his "reflections" here to lament the failure of America to produce "a great scientific tradition in the nineteenth century." This is, of course, not the only way to view the problem, as should be clear by now to readers of this volume.

15 Cohen, "Some Reflections," 667.

16 Thomas Walker, "Defense of Mechanical Philosophy," *North American Review* 33 (72): 123. Walker was writing in response to Thomas Carlyle's "Sign of the Times," in the *Edinburg Review* for 1829, which took a dim view of "mechanism" and its effects on the world.

BIBLIOGRAPHY

Aldridge, Alfred Owen. *Benjamin Franklin: Philosopher & Man*. Philadelphia: Lippincott, 1965.

——. "Thomas Paine and the Classics." *Eighteenth-Century Studies* I (4): 370–80.

American Philosophical Society. *Early Proceedings of the American Philosophical Society for the Promotion of Useful Knowledge*. Philadelphia: McCalla & Stavely, 1884.

——. *An Historical Account of the Origin and Formation of the American Philosophical Society* [1841]. Philadelphia: American Philosophical Association, 1914.

——. "Laws & Regulations." *Transactions of the American Philosophical Society held at Philadelphia for Promoting Useful Knowledge* I (Old Series): v–ix.

Anderson, Douglas. *The Radical Enlightenments of Benjamin Franklin*. Baltimore: Johns Hopkins University Press, 1997.

Arch, Stephen Carl. "Benjamin Franklin's Autobiography, Then and Now." In *The Cambridge Companion to Benjamin Franklin*, ed. Carla Mulford, 159–171. New York: Cambridge University Press, 2008.

Bacon, Francis. *The Philosophical Works of Francis Bacon*, ed. John M. Robertson. London: Routledge, 1905.

Barnett, S. J. *The Enlightenment and Religion: The Myths of Modernity*. Manchester: Manchester University Press, 2003.

Barton, William. "Essay on the Promotion of American Manufactures." *American Museum* 2: 258–59.

Bartram, John and William Bartram. *John and William Bartram's America: Selections from the Writings of the Philadelphia Naturalists*, ed. Helen Gere Cruickshank. Greenwich, CT: Devin-Adair, 1990.

Bartram, William. *Travels, and Other Writings*. New York: Library of America, 1996.

Bastian, Peter. " 'Let's Do Lunch': Benjamin Franklin and the American Character." *Australasian Journal of American Studies* 24 (I): 82–88.

Bates, Ralph S. *Scientific Societies in the United States*, 3rd ed. Cambridge, MA: MIT Press, 1965.

Becker, Carl L. "Benjamin Franklin." In *Dictionary of American Biography*. New York: Scribner's, 1931.

——. *The Heavenly City of the Eighteenth-Century Philosophers*. New Haven: Yale University Press, 1932.

Bedini, Silvio A. *At the Sign of the Compass and Quadrant: The Life and Times of Anthony Lamb*. Philadelphia: American Philosophical Society, 1984.

Bell, Whitfield J., Jr. "As Others Saw Us: Notes on the Reputation of the American Philosophical Society." *Proceedings of the American Philosophical Society* 116 (3): 269–78.

———. *Patriot-Improvers: Biographical Sketches of Members of the American Philosophical Society, Volume One, 1743–1768*. Philadelphia: American Philosophical Society, 1997.

Ben-Atar, Doron. "Alexander Hamilton's Alternative: Technology Piracy and the Report on Manufactures." *William and Mary Quarterly*, Third Series, 52 (3): 389–414.

Black, William and R. Alonzo Brock. "Journal of William Black." *PMHB* I (4): 404–19.

Bradford, William. *Of Plymouth Plantation, 1620–1647*, ed. Samuel Eliot Morison. New York: Random House, 1952.

Brasch, F. E. "John Winthrop (1714–1779), America's First Astronomer, and the Science of His Period." *Publications of the Astronomical Society of the Pacific* 28: 152–70.

Bridenbaugh, Carl. *Cities in Revolt: Urban Life in America, 1743–1776*. New York: Knopf, 1955.

———. *The Colonial Craftsman*. New York: Dover, 1990.

Bridenbaugh, Carl and Jessica Bridenbaugh. *Rebels and Gentlemen: Philadelphia in the Age of Franklin*. New York: Oxford University Press, 1962.

Brown, Richard D. *Knowledge Is Power: The Diffusion of Information in Early America, 1700–1865*. New York: Oxford University Press, 1989.

Butterfield, Lyman H. "Benjamin Rush as a Promoter of Useful Knowledge." *Proceedings of the American Philosophical Society* 92 (1): 26–36.

Butterfield, Lyman H., and others, eds. *The Book of Abigail and John: Selected Letters of the Adams Family, 1762–1784*. Boston: Northeastern University, 2002.

Campbell, James. "The Pragmatist in Franklin." In *The Cambridge Companion to Benjamin Franklin*, ed. Carla Mulford, 104–16. New York: Cambridge University Press, 2008.

———. *Recovering Benjamin Franklin: An Exploration of a Life of Science and Service*. Chicago: Open Court, 1999.

Carlson, C. Lennart. "Samuel Keimer: A Study in the Transit of English Culture to Colonial Pennsylvania." *PMHB* 61 (4): 357–86.

Chapin, Seymour L. "A Legendary Bon Mot?: Franklin's 'What Is the Good of a Newborn Baby?' " *Proceedings of the American Philosophical Society* 129 (3): 278–90.

Chaplin, Joyce E. "Benjamin Franklin's Natural Philosophy." In *The Cambridge Companion to Benjamin Franklin*, ed. Carla Mulford, 63–76. New York: Cambridge University Press, 2008.

———. *The First Scientific American: Benjamin Franklin and the Pursuit of Genius*. New York: Basic Books, 2006.

Chernow, Ron. *Alexander Hamilton*. New York: Penguin, 2004.

———. *George Washington: A Life*. New York: Penguin, 2010.

Cheyney, Edward Potts. *History of the University of Pennsylvania, 1740–1940*. Philadelphia: University of Pennsylvania Press, 1940.

Clark, Peter. *British Clubs and Societies, 1580–1800: The Origins of an Associational World*. London: Oxford University Press, 2002.

Cohen, I. Bernard. "Benjamin Franklin and the Transit of Mercury in 1753: Together with a Facsimile of a Little-Known Scientific Work Printed by Franklin." *Proceedings of the American Philosophical Society* 94 (3): 222–32.

———. *Benjamin Franklin's Science*. Cambridge, MA: Harvard University Press, 1990.

——. *Franklin and Newton: An Inquiry into Speculative Newtonian Experimental Science and Franklin's Work in Electricity as an Example Thereof.* Philadelphia: American Philosophical Society, 1956.

——. "How Practical Was Benjamin Franklin's Science?" *PMHB* 69 (4): 284–93.

——. "Prejudice Against the Introduction of Lightening Rods." *Journal of the Franklin Institute* 253: 393–440.

——. *Science and the Founding Fathers.* New York: W. W. Norton, 1995.

——. "Some Reflections on the State of Science in America during the Nineteenth Century." *Proceedings of the National Academy of Sciences of the United States of America* 45 (5): 666–77.

Colden, Cadwallader. *Selections from the Scientific Correspondence of Cadwallader Colden*, ed. Asa Gray. New Haven: Hamlen, 1843.

Cook, Harold J. "Bernard Mandeville." In *A Companion to Early Modern Philosophy*, ed. Steven Nadler, 469–82. Oxford: Blackwell, 2002.

Cooke, Jacob E. "Tench Coxe, Alexander Hamilton, and the Encouragement of American Manufactures." *William and Mary Quarterly*, Third Series, 32 (3): 370–92.

——. *Tench Coxe and the Early Republic.* Chapel Hill: University of North Carolina Press, 1978.

Cotton, John. *Christ, The Fountain of Life* [1651]. New York: Arno Press, 1972.

Coxe, Tench. *An Address to an Assembly of the Friends of American Manufactures.* Philadelphia: R. Aitken, 1787.

——. *A Brief Examination of Lord Sheffield's Observations on the Commerce of the United States: In Seven Numbers with Two Supplementary Notes on American Manufactures.* Philadelphia: M. Carey, 1791.

de Crèvecoeur, J. Hector St. John. *Letters from an American Farmer* [1782]. New York: Fox Duffield, 1904.

Curti, Merle. *The Growth of American Thought*, 3rd edition. New Brunswick, NJ: Transaction Books, 1982.

Darlington, William. *Memorials of John Bartram and Humphrey Marshall* [1849]. New York: Hafner, 1967.

Daston, Lorraine and Katherine Park. *Wonders and the Order of Nature, 1150–1750.* New York: Zone Books, 1998.

Davis, Joseph S. *Essays in the Earlier History of American Corporations.* Cambridge, MA: Harvard University Press, 1917.

Delbourgo, James. *A Most Amazing Scene of Wonders: Electricity and Enlightenment in Early America.* Cambridge, MA: Harvard University Press, 2006.

Di Lorenzo, Anthony J. "Dissenting Protestantism as a Language of Revolution in Thomas Paine's *Common Sense.*" *Eighteenth-Century Thought* 4 (4): 229–83.

Dickinson, John. *The Farmer's and Monitor's Letters to the Inhabitants of the British Colonies* [1769]. Williamsburg, VA: Virginia Independence Bicentennial Commission, 1969.

Dierks, Konstantin. "Letter Writing, Masculinity, and American Men of Science, 1750–1800." *Pennsylvania History* 65: 167–98.

Dorfman, Joseph. *The Economic Mind in American Civilization, 1606–1865*, 2 vols. New York: Viking, 1946.

Duffy, John. *From Humors to Medical Science: A History of American Medicine*, 2nd edition. Urbana, IL: University of Illinois Press, 1993.

Dugatkin, Lee Alan. *Mr. Jefferson and the Giant Moose: Natural History in Early America*. Chicago: University of Chicago Press, 2009.

Dupree, A. Hunter. "The National Pattern of American Learned Societies, 1769–1863." In *The Pursuit of Knowledge in the Early American Republic*, ed. Alexandra Oleson and Sanborn C. Brown, 21–32. Baltimore: Johns Hopkins University Press, 1976.

Earnest, Ernest. *John and William Bartram: Botanists and Explorers*. Philadelphia: University of Pennsylvania, 1940.

Edwards, Jonathan. *The Works of Jonathan Edwards*, vol. 1. London: William Ball, 1839.

Faÿ, Bernard. *Franklin, The Apostle of Modern Times*. Boston: Little, Brown, 1929.

Forman, Sydney. "The United States Military Philosophical Society, 1802–1813: *Scientia in Bello Pax*." *William and Mary Quarterly*, Third Series, 2 (3): 273–85.

Fothergill, John. "Memoirs of Peter Collinson." *London* 45 (1776), 4–6.

Fox, George. *The Journal of George Fox*, 7th edition. London: W. and F. G. Cash, 1852.

Fraser, Walter J., Jr., *Charleston! Charleston!: The History of a Southern City*. Columbia, SC: University of South Carolina Press, 1989.

Glanvill, Joseph. *Plus Ultra, or the Progress and Advancement of Knowledge Since the Days of Aristotle*. London: James Collins, 1668.

Greaves, Richard L. *The Puritan Revolution and Educational Thought; Background for Reform*. New Brunswick, NJ: Rutgers University Press, 1969.

Greene, Jack P. and Richard M. Jellison. "The Currency Act of 1764 in Imperial-Colonial Relations, 1764–1776." *William and Mary Quarterly*, Third Series, 18 (4): 485–518.

Greene, John C. *American Science in the Age of Jefferson*. Claremont, CA: Regina Books, 2004.

——."Science, Learning and Utility: Patterns of Organization in the Early American Republic." In *The Pursuit of Knowledge in the Early American Republic*, ed. Alexandra Oleson and Sanborn C. Brown, 1–20. Baltimore: Johns Hopkins University Press, 1976.

Grosser, E. Morton. "David Rittenhouse and European Astronomy." *Publications of the Astronomical Society of the Pacific* 72: 377–86.

Hall, Maria Boas. *Promoting Experimental Learning: Experiment and the Royal Society, 1660–1727*. New York: Cambridge University Press, 1991.

Halley, Edmond. "A New Method of Determining the Parallax of the Sun, or His Distance to the Earth." *Philosophical Transactions of the Royal Society of London*, 4: 243–49.

Hamilton, Alexander. *Gentleman's Progress: The Itinerarium of Dr. Alexander Hamilton, 1744*, ed. Carl Bridenbaugh. Pittsburgh: University of Pittsburgh Press, 1992.

——. *The Tuesday Club: A Shorter Edition of the History of the Ancient and Honorable Tuesday Club*, ed. Robert Micklus. Baltimore: Johns Hopkins University Press, 1995.

Heilbron, J. L. *Electricity in the 17th and 18th Centuries: A Study of Early Modern Physics*. Berkeley: University of California, 1979.

Heimart, Alan. "Puritanism, the Wilderness, and the Frontier." *New England Quarterly* 26 (3): 361–82.

Hetrick, Lawrence. "The Origins, Goals, and Outcomes of John Bartram's Journey on the St. John's River, 1765–1766." In *America's Curious Botanist: A Tercentennial Reappraisal of John Bartram*,

1699–1777, ed. Nancy E. Hoffman and John C. van Horne, 127–36. Philadelphia: American Philosophical Society, 2004.

Hindle, Brooke. *David Rittenhouse*. Princeton: Princeton University Press, 1964.

———. *The Pursuit of Science in Revolutionary America, 1735–1789*. New York: W. W. Norton & Co., 1974.

———. "The Quaker Background and Science in Colonial Philadelphia." In *Early American Science*, ed. Brooke Hindle, 173–80. New York: Science History Publications, 1976.

Hoffman, Nancy E. and John C. van Horne, eds. *America's Curious Botanist: A Tercentennial Reappraisal of John Bartram, 1699–1777*. Philadelphia: American Philosophical Society, 2004.

Hofstadter, Richard. *America at 1750: A Social Portrait*. New York: Knopf, 1971.

Holmes, Richard. *The Age of Wonder: How the Romantic Generation Discovered the Beauty and Terror of Science*. New York: Pantheon, 2008.

Hooke, Robert. *Micrographia, or, Some Physiological Descriptions of Minute Bodies Made by Magnifying Glasses* [1665]. Mineola, NY: Dover, 2003.

Hopkinson, Francis. *Account of the Grand Federal Procession, Philadelphia, July 4, 1788: To Which Is Added a Letter on the Same Subject*. Philadelphia: M. Carey, 1788.

———. "An Address to the American Philosophical Society." In *The Miscellaneous Essays and Occasional Writings of Francis Hopkinson*. Philadelphia: T. Dobson, 1792, I: 359–71.

Hornsby, Thomas. "On the Transit of Venus in 1769." *Philosophical Transactions* 55: 265–74.

Houghton, John. "A Discourse of Coffee." *Philosophical Transactions* 21: 311–17.

Houston, Alan. *Benjamin Franklin and the Politics of Improvement*. New Haven: Yale University Press, 2008.

Hughes, Thomas Parke. *American Genesis: A Century of Invention and Technological Enthusiasm, 1870–1970*. Chicago: University of Chicago Press, 2004.

———. *Human-Built World*. Chicago: University of Chicago Press, 2004.

Hume, David. *The Letters of David Hume*, ed. J. Y. T. Greig. Oxford: Oxford University Press, 1932.

Isaacson, Walter. *Benjamin Franklin: An American Life*. New York: Simon & Schuster, 2003.

Jefferson, Thomas. *Notes on the State of Virginia* [1787]. Boston: Lilly and Wait, 1832.

Johnson, Steven. *The Invention of Air: A Story of Science, Faith, Revolution, and the Birth of America*. New York: Penguin, 2009.

Jones, Hugh. *The Present State of Virginia* [1724], ed. Richard L. Morton. Chapel Hill: University of North Carolina Press, 1956.

Jones, Richard Foster. *Ancients and Moderns: A Study in the Rise of the Scientific Movement in Seventeenth-Century England*. St. Louis: Washington University Press, 1961.

Kalm, Peter. *Travels into North America* [1753–1761], 2 vols, trans. John Reinhold Forster. London: T. Lowndes, 1773.

Kaye, Harvey J. *Thomas Paine and the Promise of America*. New York: Hill and Wang, 2005.

Lawrence, D. H. *Studies in Classic American Literature* [1924]. London: Penguin, 1971.

Lemay, J. A. Leo. *Ebenezer Kinnersley: Franklin's Friend*. Philadelphia: University of Pennsylvania Press, 1964.

——. *The Life of Benjamin Franklin*, 3 vols. Philadelphia: University of Pennsylvania Press, 2005–2009.

——, ed. *Reappraising Benjamin Franklin*. Newark, DE: University of Delaware Press, 1993.

Lillywhite, Bryant. *London Coffee Houses: A Reference Book of Coffee Houses of the Seventeenth, Eighteenth, and Nineteenth Centuries*. London: Allen and Unwin, 1963.

Lingelbach, William E. "B. Franklin, Printer—New Source Materials." *Proceedings of the American Philosophical Society* 92 (2): 79–100.

Locke, John. *An Essay Concerning Humane Understanding* [1690]. London: T. Tegg, 1836.

——. *Two Treatises of Government* [1690]. New York: Hafner Press, 1947.

Lownes, Albert E. "The 1769 Transit of Venus and Its Relation to Early American Astronomy." *Sky and Telescope* 2 (6): 3–5.

Lundberg, David and Henry F. May. "The Enlightened Reader in America." *American Quarterly* 28 (2): 262–93.

Lynd, Staughton. "The Mechanics in New York Politics, 1774–1788." *Labor History* 5 (3): 225–46.

Mandeville, Bernard. *The Fable of the Bees: Or, Private Vices, Publick Benefits*, 3rd edition. London: J. Tonson, 1724.

Marx, Karl. *A Contribution to the Critique of Political Economy*, trans. N. I. Stone. Chicago: Charles H. Kerr, 1904.

Marx, Leo. *The Machine in the Garden: Technology and the Pastoral Ideal in America*. New York: Oxford University Press, 2000.

Mason, George Champlin. *Annals of the Redwood Library and Athenaeum*. Newport, RI: Redwood Library, 1891.

May, Henry F. *The Enlightenment in America*. New York: Oxford University Press, 1976.

McCoy, Drew R. *The Elusive Republic: Political Economy in Jeffersonian America*. Chapel Hill: University of North Carolina Press, 1980.

Melville, Herman. *Israel Potter: His Fifty Years of Exile*. New York: G. P. Putnam, 1844.

Meyer, D. H. "The Uniqueness of the American Enlightenment." *American Quarterly* 28 (2): 165–86.

Middlekauff, Robert. *Benjamin Franklin and His Enemies*. Berkeley: University of California Press, 1996.

Micklus, Robert. "The Delightful Instruction of Dr. Alexander Hamilton's *Itinerarium*." *American Literature* 60 (3): 359–84.

Miller, Perry. *The Life of the Mind in America: From the Revolution to the Civil War*. New York: Harcourt, Brace & World, 1965.

——. *The New England Mind: The Seventeenth Century*. Cambridge, MA: Harvard University Press, 1954.

——. "The Responsibility of Mind in a Civilization of Machines." *American Scholar* 31 (1): 51–69.

Mittelberger, Gottlieb. *Journey to Pennsylvania*, trans. and ed. Oscar Handlin and John Clive. Cambridge, MA: Belknap Press, 1960.

Montgomery, Thomas Harrison. *A History of the University of Pennsylvania: From Its Foundation to A.D. 1770.* Philadelphia: George W. Jacobs, 1900.

Moon, Jennifer Ann. "The Best Poor Man's Industry: Politics and the Political Economy of Poor Relief in Revolutionary Philadelphia." Ph.D. diss., University of Virginia, 1995.

Mr. Town [pseudonym]. *The Connoisseur* I. London: Baldwin, 1754.

Mulford, Carla. "Figuring Benjamin Franklin in American Cultural Memory." *New England Quarterly* 72 (3): 415–43.

Neale, John. *Directions for Gentlemen Who Have Electrical Machines, How to Proceed in Making Their Experiments.* London: NP, 1747.

Neel, Joanne Loewe. *Phineas Bond; A Study in Anglo-American Relations, 1786–1812.* Philadelphia: University of Pennsylvania Press, 1968.

Nelson, William. *The Founding of Paterson as the Manufacturing Metropolis of the United States.* Newark, NJ: Advertiser Printing House, 1887.

Nelson, William and Charles A. Shriner. *History of Paterson and Its Environs.* New York: Lewis Historical Publishing, 1920.

Newman, Simon P. "Benjamin Franklin and the Leather-Apron Men: The Politics of Class in Eighteenth-Century Philadelphia." *Journal of American Studies*, 43 (2): 161–75.

Newton, Isaac. *Mathematical Principles of Natural Philosophy* [1687], 2 vols, trans. Andrew Motte [1729], rev. Florian Cajori. Berkeley: University of California Press, 1934.

Norton, John. *The Orthodox Evangelist* [1654]. New York: AMS Press, 1983.

Norwood, Christopher. *About Paterson: The Making and Unmaking of an American City.* New York: E. P. Dutton, 1974.

Oleson, Alexandra and Sanborn C. Brown, eds. *The Pursuit of Knowledge in the Early American Republic.* Baltimore: Johns Hopkins University Press, 1976.

Olton, Charles S. *Artisans for Independence: Philadelphia Mechanics and the American Revolution.* Syracuse: Syracuse University Press, 1975.

Ornstein, Martha. *The Role of Scientific Societies in the Seventeenth Century*, 3rd edition. New York: Arno Press, 1975.

Overfield, Richard A. *Science in the* Virginia Gazette, *1736–1780.* Emporia, KS: Kansas State Teachers College, 1968.

Paine, Thomas. *The Age of Reason: Being an Investigation into True Fabulous Theology.* Boston: Josiah Mendum, 1852.

Pendergrast, Mark. *Uncommon Grounds: The History of Coffee and How It Changed Our World.* New York: Basic Books, 1999.

Penn, William. *Fruits of Solitude* [1695]. Philadelphia: Longstreth, 1877.

——. *No Cross No Crown: A Discourse Shewing the Nature and Discipline of the Holy Cross of Christ.* London: Mary Hinde, 1771.

——. *The Papers of William Penn*, ed. Richard S. Dunn and Mary Maples Dunn. Philadelphia: University of Pennsylvania Press, 1981–1987.

——. *Passages from the Life and Writings of William Penn*, ed. Thomas Pym Cope. Philadelphia: Friends' Bookstore, 1882.

———. *The Witness of William Penn*, ed. Frederick B. Tolles and E. Gordon Alderfer. New York: Macmillan, 1957.

Peskin, Lawrence A. *Manufacturing Revolution: The Intellectual Origins of Early American Industry*. Baltimore: Johns Hopkins Press, 2003.

Petty, William. "The Advice of W. P. to Mr. Samuel Hartlib, for the Advancement of Some Particular Parts of Learning [1648]." In *Harleian Miscellany* 6: 141–57. London: Robert Dutton, 1810.

Picciotto, Joanna. *Labors of Innocence in Modern England*. Cambridge, MA: Harvard University Press, 2010.

Potts, William John. "British Views of American Manufacturing and Trade during the Revolution." *PMHB* 7: 194–99.

Porter, Roy. *The Creation of the Modern World: The Untold Story of the British Enlightenment*. New York: W. W. Norton, 2000.

Primer, Irwin. *Bernard Mandeville's 'A Modest Defence of Public Stews': Prostitution and Its Discontent in Early Georgian England*. New York: Palgrave Macmillan, 2006.

Purver, Margery. *The Royal Society: Concept and Creation*. Cambridge, MA: MIT Press, 1967.

Ragsdale, Bruce A. "George Washington, the British Tobacco Trade, and Economic Opportunity in Prerevolutionary Virginia." *Virginia Magazine of History and Biography* 97 (2): 132–62.

———. *A Planters' Republic: The Search for Economic Independence in Revolutionary Virginia*. Madison: Madison House, 1996.

Ramsay, David. *The History of the American Revolution*, 2 vols. Philadelphia: R. Aitken, 1789.

Ray, John. *The Wisdom of God Manifested in the Works of the Creation* [1691]. London: William & John Innys, 1722.

Rede, Leman Thomas. *Biblotheca Americana*. London: J. Debbett, 1789.

Reinhold, Meyer. "Opponents of Classical Learning in America during the Revolutionary Period." *Proceedings of the American Philosophical Society* 112 (4): 221–34.

———. "The Quest for 'Useful Knowledge' in Eighteenth-Century America." *Proceedings of the American Philosophical Society* 119 (2): 108–32.

Riskin, Jessica. *Science in the Age of Sensibility: The Sentimental Empiricists of the French Enlightenment*. Chicago: University of Chicago Press, 2002.

Robson, David W. *Educating Republicans: The College in the Era of the American Revolution, 1750–1800*. Westport, CT: Greenwood Press, 1985.

Rossiter, Clinton. "The Political Theory of Benjamin Franklin." *PMHB* 76 (3): 259–93.

———. *Seedtime of the Republic: The Origin of the American Tradition of Political Liberty*. New York: Harcourt, 1953.

Rush, Benjamin. *The Autobiography of Benjamin Rush*. Princeton, NJ: Princeton University Press, 1948.

———. *Essays, Literary, Moral and Philosophical*, 2nd edition. Philadelphia: Bradford, 1806.

———. *An Eulogium Intended to Perpetuate the Memory of David Rittenhouse, Late President of the American Philosophical Society*. Philadelphia: Ormond & Conrad, 1796.

———. *A Memorial Containing Travels Through Life or Sundry Incidents in the Life of Dr. Benjamin Rush, Written by Himself*. Lanoraie, PA: Louis Alexander Biddle, 1905.

Ryerson, Richard Alan. *The Revolution Is Now Begun: The Radical Committees of Philadelphia, 1765–1776*. Philadelphia: University of Pennsylvania Press, 1978.

Schiffer, Michael Brian. *Draw the Lightning Down: Benjamin Franklin and Electrical Technology in the Age of Enlightenment*. Berkeley: University of California Press, 2003.

Schlenther, Boyd Stanley. "Colonial America's 'Un-Royal Society': Organized Enlightenment as a Handmaid to Revolution." *Journal for Eighteenth-Century Studies* 11 (1): 19–26.

Schoepf, Johann David. *Travels in the Confederation, 1783–1784*, trans. and ed. Alfred J. Morrison. Philadelphia: William J. Campbell, 1911.

Schultz, Ronald. *The Republic of Labor: Philadelphia Artisans and the Politics of Class, 1720–1830*. New York: Oxford University Press, 1993.

Shaw, Peter. *The Tablet, or Picture of Real Life*. London: Longman, 1762.

Shelley, Henry C. *Inns and Taverns of Old London*. Boston: L. C. Page, 1909.

Sibum, Heinz Otto. "The Bookkeeper of Nature: Benjamin Franklin's Electrical Research and the Development of Experimental Natural Philosophy in the Eighteenth Century." In *Reappraising Benjamin Franklin*, ed. J. A. Leo Lemay, 221–42. Newark, DE: University of Delaware Press, 1993.

Simpson, James. *Burning to Read: English Fundamentalism and Its Reformation Opponents*. Cambridge, MA: Belknap Press, 2007.

Smith, William. *A General Idea of the College of Mirania* [1753]. New York: Johnson Reprint, 1969.

———. *The Works of William Smith*, 2 vols. Philadelphia: Hugh Maxwell and William Fry, 1803.

Smith, William and others. "Account of the Transit of Venus Over the Sun's Disk, as Observed at Norriton, in the County of Philadelphia, and Province of Pennsylvania, June 3, 1769." *Philosophical Transactions* (59): 289–326.

Society for Political Enquiries. *Rules and Regulations of the Society for Political Enquiries: Established at Philadelphia, 9th February, 1787*. Philadelphia: Robert Aitken, 1787.

Speck. W. A. "Bernard Mandeville and the Middlesex Grand Jury." *Eighteenth-Century Studies* 11 (3): 362–74.

Spiller, Robert E. *The Oblique Light: Studies in Literary History and Biography*. New York: Macmillan, 1968.

Sprat, Thomas. *History of the Royal Society* [1667], ed. Jackson I. Cope and Harold Whitmore Jones. St. Louis: Washington University Press, 1958.

Stearns, Raymond Phineas. *Science in the British Colonies of America*. Chicago: University of Illinois Press, 1970.

Steiner, Bernard C. *The Life and Correspondence of James McHenry*. Cleveland: Burrows Brothers, 1907.

Stephenson, Orlando W. "The Supply of Gunpowder in 1776." *American Historical Review* 30 (2): 271–81.

Stiles, Ezra. *The Literary Diary of Ezra Stiles*. New York: Charles Scribner's, 1901.

Tolles, Frederick B. *Meeting House and Counting House: The Quaker Merchants of Colonial Philadelphia, 1682–1763*. New York: W. W. Norton, 1963.

Twain, Mark. "The Late Benjamin Franklin." In *Sketches New and Old*, 211–15. Hartford: American Publishing, 1901.

Van Doren, Carl. "The Beginnings of the American Philosophical Society." *Proceedings of the American Philosophical Society* 87 (3): 277–89.

———. *Benjamin Franklin*. New York: Viking Press, 1938.

Van Wesep, H. B. *Seven Sages: The Story of American Philosophy*. New York: Longmans, Green, 1960.

Van Zandt, Roland. *The Metaphysical Foundations of American History*. The Hague: Mouton, 1959.

Vinson, Michael. "The Society for Political Inquiries: The Limits of Republican Discourse in Philadelphia on the Eve of the Constitutional Convention." *PMHB* 113 (2): 185–205.

Victory, Beatrice M. *Benjamin Franklin and Germany*. Philadelphia: University of Pennsylvania Press, 1915.

Walker, Timothy. "Defense of Mechanical Philosophy." *North American Review* 33 (72): 122–36.

Wallace, Anthony F. C. and David J. Jeremy. "William Pollard and the Arkwright Patents." *William and Mary Quarterly*, Third Series, 34 (3): 404–25.

Walwyn, William. *The Compassionate Samaritane*. London: NP, 1644.

Waring, Joseph I. *A History of Medicine in South Carolina, 1670–1825*. Charleston [?]: South Carolina Medical Association, 1964.

Watkinson, James D. "Useful Knowledge? Concepts, Values, and Access in American Education, 1776–1840." *History of Education Quarterly* 30 (3): 351–70.

Weber, Max. *The Protestant Ethic and the "Spirit" of Capitalism*. Ed. and trans. by Peter Baehr and Gordon C. Wells. New York: Penguin, 2002.

Webster, Charles, ed. *Samuel Hartlib and the Advancement of Learning*. Cambridge: Cambridge University Press, 1970.

Weld, Charles Richard. *A History of the Royal Society*, 2 vols. [1848]. New York: Arno Press, 1975.

Wendel, Thomas. "The Keith-Lloyd Alliance: Factional and Coalition Politics in Colonial Pennsylvania." *PMHB* 92 (3): 289–305.

West, Benjamin. *An Account of the Observation of Venus upon the Sun, the Third Day of June, 1769, at Providence, in New-England. With Some Account of the Use of those Observations*. Providence: J. Carter; 1769.

Wickersham, James Pyle. *A History of Education in Pennsylvania*. Lancaster, PA: Inquirer Publishing, 1866.

Wills, Garry. *Inventing America: Jefferson's Declaration of Independence*. New York: Doubleday, 1978.

Winthrop, John [the Younger]. *Life and Letters of John Winthrop*, ed. Robert C. Winthrop. Boston: Ticknor and Fields, 1867.

Winthrop, John. *Relation of a Voyage from Boston to Newfoundland, for Observation of the Transit of Venus, June 6, 1761*. Boston: Edes and Gill, 1761.

Winthrop, Robert C., ed. *Correspondence of Hartlib, Haak, Oldenburg and Others of the Royal Society with Governor Winthrop of Connecticut, 1661–1672*. Boston: John Wilson, 1878.

Wolf, Edwin. "Franklin and His Friends Choose Their Books." *PMHB* 80 (1): 11–36.

Wolf, Edwin and Kevin J. Hayes. *The Library of Benjamin Franklin*. Philadelphia: American Philosophical Society, 2006.

Wood, Gordon S. *The Americanization of Benjamin Franklin*. New York: Penguin Press, 2004.

———. *The Radicalism of the American Revolution*. New York: Knopf, 1992.

Woolf, Harry. *The Transits of Venus: A Study of Eighteenth-Century Science*. Princeton: Princeton University Press, 1959.

Wright, Esmond. *Franklin of Philadelphia*. Cambridge, MA: Belknap Press, 1986.

Zinn, Howard. *A People's History of the United States*. New York: HarperCollins, 1980.

INDEX

A NOTE ON THE TYPE

The text of this book is set in Centaur. Centaur was designed by Bruce Rogers in 1914 as a titling fount only for the Metropolitan Museum of New York. It was modelled on Jenson's roman.